LAND OF HOPE AND DREAMS

Celebrating 25 years of
Bruce Springsteen in Ireland

Greg Lewis
Moira Sharkey

with personal stories
and photographs from
Springsteen fans
from around the world

Published by Magic Rat

The 'Magic' collection of photographs is by René Van Diemen.

The 'Slane' collection of photographs is by Thomas Quinn.

Special thanks to Andrei Talbot, Andrew Canham, Dan French and Mike Saunders.

Many fans have contributed photographs and they are credited where possible.
Please contact us if any work has been wrongly credited and we will be glad to correct any errors for the next edition.

Published by **Magic Rat**
12a Lansdowne Avenue West
Canton
Cardiff
Wales CF11 8FS
magic.rat.books@googlemail.com

www.springsteeninireland.com

© Greg Lewis and Moira Sharkey 2009

ISBN: 978-0-9562722-0-1

front cover photograph: René Van Diemen
book designed: Phil Cope and Darren Dobbs

PREFACE

During a rare quiet moment in the second of three sold-out Bruce Springsteen gigs in Dublin in 2008, a voice rang out from the crowd: "Bruce, you're Irish!" Witty, sharp and, as this book will explore, not at all far from the truth.

Through words and photographs we are going to take you on a journey from New Jersey to Navan, from E Street to Grafton. The book details every Irish show and, as Springsteen's story is about breaking down the barriers that inevitably build up between a multi-millionaire singer and his fans, *Land Of Hope And Dreams* is packed full of fans' memories and stories from the shows. As one contributor, Ciaran Gallagher of Belfast, notes: "Sense of community is disappearing. Fans go to Springsteen to get that sense of connection, not just to Bruce and his music but to each other. To stand in the pit, shoulder to shoulder, sweating and singing with people you hardly know is an amazing thing. I'm such a bad singer that I hardly sing around my own home but I have no trouble screeching at the top of my lungs in a huge stadium. In that sense a Springsteen concert is kind of a religious thing. Everyone knows what and when to sing, when to raise their arms, to pogo-dance, when to be silent and respectful. The music of course also makes you feel connected to something 'higher'."

Springsteen's most recent shows in Ireland have revealed that rock's greatest storyteller has developed a connection with Irish audiences perhaps unparalleled elsewhere. This connection is a fitting one, given that one of the significant themes of Springsteen's music is having a sense of place and belonging. In Chapter 5, the book describes in detail for the first time Springsteen's own family connections to Ireland and the story of how his ancestors sailed from their homeland to the promised land. More than a century after his ancestors left seeking a better life Bruce Springsteen returned to Ireland having made his fortune.

His 1985 concert at Slane Castle, now almost 25 years ago, was remarkable for many reasons. After almost two decades of playing live, having first started bands as a teenager to later develop a reputation as one of the greatest of all concert acts, this was to be the Springsteen spectacular.

It was his largest audience to date and his first outdoor show in Europe. It marked a moment when the island of Ireland, going through the depths of its Troubles, could welcome the person who was at that moment the most-talked-about musician on the planet. And it was remarkable too because it almost never happened.

BRUCE SPRINGSTEEN AND THE E.STREET BAND
SLANE CASTLE Saturday 1st June 1985
Gates open 3-00pm   Concert from 5-00pm
TICKETS £15.00 No Refunds, No Exchanges
No Bottles, Cans, Tape Recorders, Cameras,
ding Chairs, or Umbrellas. CONCERT RAIN OR SHINE
YONE SEEKING TO GAIN ADMISSION USING A COUNTERFEIT TICKET
WILL BE PROSECUTED

№ 1 812685

Concerts South Ltd.
Present in Ireland
BRUCE SPRINGSTEEN
and the E.STREET BAND
Saturday 1st June 1985
Gates open 3-00pm
SLANE CASTLE
TICKETS £15-00
(No refunds, No exchanges)
№ 1 812685

Slane Castle
County Meath

1 June 1985

Crowd: estimated between
60,000 and 100,000

Tickets: IR£15

Slane Castle is the home of Ireland's most famous aristocrat, the right honourable Henry Conyngham, Earl of Mountcharles – or as he is better known Lord Henry Mountcharles. His castle dates from 1785 and boasts gardens and surrounding parklands landscaped by no less a person than the great Capability Brown.

In the late 1970s Lord Mountcharles, with an eye on what was being done at Knebworth, the estate in Hertfordshire, England, which had become the "stately home of rock", saw an opportunity to bring Slane into the modern age and to turn a money-draining country pile into a thriving business. The first shows were held there in 1981 with "local" acts Thin Lizzy and U2 taking the stage. In 1985, the stonework which would provide the backdrop to the Springsteen gig was celebrating its bicentenary. Fifteen centuries earlier, it was said that here on the Hill of Slane, St Patrick had preached, lighting the fire of Irish Christianity. Now, a preacher would return, a rock missionary in jeans, taking the applause of thousands of followers, some of whom had paid five times the face-value price of the ticket to stand in the sunshine of County Meath.

Bruce Springsteen was touring to promote his seventh album, *Born In The USA*. He had been recording since 1972 and had gained a large and loyal following. His previous record *Nebraska* had been a sparse solo affair recorded at Springsteen's home studio. But this latest album had been crafted for large-scale commercial success and was backed by the brashest marketing machine dollars could buy. During the *Born In The USA* tour Springsteen was tabloid fodder, the mega-celebrity at the height of an intense fame which he had been essentially avoiding in the cult years of the 1970s and which he would spend the next 25 years trying to keep under control.

The temperatures at Slane that Irish Bank Holiday Saturday were in the early 20s, but Springsteen was much hotter than that. The Slane show has sometimes been billed as Springsteen's first outdoor show but he had played a single outdoor show in Denver on *The River* tour in 1981 and had already played a number in the early stages of the US leg and on the Australian leg of the *Born In The USA* tour, albeit in much smaller places and to much smaller crowds than Slane.

The *Born In The USA* album had been released on June 4, 1984. The tour had started in St Paul, Minnesota, three weeks later. The E Street Band which took the stage that night was missing a key member. Guitarist Steve Van Zandt had left the band during the recording sessions for the album and pursued a solo career with a more radical political message than Springsteen's. In his place was Nils Lofgren, Neil Young's former guitarist and a good friend of Springsteen's. And significantly, there was another new member of the band: a female singer from New Jersey, with – like Bruce – an Irish-Italian background, named Patti Scialfa. Scialfa got the call just five days before the St Paul show and by August she and the E Street Band were selling out 10 nights at the Meadowlands Arena, East Rutherford, New Jersey.

Springsteen had always vowed not to play stadium-sized venues, fearing that he would lose his unique sense of intimacy and connection with the audience. He always aimed to communicate as closely with those in the back seats as those at the front. At Slane, the back row was on a far off rolling hill. The concert would be a spectacular one but could it maintain the essential elements of a Springsteen show?

The *Born In The USA* tour was a rolling freight train, riding a runaway track laid by a multi-million selling album which one year after its release was still in the Top Five of the US chart. Slane was the first concert on the European leg of a tour which had already conquered the

United States and Australia. He had been offstage for a month before arriving in Ireland for the first time. The opening chords of the anthemic "Born In The USA" were some of the most familiar to radio listeners. Now, at two minutes past five, they rang out for real and, as the sun shone down over the west battlements of the castle, the hands of thousands who gathered across the rolling hills of Meath, punched the air. It was easy to forget at that moment, that only a few weeks before, intense efforts were being made to stop the show. The battle to ban Bruce from Slane was a very real one, although in truth it was a struggle of David versus Goliath proportions in which the Slane Village Householders' Association (SHA) was most definitely the little guy. The association had been set up specifically to oppose the concert.

It is probably fair to say they did not know too much about Springsteen himself. Their objections were mainly based on the "malicious damage" resulting from "disturbances" at the Bob Dylan concert at Slane the previous year. That show had taken place on a Sunday and the small Meath village had been over-run the previous night by crowds of drunken yobs.

In the middle of April, Bernard C Angley, from Limerick, wrote a letter to the *Irish Times* which succinctly summed up the debate about Slane. He sympathised with the villagers but felt "their stance on the issue is very unfair and discriminating against young people" who may be "deprived" of seeing Springsteen "in this international youth year". He suggested a compromise with the promoter Jim Aiken to make sure that there were enough facilities on site so that the concert-goers would not need to go into the village and so that "the concert of the year" could continue. Mr Angley's proposals did signal the way forward, although the residents did not know that yet. They pressed ahead with their legal challenge, after a vote at a meeting which SHA spokesman and village chemist Gerald Breen said 70 per cent of the village attended. The villagers he said had been unimpressed by a promise by Lord Mountcharles to "massively increase" the number of security men in the castle grounds and not to hold a concert in 1986. Onlookers reckoned the legal action would cost villagers £2,000 and was unlikely to succeed. Lord Mountcharles and Jim Aiken met with Garda officers in divisional police headquarters in Drogheda and Lord Mountcharles told the *Meath Chronicle* on April 20, 1985, that reading between the lines it was "an extremely high probability" that Springsteen would appear.

Born In The USA
Badlands
Out In The Street
Johnny 99
Atlantic City
The River
Working On The Highway
Trapped
Prove It All Night
Glory Days
The Promised Land
My Hometown
Thunder Road
Cover Me
Dancing In The Dark
Hungry Heart
Cadillac Ranch
Downbound Train
I'm On Fire
Pink Cadillac
Rosalita (Come Out Tonight)
When I Grow Up (To Be A Man)
Born To Run
Bobby Jean
Ramrod
Twist And Shout

To add to the mix, Lord Mountcharles was now receiving telephone calls from a growing group calling itself the Silent Majority who were in favour of the concert. "I am apologising for the hassle that this caused last year and I am asking for the chance to prove it can be done right this year in the best outdoor site," said the peer.

The *Irish Times* did a phone-around and found that local residents and businesspeople were "believed to be nearly equally divided on the issue". The stand-off came to a head during the last week of April. The promoters met with Springsteen's management in New York and signed for the concert to take place on June 1, a Bank Holiday weekend. (Springsteen and the band's estimated earnings from the show were to be £500,000-£600,000, while the promoter was reported to be looking forward to a six-figure payday from an evening expected to gross a cool £1m.)

Tickets went on sale almost immediately and, at the same time, the SHA prepared its papers for its day in court. Then Mr Breen, Lord Mountcharles and Mr Aiken met again. They talked late into the night of April 24, finally coming to an agreement at around 2am the next morning. After the six-hour meeting the SHA had "agreed unanimously" not to oppose the concert, with Jim Aiken promising to make a reported donation of £10,000

MAXPIX

to village charities as a gesture of goodwill and to stay in the village until the end of the concert to act as liaison officer for the villagers.

The offer to charities, it later emerged, was rejected by the association. However, Mr Aiken's long list of concessions also included a ban on camping in the area of the concert; to provide sanitary facilities and extensive first-aid facilities on the site; to employ sufficient numbers of people over four days to "clean the village and surrounding area"; and to replace and repair any damaged community property.

There would be the usual undertaking to follow police requests over traffic and, more unusual but no doubt important, a promise that "elderly people will be given IR£20 per night of the concert weekend to pay for relatives to stay overnight".

The debate over the concert apparently took its toll on the local community. The press officer for the community council, having received numerous anonymous phone calls and under continual pressure from eager journalists, stood down and Lord Mountcharles admitted he had "had it up to my tonsils" with the controversy over the show. "I have worked very hard and so did Jim to put this together. An awful lot of work has gone into it. I have no sense of victory at the moment, none at all."

The build-up to the Slane event was massive. Every second song on the radio was Springsteen and there was lots of coverage in the Press. At that time concerts really meant something in Ireland. It was a major event. It felt like most of the country was gripped by Springsteen-mania and everyone wanted to be part of it. When he was in Slane the weather was brilliant. Myself and three friends sat in Slane and waited for hours and hours before he went on stage. We got badly sunburned. At approx 5pm on Saturday we were suddenly aware that there was 65,000-plus fans in the one place, all there for the same reason as us. I remember a couple close to us had somehow managed to bring in a video camera. It was an absolutely brilliant day; the natural arena was ablaze with colour. I think his songs appeal to Irish people because he sings about issues that affect us all at some stage in our lives and he also comes across as a genuinely nice person.

Alison English, Sligo

I was enjoying a few pints in the Roundwood Inn in County Wicklow with a few friends when in walked Bruce and a big guy friend. They sat up at the bar and started drinking Guinness, trying to ignore people. Being Irish we instantly decided to ignore this superstar in return. "If he thinks I'm going to make a fuss of him, he can forget it", kind of vibe. We continued on ignoring him and enjoying our Guinness, when we notice him in deep conversation with an old farmer we knew, at the bar. Later in the evening the farmer joined us at our table. I asked him, "Do you know who that was that you were talking to?" "Some effing yank," was the reply. On the way out of the pub much later, I bumped into Bruce, and he asked, "Hey, what's the name of your farmer friend? I'll look him up."

Jon Buckley, Wicklow

My best friend from school, Helena Naish, and myself liked American rock music, and it was her idea to go to the gig in Slane. Neither of us had been to a gig before and there was much excitement. We bought our tickets but weren't sure how we were going to travel out to the gig. Then Dublin Bus, or CIE as it was known then, announced that for IR£5 extra you could catch a return bus from Mountjoy Square in Dublin to Slane. As 21-year-olds with no other transport it sounded like a great deal to us. We set off early from home in Beaumont, Dublin. It was bright and sunny and we had an unremarkable journey till we got within a mile of Slane village. The bus came to a stop and it was bumper to bumper all the way. There was a great atmosphere and at various times people would get off the bus and walk alongside for a while, chatting and singing Springsteen songs at the top of their voices. Eventually we got to the village. I remember us walking along the bridge up to the gates of the castle, everybody in a hurry to get a good spot to watch the gig. ⬇

Mr Breen agreed that Jim Aiken "bent over backwards" to placate the objecting villagers, but added: "We have had a mutual victory and we have proved the point that concerts cannot be imposed on us without proper consultation."

Within a couple of days tickets, priced IR£15 and with a maximum of 10 allowed per person, were "selling briskly" but the SHA felt they had won a moral victory. They had certainly made the promoter consider the wishes of the community, and stood up to their principles while as the *Irish Times* reported "accepting no money for allowing (the) Bruce Springsteen concert to go ahead".

One reported condition of the agreement was that the Springsteen show would be the last at Slane. A spokesman for Mr Aiken said that "bar being asked by the local people it's unlikely that we will promote another concert in Slane" and the owner of Slane said "God only knows" what the future holds. "1986 is not under consideration at all at the moment."

Concerts at Slane, of course, would not end with Bruce. David Bowie, Guns 'n' Roses and Madonna were among those to follow in coming years.
The gig settled. The debate ended and the excitement began. Springsteen had been sent a video of the lay-out of

Slane and was said to be "highly impressed". But what would Ireland make of the man described as an "all-American rocker"? Ahead of the show, journalist and fan Joe Breen predicted Springsteen would cope with the scale of Slane. "No matter what the venue or the place his performance will never be anything less than honest.

John Markey

Some concerts will be better than others but the bottom line is that Springsteen, the perfectionist, feels a responsibility to his audience …"

The show was quickly creating a buzz with tickets selling for IR£75 to IR£100 on the black market. Dealing with legitimate demand, Jim Aiken said: "I have never known so much excitement about a single concert."

Two Dublin-based helicopter companies were competing to offer the most luxurious trips to Slane. Aviation Promotion and Dublin City Helicopters combined to do special return trips for

IR£149 while Irish Helicopters Limited was due to fly over 200 people from Dublin to the VIP areas of the venue. However, they were catering more to high-fliers than old fans. A spokesperson for Aviation Promotion said: "The buyers are mostly trend setters getting in on what has been sold as the social event of the summer. I wouldn't say we've sold one ticket to a true Springsteen fan but there's certainly a big demand for the flights." In the United States, Springsteen was pretty busy himself. On May 13, 1985, the man who vowed he would never settle down married model Julianne Phillips in a private midnight ceremony at a lakeside church near Portland, Oregon. Springsteen had met Julianne backstage during a concert in Los Angeles seven months previously.

During the last week of May he recorded the video for the new single "Glory Days" and started pondering over the set lists for 18 shows in Europe at which he would play to a total of almost one million people – starting in Ireland. As the countdown to the show entered the last week, all 60,000 tickets had been sold. Many more had passed hands on the black market and thousands more fans without tickets were getting ready to storm the peaceful green fields around Slane in the hope of getting in to see Bruce.

This massive demand at first must have been music to the ears of both artist and record company – but it was to have a sobering effect on the way Springsteen approached the concert.
He had always been concerned that every member of his audience had the night of their lives – whether it was their first time at a Springsteen show or their 112th. Now events elsewhere would convince him to become concerned for their safety as well.

On Wednesday, May 29, more than 60,000 supporters of Liverpool and Juventus converged on the ageing Heysel stadium in Brussels for the European Cup Final. Shortly before kick-off the atmosphere turned violent and a group of Liverpool fans charged through a thin line of police to attack Juventus supporters. There was a panic and a retaining wall collapsed. Thirty-nine Italian and Belgian fans died and hundreds were injured.

The tragedy unfolded on television screens across Europe and made headlines around the world. The next couple of days' newspapers were packed with photographs of the tragedy and the event was something that Springsteen had in his mind when he arrived in Dublin by Aer Lingus jumbo on the morning of Friday, May 31.

It was a fairly low-key arrival captured by a couple of paparazzi at the airport.

There was a crew tower and a small tree in front of it, and we parked ourselves against it and watched the stage from there. I remember at some point looking back up the hill and being shocked at the number of people that were behind us, it was a huge crowd. Thankfully we didn't get caught up in the surge forward when Bruce and the band came on stage. There was huge audience participation in "Born In The USA", "Dancing In The Dark" and "I'm On Fire". I remember being able to sing along to only a few songs but I thought that Bruce and the band were fantastic. They used the whole stage and spent lots of time running up and down from one side to the other. What a showman.
The Saturday after the Slane gig saw me in town, walking up Talbot Street and by the time I got to O'Connell Street I had bought the entire back-catalogue of Springsteen albums from various vinyl record shops along the way.
I still play all of these albums today. The music sounds as good as it did back then.

Jocelyn Kelly, Dublin

Recent concerts I can remember in great detail. I know what Bruce played nights 1, 2 and 3 in Dublin '08. I know what differences there were between the set lists of *Seeger* Dublin and *Seeger* Belfast. But Slane, in 1985, I remember more as an 'event', a day which set me on a

musical course from which I have never diverted. I was 16 and had never been to an outdoor concert before. That day was a big deal in our household because I was travelling to the show along with my older brother Ciaran and his girlfriend (now wife) Margaret, and with my sister Una and her friend Alison. My mum prepared a good old Ulster Fry breakfast while we played *The River* album from the next room.
I remember the sunshine, I remember the long journey down and I remember the buses. There were rows and rows of buses lined up in car parks. The headlines the next day said there were 100,000 people there and the majority seemed to me to have arrived in buses from the North.
I remember Bruce being anxious about the crowd and the jostling at the front. At one stage me and my sister ventured towards the front and when I looked over my shoulder I was almost overwhelmed by the scale of the crowd behind us. I remember vividly "The River" being played passionately while the River Boyne flashed up on the big screens, and I remember the introduction to "I'm On Fire" and the excitement of "Born To Run".

The concert was a Saturday and on the Monday my O-levels started. How the hell did my mum let me go to the show? First exam up was English language which required students to write an essay from an assorted selection of titles. ⬇

all photos Thomas Quinn

Springsteen wandered through customs with Julianne, walked past two black limousines (which turned out to be for somebody else) and hopped into a yellow van. By 6pm he was at Slane Castle for a sound-check. First he wandered through the tented village next to the River Boyne which had been set up to provide hospitality and changing facilities for the band and guests, then he walked across the field in front of the stage to listen and look from the fan's perspective.

He then took to the stage to play "Born In The USA", "Dancing In The Dark" and what the *Evening Herald* described as a "soulful rendition" of "Danny Boy".

Then, according to the *Evening Herald* and later *Rolling Stone*, in the drawing room of the castle, Springsteen jammed with Debbie Harry, Pete Townshend and Eric Clapton.

In a rare interview in 2004, Lord Mountcharles told *Hot Press* that Springsteen played a full set which was all about overcoming pre-show nerves.

"Everyone reacts very differently when they're going to go on stage, because I mean it is a hell of a thing," said the castle owner. "Slane is a very dramatic place to play. When you go out on that stage, it's just a massive audience.

"For example, Springsteen was actually rather freaked when he went out ... Yet, the night before ... He was so intent on putting on a stunning performance – which he did, an absolutely stunning performance – that he actually did the entire set the night before in the castle.

There were only six of us watching so it was rather special."

Springsteen arrived back in his hotel, the Gresham, in Dublin, in the early hours of Saturday.

He got up late the next day, had a late lunch and travelled with Julianne by helicopter back to Slane.

At the castle, it was said, his demands, unlike Dylan and the Stones before him, were simple: a small functional dressing room by the banks of the Boyne and a few minutes for him and Julianne to take a stroll and enjoy the scenery.

A few minutes of peace and tranquillity before a roar that would be heard across the countryside. Outside the venue village residents had been given special passes to get through the roadblocks surrounding the area. Farmers were turning fields into car parks and charging accordingly. Hundreds of Gardai were on the streets.

The Garda's advice to fans to stay away from Slane until the gates of the castle opened at 3pm was largely ignored. Many, included a large number from Northern Ireland, had arrived in Slane on the Friday, around the same time as buses of Gardai appeared to set up base in a parochial hall and an old technical school. The country village they arrived in had shut up shop. Many windows on the main street had been boarded up; some people had even removed plants from front gardens.

Mike Saunders

Jim Page

Mike Saunders

Jim Page

Jim Page

Dave Percival

On the Friday night many fans bedded down in sleeping bags on the grass, and there were more than a few who would have a restless night worrying whether they would get a ticket. There were warnings against forgeries with a number of forged tickets being discovered in Birmingham, England, on the Friday. Three hours before the show was due to begin, 4,000 extra tickets went on sale and were snapped up by eager fans. The police later put the crowd in six figures.

Joe Breen described the hullabaloo in *Rolling Stone*, noting that the huge demand for tickets rested not on Springsteen's previous six albums but on the success of the singles "Dancing In The Dark" and "Born In The USA". The album *Born In The USA* had become a phenomenon, even the fact that the sentiments of its title song were largely misunderstood made it a talking point. Springsteen was a man in the news as well as the entertainment pages. "Newspapers and TV and radio stations from all over Europe had been pumping out Springsteen bios all week, while their reporters scurried about to find some fresh angles on New Jersey's most famous son," wrote Breen.

Away from the throng, the VIPs, the "champagne set" mingled outside the castle. They were 800-strong, and included Pete Townsend, Eric Clapton, Spandau Ballet (who had been flown in on a giant Sikorsky helicopter), Seamus Healy, Springsteen's friend Elvis Costello, a former Lord Mayor of Dublin, Michael Keating, politicians Dick Burke, Monica Barnes and Liam Skelly, the young Haugheys, 200 VIP pass holders from RTÉ and, of course, members of Lord Mountcharles' family. There were rumours that David Bowie was there too.

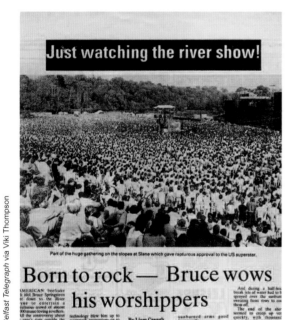

Belfast Telegraph via Viki Thompson

Fifty personal guests of Springsteen and his wife were fêted in a nearby tent before his performance. Slane buzzed like an army base all afternoon as choppers brought in VIPs with tickets for the social event of the summer and finally the band.

One of the titles on offer was 'The Music Makers' and that was when I wrote my first music article. I would love to get a hold of that paper now to read it again. I passed the exam anyway, so thanks Bruce!

Brendan Mulgrew, Belfast

We travelled down in a minibus, maybe a group of 10 of us, all fans to a greater or lesser degree but only I had seen Bruce before. I had been to a 1981 *River* show, when myself and good friends Rab McConaghy and Willie Ireland travelled over to Birmingham. The memories of Slane are of huge crowds and sunshine and a long journey home after the biggest gig ever in Ireland.

We sat on the slope at the castle side and had a great view even if it was more big screen than stage that we watched. I remember stories of people breaking through gates and holes in hedges. We could see people trying to access backstage by paddling and swimming across the river. The crowd seemed to grow all day and once Bruce was on stage there was no "floor" visible. On the way out, we just climbed over ditches and through hedges and fences. There were no organised exits. Bruce was overawed by the size of the crowd.

Highlights for me were the long story about the Garden of Eden before "Pink Cadillac", and the almost solo performance of "When I Grow Up (To Be A Man)" and sensing that it was some kind of personal statement by Bruce, now a married man. A great day, like summers as a child all the bad bits are lost in the telling and it was all sun and songs, but since then everyone you speak to claims to have been there, and while the crowd was big I really don't think everyone between the ages of 17 and 50 really made it into the Slane amphitheatre that day.

Nigel Flynn, Ballymoney

AMERICAN DREAM

When I was 14 years old my mother Kathleen (RIP, one of the "Souls Of The Departed") bought me a radio which picked up Radio Luxemburg. This radio was to change my life in many ways! When I heard it blasting out the story of Spanish Johnny driving in from the Underworld, every bone in my body shook with astonishment and longing for more of this music.

I called the radio station and asked them about the song and the guy singing it. The DJ was taken aback that a 14-year-old kid had called in about this. He sent me all this stuff on Bruce Springsteen. That was 30 years ago and I have had the pleasure to have seen Bruce more than 100 times. Music and a couple of American TV shows were my escape from everything, if I did not have a football at my feet. I was so enthralled with Bruce's music and the freedom he spoke of that I wanted to see this 'promised land', so I made up my mind to make my way to America! ⬇

According to Springsteen biographer Dave Marsh: "Slane was the place to be that Saturday, whether you were a big Springsteen fan or not."

When Springsteen bounded on stage at 5pm he was a different man from the thin-bodied, pale-faced rock 'n' roller of *The River* tour three years earlier. He was muscular and gym-toned in his jeans and maroon and white striped polo shirt. Cathal Dervan described in the *Meath Chronicle*: "Grown women and some men cried, swooned and fainted as the Boss appeared in t-shirt and jeans. For some the excitement was just too much and they were carried away by the ambulancemen to the great rock and roll hospitals."

"Born In The USA" opened the 80-minute first set with the band then driving headlong into *"Badlands"* and *"Out In The Street"*, and Bruce finished his song of friendship with "Hello, it is nice to be in Ireland."
He had also already been spooked by the crush at the front. According to Dave Marsh, even before the show started the hundreds who jostled close to the stage "included dozens of drunks whose enthusiasm was expressed primarily by shoving forward; on the fringes, but within Bruce's view. Some got into fistfights." This wasn't what a Springsteen show was about. "How could you sing about self-respect

Irish Times

18

before an audience that threatened to become a mob? How did you re-adjust their focus and get them to listen?"

Thomas Quinn

Maybe Bruce was over-reacting (after all there would be no serious injuries and, as Pete Townshend was heard to say, "It's always like this when you play outdoors") but three songs in he looked down anxiously at the first few rows, where the fans were packed together against the barrier and were being pushed by the waves of momentum coming down through the crowd.

I grew up in Coalisland, County Tyrone, where it was the IRA or the highway. I had three older brothers, Damien, Nick and Thaddeus, an older sister, Siobhan, a younger sister, Lorrainne, and a younger brother, David. We were all two years apart in age so we listened to the same music. When I was 17, I came home from school and said, 'This is not happening for me. I am out of here. I am going to America and that's that!' I broke my mother's heart.

It was 1982. I knew the States from *The Dukes Of Hazzard*, all that American freedom and racing cars and, of course, the music of Bruce Springsteen. My friend, Davy Curran, and I made our way there. I started bartending in this country music bar when I was not even 18-years-old, right in the thick of Manhattan. One day, I noticed this girl pull up in a Corvette convertible. She came in the bar and, man, she was a lovely looking blonde. It was just like "Racing In The Street"! Next thing I saw the Jersey registration plate. "This is unreal," I said to her. "Where do you live?" "Jersey, baby!"

I said, "Jersey! I have always wanted to go over there."

"What time do you get off work?"

"4 am," I said. "But let me ask the other guy."

I went over to the cool guy running the bar. His name was Malachy Smyth, from Belfast. I asked him if I could get away early.

He took one look at this hot blonde and her awesome car and said, "Get out of here, kid, and enjoy yourself."

"Do you wanna drive, babe?" she asked when we were at her car.

"Maybe in a little while," I said. "But would you mind if I picked something up from my apartment first?"

I got my four track cassette tape, I think it was *Greetings From Asbury Park*. She laughed and said, "Where to?"

"Take me to where Bruce comes from," I said. "Jersey!"

I remember going over the bridge and putting in that tape. I had never felt freedom like that. Pure magic.

Iggy Hughes, New York (formerly of County Tyrone)

It all started for me in 1984 when I met my future husband John. He was a massive fan of Bruce Springsteen since 1979. I had never heard of him. The *Born In The USA* album was constantly played in the car.

When the Slane concert was announced I wasn't interested. On the day the tickets went on sale John phoned me at my work and said: 'Last chance, do you want a ticket or not?' There was a spare seat in the car as John was travelling with his mates, Martin and Neil. I said, 'Okay, it will be a day out.'

Finally, the day of the concert arrived. We couldn't believe the sky was blue: it was to be the warmest day of the year.

We left Donegal with Bruce playing all the way. The traffic was bumper to bumper for miles on the approach to the village; there were cars, coaches, mini-buses and motorbikes parked everywhere. ⬇

"What you got to do down here, if you can, is push back a little bit from barriers so the people that are crushed up against the barriers don't hurt themselves," he said nervously. "Make sure everybody is back up on their feet there and if you can try and stay in one place. If anybody needs help to get out of there raise your hand and somebody will pull you out."

He paused as security tried to help some people at the front who had been overcome by heat or had become tired and emotional from partaking of refreshment. "What you got to do is stop that swaying back and forth because it is knocking people down." Then, as the sun continued to blaze down, he played "Johnny 99" and "Atlantic City", two songs from his acoustic, folk *Nebraska* album which, taking inspiration from Woody Guthrie and Flannery O'Connor, seemed a world away from the lush lawns of a castle.

Next up was one of the highlights of the show. "When I was a kid my old man used to sit in the kitchen and late at night he'd lock up the front door so you could not come in," he said, laughing self-consciously at the memory. "We would have to come in the back porch and some nights if you were coming in too late you were better off waiting 'til morning …"

all photos Thomas Quinn

The crowd may have been stretching back beyond the horizon but Springsteen was determined to use the intimacy of his story to create a connection. "I used to have a sleeping bag I used to stash out on the side of these woods and sleep in somebody's car or somebody's porch. I guess those places felt more like my own home than my own house. This is for everybody who needs some place to go when you can't go home."

Springsteen's mournful harmonica rang out the opening bars of "The River". It's a painful tale of love and longing but here in the sunshine of an Irish bank holiday it was given a new twist as the huge video screens each side of the stage flickered with images of the Boyne. It was a moment which would remain in the minds of many fans for years afterwards. And this footage of the Boyne would be used during the song throughout the rest of the tour.

"Working On The Highway" then picked up the pace before Bruce played Jimmy Cliff's "Trapped", a song from the *USA For Africa* album, which had already become a favourite with fans, and "Prove It All Night". Going back to a concert classic from the days before the real big-time seemed to put Bruce well at ease.

"Are you alright out there?" he asked the audience before starting the next song. This time it was a fun question, his tone had lightened a little.

"*Yeess*," came the reply. "Are you sure?" He smiled. "Alright. This is a song about old times. It's sentimental. It's kind of nostalgic. Now, I got my share of old times. But now the big man, Clarence, he's got quite a few more old times than me. But as you can see he has maintained his youthful beauty."

A huge cheer rose from the crowd. "Every time you go out on a Friday night there is always someone who comes up to you and says, 'Hey remember me? We went to high school together. Back in high school – remember the guy who dumped the pizza on your shirt in study hall? Yeah, that's me! Ahh, how you doing?' Everybody tells you what a great time you had in high school and stuff … I hated high school! I could not stand no high school. I mean I DIDN'T LIKE IT! Every time eight o'clock comes at night I'm *still* glad I don't have to do my homework. At high school I was only interested in two things: one was playing guitar, the other was ... was … ah, was … you know that one. Anyway the only one I became really good at was the guitar. The other one I am still practising, practising, practising. This is a song about time's winged chariot, Father Time and how all things must pass …" Springsteen turned to Clarence: "Are you ready, Big Man? ..." … And into "Glory Days".

Springsteen, 35 and already obsessed with the passage of time, ended the song with a plea to the crowd, "Don't let me down now.

On our way down to the castle we were greeted with a sea of stalls selling Bruce merchandise, including t-shirts, bandanas, American flags, etc, and there were fast food stalls everywhere.

When we got to the venue we made our way up close to the stage. When Bruce came on at 5pm, there was a massive surge of people, pushing and shoving. During the concert the security staff were very busy hosing the crowd down with water and taking out people who had fainted from the heat and the crush. We made our way up as close as we could get, but moved back as it was very rowdy. One memorable moment was during "The River" when the big screens showed a picturesque River Boyne. At that stage we looked behind us at the crowd on the hill, over 80,000 people. It was an awesome sight, one I will never forget. Bruce and the E Street Band were fabulous.

Bruce was 'King of The Castle' for that day. I was definitely hooked.

Tina Gill, Quigley's Point, County Donegal

I am a big fan of Bruce. I first saw him in Slane. I thought he might dance with me as he sung "Dancing In The Dark". I believed it then and believe it now … It's going to be!

**Liz O'Céannubháin
of Lavey, near Magherafelt**

I first saw Bruce live in Slane Castle in 1985. I was so gripped by his music and stage presence that I promised myself if he ever played in Ireland again that I would have to go to see his shows. True to my promise I've been lucky enough to have seen every show he has played in Ireland and needless to say it has been a memorable journey.

Bruce is a true legend and his music and lyrics touch so many people's lives and he puts so much energy and passion into his live shows it's a spine-tingling experience for me. I went to Slane not knowing anything of Bruce except his classic song "The River". I had no trouble getting a ticket it was included with the bus trip for only IR£22 pounds, what a bargain. My biggest problem was getting the day off for the concert as I was working as an apprentice butcher and the concert was on a Saturday, our busiest day. But, thank god, I persuaded the boss to let me go to see the real Boss.

I didn't know what to expect but, boy, what a show we were lucky enough to witness. The moment Bruce came out on stage and opened with "Born In The USA" I was converted to becoming a Bruce tramp.

He played with such heart and passion he just blew the crowd away. He also donated £10,000 to the Simon Community in Dublin as he always made a donation to a charity in every country he played on the *Born In The USA* tour. What an ambassador for the poor as well as a rock and roll legend!

We travelled most of the night to get back to my hometown and finally got back at eight in the morning but I didn't mind as I was on a high for days after my first Bruce gig.

John Flannery, Ballymote, County Sligo

"IF I WERE YOU, I WOULDN'T START FROM HERE"

It took weeks of meticulous organisation to get our group together. A few of us met up in London on May 30 and then met up with the rest at Coventry, Birmingham and Liverpool. We were Mike, Dan, Mick, Neil, Tony (number 1), Robin, Tony (number 2), Dave, Denise, Jim, Jeff, Kev, Marge, Catharine and Janice. We were Bruce's Fabulous Fifteen Fanatics.

We divided ourselves up into a car and a 12-seater yellow minibus festooned with "I'm A Rocker" stickers. This was to be our mobile home for the next seven days and for the 1,000 miles to Dublin and back.

Taking the 2.45 ferry, we drove onto Irish soil around 6.30. Feeling confident with three different maps of Dublin, we set off in search of our pre-booked guest houses.

That evening, we carried out several sneak attacks on local newsagents, stripping the shelves of anything featuring Bruce. In those bygone days of megastardom and total media overkill, he was everywhere, and it was a full-time team effort to check every music paper, national paper, local paper and magazine. Having agreed on an early start, we piled into the minibus at 4.30am on what was now Saturday, June 1, Dave's birthday, and set off in search of a 24-hour petrol station. By now, getting lost in Dublin was inevitable and all part of the fun. As we crossed the Liffey for the umpteenth time, we switched on the radio in time to hear "Trapped" (from the *We Are The World* album) blasting out.

While filling up, we decided to ask the taxi driver next to us for the directions to Slane. "Well, the quickest way is to go up to those lights and turn right," he began. "The only problem is you can't turn right there, cos you'll end up in the harbour."

Legend has it that he also said, "If I were you, I wouldn't start from here," but we can never be sure.

As the outskirts of the city gave way to the fields and farms, it was hard to imagine that a vast rock concert could be taking place in such tranquil surroundings. The only indications that this was not an elaborate hoax were the occasional yellow A4 signs fixed to trees which read, 'Bruce Springsteen Concert'. Naturally, we took one.

After around 20 miles, we encountered a police checkpoint. We passed over our tickets to an officer for inspection. "Sorry, lads," he said, poker-faced, "these are forgeries." We had a collective heart attack before, with natural comic timing, he continued, "Only joking. Enjoy the show!" Breathing a giant sigh of relief, we drove on before he changed his mind.

Two miles from Slane, a second checkpoint and the end of the road as far as concert traffic was concerned. Farmers were allowing the surrounding fields to be used as car parks, charging £2 a vehicle. We pulled off the road. It was still only 6am.

We walked slowly up the valley into the village. It was then we discovered that we were not quite the first to arrive. A number of fans, traders and experienced boozers had turned up the night before. ⬇

I can see that big clock ticking every minute of every day … No matter how old you get you keep on searching." The end of "Glory Days" set up perfectly "The Promised Land".

Despite the vast size of the Slane crowd, Springsteen still spoke to them as if they were one person, as if he was back in a club in New York City or Boston, and as he introduced the next song he again began to describe something of himself.

"I grew up in a little town, it's kind of small-minded," he said. "I guess everybody kinda has a love-hate relationship sometimes with the place they were born in. I know when I was 17 I couldn't wait to get out of there and I was sure when I left I'd never miss it. I wouldn't miss the friends I had there and the folks. I would never want to go back.

"So I got a chance to go out on the road and for a long time I really didn't miss it, but then as I got older I started to come home and get my car and drive back through the streets I grew up on and see what my old friends' lives were like.

"And I guess one of the things I was afraid of when I was younger was of belonging to something. Because if you belong to something that means you have got some responsibility towards it. I guess it is hard to find some place to call your home very easily. Anyway this is from my hometown to your hometown …"

all photos Thomas Quinn

Dave Marsh suggests that as Bruce spoke he believed he was not being listened to (he left out mention of the Simon Community, the homeless organisation in Dublin which he was supporting) because of the continuing jostling at the front. "(But) those who sat well back in the crowd experienced no problem," wrote Marsh. "The problem only existed where Bruce would be most aware of it."

Springsteen moved from "My Hometown" into the absolute fans' favourite, "Thunder Road", and at the song's wonderful play-out, Springsteen found himself (as was customary) in Clarence's arms.

The first set down, Springsteen had already won over the crowd and an army of new Irish fans.

The second set opened with two of the *Born In The USA* tracks which had been filling the airwaves in the lead up to the concert, "Cover Me" and Dancing In The Dark" (during which Patti Scialfa was his dancing partner), followed by the sing-a-long of "Hungry Heart" (including a brief dance with someone from the crowd) and the high jinx of "Cadillac Ranch" and the minor key pathos of "Downbound Train".

Introducing another number from *Born In The USA* Springsteen muttered, "I remember my dad was sitting around thinking about everything he wasn't ever going to have. He gets you thinking like that too. I can remember standing down on the corner watching the girls and the cars go by waiting for one of them to stop …" The guitars picked up the smouldering, desire-laden opening bars of "I'm On Fire".

Then, more tomfoolery to introduce "Pink Cadillac", a variation on a piece of cod-evangelist spiel which would become central to the *Born In The USA* shows – even in Ireland, Europe and Japan where few had any experience of television evangelism. Springsteen had studied Reverend Jimmy Lee Swaggart, of Louisiana, enough to produce a perfect impression, at once ridiculous, comic and almost insightful. "Well, now, this is a song about the conflict between worldly things and spiritual health," Springsteen blustered. "Between desires of the flesh and spiritual ecstasy.

"This is a song about temptation. Now, where did this conflict begin? Well, it began in the beginning in a place called the Garden of Eden. That's right, and the Garden of Eden was originally believed to have been located in Mesopotamia. "But the latest theological studies have found out that its actual location was 10 miles south of Jersey City, off the New Jersey Turnpike. That's right.

"But now, understand, in the Garden of Eden there was none of the accoutrements of modern living. They did not have no TV.

The results of this all-night session were all around us – lifeless bodies huddled in sleeping bags at the side of the road or laid out on garden walls.

We followed the stone perimeter wall of the castle grounds to the main entrance of the concert site, joined a small group of others at the front of the queue and sat down. It was now 7am, a mere eight hours before the gate was due to open.

As the morning ticked slowly by, the sun rose in a cloudless sky and the crowd grew larger, queuing peacefully three or four deep either side of the entrance and down the road in both directions for as far as the eye could see. Some of our group passed the time by playing Boss-opoly, a specially-adapted form of Monopoly featuring place names like E Street, Thunder Road, Mansion On The Hill, My Father's House and Tenth Avenue, and using alternative banknotes with Bruce's face on them.

Now and again, small groups of us walked off to investigate the army of unofficial merchandise stalls. We counted up to 40 different designs of t-shirt alone! While chatting to one programme seller, we jokingly questioned the authenticity of his obviously home-made produce. "That's not official," we said. "Isn't it?" he replied, appearing genuinely surprised. We bought one anyway, just for posterity, because printed on the front cover were the immortal words 'Bruce Springsteen, Slane Castle 1*th* June 1985'. Because of this we will always remember Slane as the Firth o' June.

Around 12 o'clock, some frenzied activity at the front signalled that the tarpaulin

sheet at the gate was about to be opened three hours early.

Once we were inside, a breathtaking panorama opened up before us. From the entrance, the vast cow pasture which formed the concert venue sloped steeply, then more gently down to the River Boyne, flowing peacefully across the site in the middle distance. At the bottom of the hill, backing onto the river, stood the giant stage, flanked on either side by massive PA stacks and video screens. Trees bordered the area and covered the slopes of the opposite bank. To the right, dominating the scene, stood the castle.

It was a truly beautiful setting, and the weather was perfect. Pausing momentarily to take it all in, we ran down the hill as U2's "Pride" played over the PA. Fearing a crush at the very front, we based ourselves directly in front of the mixing tower, itself a multi-storey building which could have housed several families. Accommodating the sound desk, spotlights and a video cameraman, it was connected to the stage by a long umbilical cord of wires, slung high above the crowd. The stage itself was multi-levelled and had no backdrop, enabling us to see across the river. Catwalks extended out at either side for Bruce to run along, and extra sets of back-up speakers had been positioned at intervals further up the hill. Various official merchandise stalls, food and drink vendors, toilet blocks and first aid posts hugged the perimeter.

Soon, the site was a colourful mass of humanity, packed with fans from the stage right back up the hill to the road, with barely a blade of grass visible. ⬇

You could not go home and crawl up in your little bed and put your head on that little pillow and put on the television and watch it all night long.

"They did not have no hamburgers. You couldn't go on to the highway and buy a cheeseburger if you wanted one. They didn't have none of that shepherd's pie – no, sir, in the Garden of Eden there was no sin. There was no sex. Man lived in a state of innocence.

"But, now, when it comes to no sex, I prefer the state of guilt that I come from.

"But just before the tour I decided to hitchhike out to the location of the Garden of Eden to find out the answer to some of these mysteries. And so I got on out there. And that place is now occupied by Happy Dan's Celebrity Used Car Lot.

"I walked in. The man said to me 'Son, you need [*rapid fire sales pitch*] a-yellow-convertible, a-four-door-DeVille, Continental-spare, wide-chrome-wheels, air-conditioned,automatic-heat-and-a fold-out-bed-in-your-back-seat, eight-track-tape-deck-TV and a phone so you can speak to your baby when you are driving all alone …'

"I said: 'I'll take two.'

"And I said, 'But, Dan, that's not the reason why I came. You see I want to know the answer to this temptation. Why does my soul pull me one way and my flesh pull me the other? Why do I feel this guilt all the time?'

"And he said, 'Son, well that's easy, because right here on these 10 beautiful commercially-zoned acres was the sweetest little paradise that man had ever seen. In the Garden of Eden there were many wondrous things. There was a tree of life, there was a tree of knowledge of good and evil. There was a man Adam, there was a woman Eve, and she looked so fine. And when Adam kissed her it was the first time that a man had ever kissed a woman. And she had legs that were long and soft to the touch.

Thomas Quinn

And when Adam touched her it was the first time a man had ever touched a woman. And then they walked out into the green fields and then they laid down and when Adam … [*knowingly*] let's just say it was the first time.'" The preacher's voice rose, filled with fire and brimstone. "'But there was something else in the Garden of Eden on that day! Old Satan came slithering up on his belly and somehow he turned their sweet love into a betrayal and sent them driving down into the darkness below.

It was an amazing sight, at once both exciting and overwhelming. At 4pm, Jim Aiken announced that Bruce would be on stage at five. This proved to be the signal for the dream to turn into a nightmare. The natural slope of the site, combined with the inevitable human desire to move closer, soon resulted in a dangerous crush at the front. When Bruce hit the stage at five o'clock, thousands more surged forward, increasing the pressure and causing a steady stream of limp bodies to be pulled over the barrier.
Standing in front of the mixing tower, we were spared the pressure from behind and could maintain our position without being carried forward into the mob.
At one point, Jon Landau appeared at one side looking concerned, while Bruce himself asked the crowd to move back on a couple of occasions, his requests falling on deaf ears.
There was actually very little the security staff could do to reduce the crush, beyond training hosepipes on the crowd to combat the effects of the searing heat. At one point, there were so many water droplets in the air that a mini-rainbow formed above our heads.
The show passed by in a blur. The song selection was fairly typical of the latter stages of the *Born In The USA* tour, consisting mostly of material from *Born In The USA*, *The River* and *Darkness On The Edge Of Town*, plus regular non-album inclusions like "Trapped", "Pink Cadillac" and the closing medley of "Twist And Shout/Do You Love Me"? Essentially no surprises except, that, is for Bruce's choice of first encore, a solo electric version of "When I Grow Up (To Be A Man)".

Throughout the show, Bruce sweated a lot, ran out along the catwalks several times, sang with Patti, kissed Clarence, danced with a girl from the audience, turned his baseball cap back to front and walked to the back of the stage to wave at the fans perched in the trees on the other side of the river, watching the show for free.
Having been used to seeing the E Street Band dressed in dark suits on the *The River* tour, it was a stark contrast to see them wearing brightly-coloured shirts for maximum noticeability. The sight of Roy Bittan actually dancing lingers in the mind, as does Nils Lofgren's huge styrofoam stetson (worn during "Cadillac Ranch"), and the use of a panoramic view of the Boyne flowing into the distance during – what else – "The River".
As the final strains of "Twist And Shout" died away, the massive crowd began to disperse and we regrouped to count our bruises. Deciding to rest and relax until the majority of the fans had gone, we were able to witness the aftermath of the front-stage chaos. The ground was a sea of rubbish – paper, discarded clothes and thousands of empty plastic bottles.
Around 9.30pm, as the sun set behind the castle and the evening chill set in we began to make our way back, dragging our sunburnt skin and aching bones up the hill with considerably less energy and enthusiasm than we'd had when running down some nine hours earlier. ⬇

"'But that's alright [*the full evangelist ready for saving souls*] because right here today on this back lot for 99.95 and no money down, and don't worry if you got bad credit it's good here, I've got the keys to the getaway car … And if you've got the nerve to ride, I've got the first Pink Cadillac …'" From "Pink Cadillac" into the song of the youthful Springsteen, the young singer-songwriter from the early '70s with a new record deal in one hand and a band of friends from the Jersey shore following behind him: "Rosalita (Come Out Tonight)".

The song had ended concerts for a decade and was the moment Springsteen introduced the band. Midway through a 12-minute version of the song, he said: "Alright, ladies and gentleman, and all you Irish people out there, it is now my honour, my responsi-bility, my duty, and if I don't do it they'll be real pissed off … On the piano, Professor Roy Bittan. Next an alumni of Southside Johnny and The Asbury Jukes, on the vocals, Ms Patti Scialfa. On the drums, the man who puts the beat that gets you moving your feet and out of your seat, the mighty Max Weinberg. On the organ, Phantom Dan Federici. On the bass guitar, the man with the thunder from down under, Mr Garry W Tallent. And on the guitar, Mr Nils Lofgren. And last but not least, the king of the world, the emperor of the universe, the master of disaster, in this corner, coming in at 265lbs, the most handsome and the biggest man you've ever seen, 'Big Man' Clarence Clemons on the saxophone."

After closing the second set with the wild dance of "Rosalita", more concerns for the crowd. "Wherever you are, don't hurt yourself. Come on out of there! Thank you, everybody."
The band disappeared, but this would not be a Springsteen concert without a blistering encore which went on until the fans *could not take it no more.*
The Slane encore began on a reflective note, with Springsteen's voice cracking with emotion. After all, the concert struck Springsteen on a gut level for three reasons.
It was his first show in Ireland, the land of so many of his father's ancestors. It was the show at which he left behind a part of himself. He had now stepped completely into the full glare of celebrity, right into that darkness on the edge of town, where you left behind that bit of yourself which was part of the community and became everybody's property, *the superstar.*
And, thirdly, it was his first concert since his marriage to Julianne. Bruce started his encore with the usual thanks but what was to follow was a song he had never performed before, and has not performed since. It was special to Slane because it encapsulated all the reasons for which the show was a milestone for Springsteen.
"I'd just like to take a minute to thank everybody for coming down to the show today," he said.
"Thanks so much. This is the first time we have been in Ireland. I had a grandmother from here, McNicholas, and I don't know how to thank you. This is, I guess, the biggest crowd we have ever played to." A huge, long cheer. "There sure is a lot of you! You guys got to be a little gentler with each other down there. Well, I have been thinking a lot of different things standing here today. I guess this song kinda sums it up."
And with that he launched into a virtually solo version of "When I Grow Up (To Be A Man)" by The Beach Boys, another song about the passing of time and about understanding what it means to be an adult. Springsteen has spoken about trying to deal with growing up in a rock 'n' roll world, a life which extends adolescence and retards maturity. This was the rock star declaring here, in front of the world, he had come of age. It was a moment in which Springsteen appeared vulnerable, laying himself open before so many, so much so that according to Dave Marsh when it was finished he turned to the band "with a look almost of supplication, and in the next few minutes you could see what they were really worth to one another". Springsteen shouted for "Ramrod" and

then tore into "Born To Run", the Fender and sax echoing across the countryside.

"I can see that lovely sun is sinking low, that must mean it must be time to go," Springsteen joked afterwards, half singing to himself. The crowd shouted "NO!"

"But I feel like I am just getting warmed up … so …" And the E Street Band struck up "Twist And Shout/Do You Love Me?" – Springsteen's extra long version, a series of crowd sing-a-longs and false endings which transformed a three-minute pop song into a ten-minute epic.

"I'm not here looking for any romance," said Springsteen, with Julianne in the wings. "I want you to take this last chance – cos all I want to do is dance now …" and off the band went again.

The sun was finally disappearing.

"How're the people way back up there on the hill now? You guys alright over there?" The band played on …

"How about you guys way back there?" And on.

Bruce studied the guys at the front. "How's the people down here on the dance floor? Did you survive, *that* is the question?"

He turned to Clarence Clemons, his main foil.

"Big Man, how you feeling man?"

"I'm feeling groovy," Clarence replied.

"Is the Big Man alright?"

"I'm alright!"

"If the Big Man's alright then we can continue!"

Another verse before Springsteen turned to the crowd again.

"Before I go there's one thing that I gotta know," he giggled. "There's one question that I need an answer to. We flew all the way over here, over the ocean, it was a long flight! There's one question I need an answer to … What I wanna know is, the only thing I need to know is … what I really want to know is … what I came all the way over here to find out is, I mean what I came to Ireland to see is … DO YOU LOVE ME?" And finally one last chorus: "Don't make me do it! Don't make me hurt you now! I'm warning you I'll do it. That's the kind of guy I am."

And then the connection with what had gone before, Springsteen's call that had ended shows since, well, who could remember when? "I'm just a prisoner ... *of rock and roll*!"

Springsteen and the band had pulled it off. "Thank you," he shouted from the stage. "Happy birthday, happy Halloween, happy the rest of your life. God bless you. Thank you, Ireland. We love you. Have a safe trip home. Thank you."

It was all over. Springsteen and the E Street Band rushed from the stage. The band attended a dinner at the castle but Springsteen and his manager Jon Landau got the first helicopter back to Dublin.

The road was a solid mass of bobbing heads disappearing into the distance like the start of the London marathon.

We made it back to the guest house by around 2am after a shattering 22-hour day. Heads hit pillows and sleep came almost immediately.

The next day we reluctantly boarded the ferry at Rosslare and went up on deck to watch the coast of Ireland disappearing slowly into the sunset. Although we'd only been in the country for two days, we'd definitely got the bug, and had fallen in love with the people, their unfussed approach to life, their hospitality, generosity, unique sense of humour and illogical logic.

The Guinness wasn't bad, either.

Vowing to return one day, we sailed off into the night, on our way to Bruce's two shows in Newcastle, but that's another story.

Mike Saunders
(with Dan French and Linda Gilder)
Hove, England

Landau recalled: "I wouldn't say Bruce had a good time, but he was not feeling bad when the show was over. We had stuff to talk about, you know … "We got the wildest crowd in the first 15 minutes of the tour. And the frightening thing was not what was happening here, but is it gonna be like this every night? Am I gonna have to go through six weeks of that, because that would have been a little difficult." Springsteen left the stage at 8.30pm and was quickly back in his Dublin hotel suite eating his evening meal.

Springsteen had had his last word from the Slane stage. "Thank you, Ireland." But there was so much more to say about that long summer's evening at Slane. The *Meath Chronicle*'s Eamonn Holmes wrote a colour piece, describing how, "Love stories began in Slane as the sun shone and Bruce Springsteen played his heart out.
"As the roads outside the site filled up the carnival atmosphere increased. Everyone was out to have a good time … Two lads who had 'borrowed' the Kodak girl from a local chemist and christened her Agnes were offering to buy a t-shirt for her but were anxious to learn her size.
"There was no trouble during the concert, some of the stewards who were guarding the towers holding the auxiliary speakers were enjoying themselves just as much as the paying customers.

For anyone who has been at concerts before it was good to see them having fun rather than scowling and making others sit down or stand up or whatever. "Indeed two nearby were having such a good time that their supervisor came over to tell them to cool it."

So, in places, Slane looked like Woodstock. Springsteen, worried about the crush at the front and concerned that he would fail to connect with and control the audience in the way he did in smaller venues, had replaced some of his quest for intimacy with a high-energy and hard-rocking performance. Holmes' colleague Cathal Dervan described the gig as the "most energetic, charismatic and brilliant stage show yet seen in this country" and picked out "The River" – as many fans would – as a highlight.

The *Sunday Independent*'s headline claimed "Springsteen's fire lights up the hill".

Joe Breen, one of a minority in the audience who had seen Bruce prior to the *Born In The USA* hype, hinted at the limitations inherent in playing to such a huge crowd, but was blown away all the same: "Against a backdrop of lavish praise and high expectations Bruce Springsteen justified his reputation on Saturday with a performance that, while restricted in its emotional range, was never less than powerful and convincing." He said the band would

surely get better and better as the European leg of the tour progressed, but the show would "go down in memory as the finest at the venue".

All Springsteen fans have views on which setting they prefer: the large or the small venue. Stadiums might feel like an event, but clubs and theatres have an intimacy which is just as memorable. Breen said of Slane: "In front of 65,000 people in the broad daylight of the open air (intimacy) is just not possible. The added distractions of the sound delay and the video screens do not help either, though the clever use of the video cameras and the excellence of the sound were essential to the overall success of the concert. "Basically by playing such huge venues, Springsteen had to sacrifice one of the most important elements of his live performance – total contact with and control of his audience.

"In compensation he rocks a lot harder and the show adopts a much more 'up' profile." He concluded: "Anybody who still believes Bruce Springsteen and the E Street Band are rock 'n' roll hype should think again. They are the real thing."

The real thing, and no trouble. Slane villager Gerald Breen, who had led the initial opposition noted that "sunshine and Springsteen go together" to make a success. Chief Superintendent Michael Bohan said the good behaviour

of the crowd "showed to the world that the Irish can organise a rock concert which can accommodate thousands of fans without incident."

From the estimated crowd of 100,000, the police made only a few arrests (mainly for touting or minor drug offences), noting only two cases of malicious damage to parked cars and some minor thefts, and despite the amount of people noted to have been unsteady on their feet only three people were arrested for drunkenness. Over at the first aid tent, 100 members of the St John Ambulance Brigade had dealt with 400 people. Most had been sunburnt, others had cuts and bruises, and 35 were serious enough to be taken to hospital.

And so despite the legal battle and fears which preceeded the concert the *Meath Chronicle* was able to report that Slane was "sure to rock again" following the incident-free Bruce Springsteen concert.

Leslie Horgan reported: "More than 100,000 people crowded into the natural amphitheatre and Gardai, promoters and the erstwhile objectors were more than pleased with how peacefully the event went off ..."

Jim Aiken donated £5,000 to the local Tidy Town Committee and a similar sum to the Mount Argus Dublin restoration fund in recognition of the services rendered by the Gardai.

A spokesman for the promoter said that local opinion could result in Mr Aiken being released "from his undertaking not to be involved in future concerts". Mr Breen, who had been the spokesperson for the concert's opponents, said he imagined that a more sympathetic hearing would be given to calls for future concerts.

Chief Superintendent Bohan described the young rock fans as a "credit to themselves and their parents."

While at the Bob Dylan concert in 1984 the Garda station had been attacked by rioters, after the Springsteen gig several groups of people had stopped outside the tiny Slane station and chanted: "Garda Siochana, we love you".

On the meadows in front of the castle after the end of the show, a Garda spokesperson read a message thanking the crowd for behaving itself so immaculately, and the very last word came over the public address system from promoter Jim Aiken: "Youse have been absolutely wonderful!"

Springsteen, moving on to the UK and Europe and eventually closing the tour in Los Angeles in October, would never forget Slane. Later, according to one UK newspaper, he would call it the "scariest" concert he had ever played.

But a relationship with the Irish fans had started which would grow and develop over the coming years.

Indeed, only a short time later, after three sell-out concerts at Wembley Stadium, Springsteen was making his own appeal to one fan.

Billy Jeffries, a 16-year-old from Dublin, had followed Bruce to London and been turned away from the star's hotel by a security guard. He had been waiting patiently for an autograph.

Springsteen had heard the story and wanted Billy to get in touch. Springsteen's relationship with the Irish fans had started alright, and it was going to be a beautiful one.

Thomas Quinn

RDS
Dublin

7 July 1988

Crowd: 33,000

Tickets: IR£15.50-£20.50

37

The *Born In The USA* tour had been a spectacle played out across tabloid newspaper pages as well as stadia stages. During 1984 and 1985 Springsteen's life - his exercise regime, his visions of an apparently-quaint small-town America and his marriage - was dissected and reported across spreads in national newspapers.

By the time the tour finally ended fans were asking what on earth would, *could*, Springsteen do next? How could he top *Born In The USA*?

He provided the answer in 1988: he did not strain to go bigger or more dramatic; he aimed for the more intimate and more personal. *Tunnel Of Love* was pitched somewhere between the skeletal arrangements of *Nebraska* and the grandiose *Born In The USA*.

And although the tour was dubbed the *Tunnel Of Love Express* it was more of a fairground ride, on which the rider would struggle with new love, would have some fun but would spend an awful lot of time looking in the mirror to analyse what was staring back.

It was a shorter tour. The album came out in October 1987, Springsteen tinkered with the live show for a few months and only kicked off the tour at the end of February 1988. And it closed on August 3.

It all started off kind of quiet, without the media attention given to the previous tour – but by the time it arrived in Europe things were beginning to hot up.

Because the fairground ride in question was love. And that, by 1988 was not going smoothly for the Boss.

The album looked and felt different to *Born In The USA*. Springsteen now wore a black suit, white shirt and bootlace tie on the cover, and the songs inside contained new levels of introspection and an analysis of something new: marriage. *Tunnel Of Love* was Springsteen's first recording since his marriage to Julianne, and although Springsteen carried a bunch of red roses in some promotional photographs for the album, sadly all was far from rosy at home.

The theme was clearly established in the album's hit single "Brilliant Disguise", in which the singer moved around in a world with which he was not quite familiar. Dancing in the dark, perhaps, and it was a slow dance in which neither partner was quite sure of the other – or of themselves.

He had recorded the album alone and found himself with a collection of country-inspired ballads, around which he might strain to create a high-energy stadium show. But by the time the tour started he had come up with not only a raft of new songs but had also supplemented the band with a horn section led by Richie "La Bamba" Rosenberg.

The tour kicked off in Massachusetts on February 25, 1988, and wound its way through the United States.

Early in May, while on the West Coast,

Bruce and Julianne separated, and everyone backstage was in on the story that he and Patti Scialfa were now a couple.

The news did not go public until early in June when the tour arrived in Europe and an Italian photographer caught the couple in a clinch. The story hit the tabloids as the show moved through northern Europe. On July 3, the band played Stockholm and then the *Tunnel Of Love Express* turned towards Ireland.

Some of the excitement about Bruce's private life followed it.

On the day of the show, to be Springsteen's first at the RDS in Dublin, a gossip column in the *Irish Independent* reported on a "Kerry Hideaway for Bruce". According to James Mulchahy, Springsteen and "current love of his life, Patti Scialfa" had headed off in a minibus with a minder two days before the show "for a quiet sojourn to a guest house near Killarney".

"Amazingly," wrote Mulchahy, "they were unrecognised by locals.

"Apparently unlike some superstars who rant and rave during flights I hear Springsteen is a most charming passenger utterly polite to the Ryanair crew, he slept and wrote letters on the journey and invited the crew to a BBQ at Carton House, Co Kildare, which was being thrown by CBS, his record company, on Monday night.

"Upon arrival back from Kerry on Wednesday night he was seen having fish and chips in the take-out opposite Blackrock College. Tonight after the concert he booked to have dinner in restaurant Na Mara in Dun Laoghaire with Jim Aitken (sic)."

The sun may have blazed at Slane but downpours were forecast over Dublin and fans were being warned to bring raincoats to the RDS.

According to the *Evening Herald*, Bruce prepared for the show with a work-out at a local gym and a walk around the area outside his hotel, the Berkeley Court.

Around 33,000 fans were at the RDS, paying IR£20.50 and IR£15.50 to see the show.

And they had much to celebrate. A great and marathon four-hour show, and the raincoats were not needed.

As Paddy Murray wrote in the *Evening Herald*: "It didn't even rain. It wouldn't have dared. They don't call Bruce Springsteen the Boss for nothing."

Murray said that from the moment Springsteen stepped on to the stage "he gave everything to an audience that gave everything back".

"You can't help but enjoy a concert when you know the star is having just as good a time as you are," he said. "Anyone who was in Slane that balmy summer's day in 1985 felt they had been to the best concert ever. Those who missed Slane were made to feel they had missed a once-in-a-lifetime opportunity.

"But at the RDS last night Bruce Springsteen surpassed his performance in Slane. It was no wonder that people said afterwards that the best two concerts they have seen were Bruce Springsteen and Bruce Springsteen.

"The sheer energy and power from the stage not just from the Boss but from the brilliant saxophonist Clarence Clemons, the superb brass section, Nils Lofgren and the whole band, helped make a brilliant concert one to remember forever and one to judge all others by.

"At the RDS last night he was in charge. Some might think that IR£18.50 is a lot to pay to see a rock star. It was cheap at the price."

Better than Slane?

Well, like Slane this certainly was going to be a *show*. Springsteen might have eschewed the rolling hills of Meath for the streets of Ballsbridge but the excitement remained palpable.

Mary Maher, of the *Irish Times*, described a sea of vendors elbowing for space outside Jury's Hotel, so that "by the Horse Show House the street was nearly impassable. There was still half an hour to go and they'd been pouring in since 3pm."

Inside, a huge stage was topped with a high banner bearing the words 'Tunnel Of Love'.

Tunnel Of love
Boom Boom
Adam Raised A Cain
The River
Seeds
All That Heaven Will Allow
Downbound Train
Cover Me
Brilliant Disguise
Tougher Than The Rest
Spare Parts
War
Born In The USA
Chimes Of Freedom
Paradise By The C
She's The One
You Can Look (But You Better Not Touch)
I'm A Coward (When It Comes To Love)
I'm On Fire
Because The Night
Dancing In The Dark
Light Of Day
Born To Run
Hungry Heart
Glory Days
Bobby Jean
Cadillac Ranch
Tenth Avenue Freeze-Out
Sweet Soul Music
Raise Your Hand
Twist And Shout

"The crowd milled and swirled and watched the vast mega screen for the first close-up genuine proof that he was really there," said Maher.

Then the E Street Band bounded on stage, one by one, to the opening strains of "Tunnel Of Love". Patti was carrying a bouquet of scarlet heart balloons. There was a slight hush and in the gap Bruce ran on and "the whole 30,000 went ecstatically berserk."

"Are you ready for a ride?" Bruce called out, as a warm evening sun broke through the clouds over Ballsbridge, and the music "blasted off", according to the *Irish Independent*, at such a pace that the crowd was quickly "jumping".

The set was a familiar one. "Tunnel Of Love", then straight into "Boom Boom" and, after slipping off his jacket to reveal a dark waistcoat, "Adam Raised A Cain".

Those who had seats were already on their feet. Those standing, danced. One girl waved a flag which had a Stars and Stripes one side and a Tricolour on the reverse.

By the third song, wrote Mary Maher, the "stewards began hauling the overexcited from the front row, two first, then another, then three more felled by exuberance and crowd pressure and removed to the safety of the enclosure where they were revived with cups of water."

Those were not the only flashbacks to Slane. Now, with Springsteen hunched over the microphone in a "steelworker's slouch", images would come rushing back for many as he played the bluesy harmonica opening to "The River".

"Seeds" allowed the band to shine. Afterwards, Springsteen looked skyward. "So this is what summer in Dublin's like?" he asked. "First the sun shines, then it rains, the sun shines and then it rains …"

The cheery "All That Heaven Will Allow" was his way of telling the crowd "what summer was like in the States".

"Here she comes walking," he sang, with an eye on Patti. "Should I listen to my heart …? Well, should I?" "Yes" came the crowd's knowing response.

Maher drew on James Joyce's *Ulysses* and one of his story-telling characters to describe the Springsteen effect: "Molly Bloom couldn't have done it better," she wrote.

Patti, dressed in a skin-tight mini skirt, black tights, ankle boots, black top and a huge silver necklace which contrasted sharply with her fiery red hair, was very much stage front as the first set steamrollered through "Downbound Train", "Cover Me", "Brilliant Disguise" and "Tougher Than The Rest". During the latter song, Bruce and Patti's eyes fixed on each other.

Then came "Spare Parts", and the political double-whammy of "War" and "Born In The USA", a "mind-blowing version" with Springsteen "holding up his guitar like an icon before crashing into the frets". Springsteen's next project was a tour for Amnesty International, one of the organisations which held collections at his shows.

He dedicated the next song, Bob Dylan's "Chimes Of Freedom", played for the first time on that tour only three concerts earlier (although first performed 10 years earlier on the *Darkness On The Edge Of Town* tour), to Amnesty.

During the second half, the band turned up the heat even further. "Paradise By The C", by now familiar to new fans through the *Live 1975-85* box-set but only recently played live for the first time in 10 years; "She's The One" and then a double-header in which the sparks flew between Bruce and Scialfa: "You Can Look (But You Better Not Touch)" and "I'm A Coward (When It Comes To Love)", each introduced with stories which jokingly underpinned the mix of raw desire and bad jokes which ran through both songs.

The first had Springsteen learning a perpetual but unwelcome lesson in restraint, starting when he was a baby and he was "crawling across the floor heading for my television set ... and I remember my mama saying ... 'Oh, son, don't you touch that thing'" and ending, of course, with a girl in a parked car telling him something similar only under different circumstances.

The second was also familiar to tourgoers, another lecture performed TV evangelist-style on the difficulties of love. A call for brave men: "Do we have any macho men out there? Because I've known men that would swim rivers, that would climb mountains, that would wrestle with the beasts of the jungle but ... there was one thing that they was afraid of, there was something that scared them to death, do you want to know what that one thing was? Well, what I'm talking about is: L-U-V. I'm talking about love. Love scared those men to death."

There was the same warning for the "courageous Irish girls" because he'd "known women that when they got next to love ... they ran home back to their loneliness and to their isolation."

Then, of course, the preacher linked himself to the crowd. "I'm not down here tonight just pointing a finger, I'm down here because I've got something that I've got to confess!" A throw of the arm and a raise of the voice.

"And what I want to tell you is that I have sinned." A slight, nervous laugh. "And I don't need no Jimmy Swaggart or Jerry Falwell to forgive me, them boys can kiss my ass.

"I want to say that I'm a brave man, if I don't say so myself, but what I've got to confess to is that I'm a coward when it comes to love …"

And off goes the band. "I'm A Coward" was a major set-piece in the tour, played for every laugh and bad piece of dancing Bruce could get out of it.

I'm a year or two older than Bruce and have been a fan since 1984. There was a programme on RTÉ television every Sunday afternoon at the time called MTUSA (a kind of a forerunner to MTV). It was presented by a guy called Vincent Hanley aka Fab Vinnie.

My 11 and nine-year-old daughters were beginning to find their 'pop' feet. They were big fans at the time of Madonna and used to watch this show every week.

It was on this programme that I began to see videos from Born In The USA. I think "Dancing In The Dark" was the first one. I liked what I was hearing and bought the album (vinyl) which I virtually wore out. Since then I've been a huge fan and during the period between the release of Born In The USA and its follow-up, Tunnel Of Love, I had bought all of the back-catalogue.

My first time to see him live was in the RDS on the Tunnel Of Love tour in 1988. I was in one of the stands in a fairly good viewing position and I also had binoculars with me. From memory, there were no big video screens then.

The show opened with "Tunnel Of Love", followed by "Boom Boom" and "Adam Raised A Cain" and I sat there feeling nothing special: I was probably still in shock at actually being at the show. Then the magic occurred, the harmonica strains that announced the introduction to "The River" and the hairs on the back of my neck literally stood up and I stayed in that ecstatic state for the remainder of the show.

Dan Kavanagh, Dublin

After Slane, Bruce left us waiting three years before he came back, but it was worth the wait.

He played the RDS as it was a smaller venue, but what a show. It was the Tunnel Of Love tour and it was an even better show than Slane.

I was at the very front of the stage and Bruce and the band were on fire. He put on one of the best Bruce gigs I have been to. He mixed the show with hits from the Tunnel Of Love album and some of his older classics and I danced and rocked to Bruce for over four hours of rock and roll heaven.

He ended the gig with an astounding acoustic version of "Born To Run" and I still remember the tears running down my face as he left us to ponder just what we were lucky enough to see.

John Flannery, Ballymote, Co Sligo

We've four kids, aged from 12 to 27. But come Boss time we feel so youthful ourselves.

Tunnel Of Love was our first Springsteen concert experience, fourth row from the barrier. Carol fainted with the crush of the crowd and got pulled out by security. I followed (reluctantly), out the side and straight to the back once Carol recovered. Then we got back to the front. And we were bitten with the bug.

From then on we planned every concert trip. For every Irish concert we queued long hours and headed straight to the front barrier.

John and Carol Mahon
Lifford, County Donegal

It was where the five-part brass section which accompanied the E Street Band got to goof as well as blow their lungs out.

Then he returned to more serious explorations of love, desire and loneliness, "I'm On Fire", "Because The Night" and "Dancing In The Dark", complete with a guest dancer from the crowd, before rocking it out with a fantastic finale.

The band introductions were threaded through "Light Of Day" and included "the most handsome Irish man you've ever seen – I'm talking to you about the one, the only, the inimitable, the incredible, the unbelievable Clarence 'Big Man' Clemons".

Wrote the *Irish Independent*, "A packed arena greeted every new anthem with wild appreciation and there was a huge Northern contingent adding to the noise."

Tony O'Brien noted that the sun was finally setting but, "in the presence of this marvellous New Jersey-born entertainer nobody noticed the gathering chill."

Then an acoustic "Born To Run" – "I hope this song's kept you as good company on your search for your answers as it has me on mine," said Bruce. "I wanna do this for you, wishing you all love, hope and happiness" – and the sing-a-longs of "Hungry Heart", "Glory Days", "Bobby Jean", "Cadillac Ranch" and "Tenth Avenue Freeze-Out", and, in a night that seemed like it was never going to end, the triple-headed tour closer of "Sweet Soul Music", "Raise Your Hand" and "Twist And Shout". (Before the Beatles classic Springsteen took out an old fashioned pocket watch to check the time … and, of course, there was time for one more song.)

In *Backstreets* magazine, Northern Irish fan Paul Trimble picked out "Cadillac Ranch" as a highlight. "By this time Bruce had the audience in the palm of his hand and this seemed to inspire him all the more," he said, and added: "During 'Twist And Shout' the look of pure enjoyment on his face was that of a man who was really having a good time. His beaming face filled the screen as he said: 'I don't want to go home'. And I believed him."

It was a show that Bruce did not seem to want to end. It had started at 6.45pm and finished just before 11pm. Tony O'Brien in a review in the *Irish Independent* described it as a "marathon four-hour display of non-stop music (which) showed why he is still the King of Rock in the 80s". According to O'Brien, this "tour de force" was the "longest single show ever seen by an Irish audience".

The next day, according to Paddy Murray: "Bruce Springsteen walked out of his Dublin hotel to buy the morning papers.

"Nobody gave him a second glance, not even those who had been among the 30,000 who packed the RDS Jumping Enclosure last night.

"No other rock star could do it. No other rock star could put on the cloak of anonymity less than 12 hours after presiding over what is arguably the world's greatest travelling rock circus.

"But then no other rock star could do what Bruce did last night at the RDS."

The *Irish Independent* played up many people's interpretations of the *Tunnel Of Love* shows, under a headline describing the concert as a "high decibel serenade for secretary Patti".

It reported: "It was the night The Boss got caught smooching with his secretary. Bruce Springsteen and Patti Scialfa made no secret of their love at the RDS last night.

"Gazing longingly at each other and rubbing up close in front of 35,000 fans. But it was more than that, much more than that. A powerhouse high-decibel total energy performance by the man from Freehold, New Jersey.

"A good-humoured uninhibited crowd enjoyed the fine weather and the anthem of a former altar boy whom the nuns dubbed a WBP – a wastepaper basket pupil."

The nuns might have taken a different view now for as the *Sunday Independent* noted the mood at the concert was one of "joyous, almost born-again intensity".

For Kevin Courtney, the reviewer for the *Irish Times,* the E Street Band "pounded a collective heartbeat and seemed to breathe life into the whole city". "The spectacle," he wrote, "was a reaffirmation of the ability of rock 'n' roll to achieve intimacy, a sense of kindred."

The shock of the magnitude of the Slane experience behind him, Springsteen had quickly found the connection again with the large audiences and was "capable of projecting a sense of true values as he always has been".

Courtney added: "Watching Bruce Springsteen play you begin to feel, like he does, that the little things are the most important: the search for home and happiness, the maudlin memories of the past as shown in "Glory Days", even that simple word 'love'."

He concluded: "Amidst the humour, the excitement, even the sentiment and the sorrow, the reaffirmation is always there. Springsteen is a performer who is looking for solidity in both life and love, and so he sets out to strengthen the foundation on which those two delicate qualities rest and ends up giving his audience something firmer to stand on."

The Star reported: "Springsteen was perched on a 20ft podium for much of the concert but occasionally went down steps of the stage to shake hands with fans."

I have seen Bruce nine times since 1985. I knocked his front door in Rumson, New Jersey, in 1987. My friend Paddy and I just walked straight up the gravel driveway and knocked the front door. We were told by a guard that he was not at home. He said he was in the city working on his new album, *Tunnel Of Love*.

I heard Bruce telling the story about knocking Elvis' front door in 1976, so I expected him to understand.

I was in my early 20s then and full of the enthusiasm of youth.

I wasn't Bruce hunting on May 24, 2008 in my mid-40s and haven't done so since that day in 1987 but what happened shows how, "Everything comes to those who wait".

I was in the pit on Friday night (May 23, 2008) with my wife Mary and again on Sunday night with my two sons, Stephen and Paul. Fantastic shows.

My wife and I were waiting on Grafton Street on Saturday for Stephen to meet us after doing one of his 1st year maths exams at Trinity College.

We were just chatting when I looked up and saw Miami Steve walking up the street. I walked over to him and told him Friday was fantastic and that I was going again on Sunday.

I asked for a picture. He said it would create too much of a fuss but said he would shake my hand. I shook his hand and thanked him.

My son then phoned and said he was in a nearby church just off Grafton Street. We met him and I was so excited telling him about Steve.

We returned to Grafton Street to talk about our meeting with Steve and how he got on with his exam. I couldn't stop thinking how lucky we were to meet Steve. Then the unbelievable happened, I looked again and said to my wife, "There's Bruce!"

"Where? *Where?*" she said, and I walked straight over and stuck out my hand and told him how much we enjoyed the show on Friday and that we would be going again on Sunday. He thanked me. My son and my wife were a few feet back and my wife still can't believe it.

I've often thought what I would say to Bruce if I met him but never expected it to happen. I just wish I had asked him to sing "Incident On 57th Street" as it is both my wife's and my favourite.

Stephen Friel, Coleraine, County Derry

I remember my neighbours in Co Donegal coming around before they set off for Slane and me not being able to go as I was 15 and sitting exams. I swore revenge, like it was their fault!

A friend and I hatched a plan where we would fail our intercert but get to see Bruce but sense prevailed in the end.

For *Tunnel Of Love* I travelled up and back in the same day. I can close my eyes and see the stage with the ticket booth, etc. The bass in those days was much bigger than today and you could feel it reverberate through your whole body.

As a first concert it was just amazing. I'm not one for going buck mad and just stood there for about three hours with my mouth open thinking, This is it. ⬇

"The four-hour long party finished in the floodlit showgrounds with Bruce thrilling Beatles' fans with an energetic "Twist And Shout".

"When Bruce played Slane in early June 1985 he said that the pushing and squashing at the front sections of the 100,000 strong crowd made his first Irish concert the scariest he has ever played.

"But during the Boss' flight to Sheffield this morning he will be reflecting on his second Irish concert as one of the great successes of his 16-year musical career."

Springsteen, promoter Jim Aiken said, enjoyed the RDS – and there is no reason to doubt that, considering the number of times he was to return over the coming years.

The US-based *Backstreets* concluded simply: "The Irish audience adores Springsteen."

This is the music I play when I'm happy, sad or just thinking, and that man not 50 yards away created it all. For a boy from Donegal it was my second trip to the big smoke and I vowed to catch Bruce there as much as possible in the future.

Eddie Barron, Liverpool

I first discovered Bruce when I was 16 through watching MTUSA on Sunday afternoons. This was around the time of *Born In The USA*.

I remember sulking and crying for the entire day that Slane was on: my parents (rightly, I suppose, in hindsight!) would not let me attend as I was so young. They did, however, get me tickets for my birthday to see him in the RDS on July 7, 1988. I took my little sister who was not a fan at all and to say we both floated back to our hotel after the concert is an understatement. I was blown away and she was converted.

Tracy Hegarty, Limerick

When the *Tunnel Of Love* tour was announced, Bruce was coming to play the RDS, outdoors in July, I knew that I had to get tickets. I persuaded my husband Paul to go to the gig with me. It didn't take too much pressure as he had heard me going on and on about Slane and also listened to a lot of Springsteen music as I was playing it quite a lot at home.

My mum and dad were 25 years married in 1988 and went off sometime in late May early June for a holiday in Greece. They spent some time island-hopping and on one of their boat trips they met up with an American woman, Carol Dodds, who was having a week's holiday in Greece before she started as a video director for the Bruce Springsteen *Tunnel Of Love* tour. They got on very well and my mum and dad gave her their address and she promised to visit when the tour was in Ireland.

I got to meet her and she offered us complimentary tickets for the gig, which we took, my original tickets I sold for face value to another Bruce fan. I collected the complimentary tickets on the day of the gig in the Westbury Hotel and as we entered the lobby area the E Street Band was making their way to some white Ford transits that were laid on to take them to the gig. I am sorry to this day that I didn't say 'hi' and get some autographs.

Bruce wasn't in attendance but he later passed in another van sitting in the back with Patti on their way to the venue.

The gig itself was fantastic. It was a proper Bruce show. The opening sequence of the admissions booth selling tickets to the band for some carnival rides set the atmosphere. I really liked listening to *Born To Run* and the "She's The One" track off that was also played, it was great. The version of "Spare Parts" was also a standout, it had been changed around and given the "live" treatment, which Bruce and the band do so well. There was great rapport between the audience and the band.

If I was mad about Bruce and the E Street Band after Slane they went up several notches in my estimation after this show.

Jocelyn Kelly, Dublin

Another tour, and this time more friends and another bus heading for the Anglesea stand in the RDS. We crashed the van in Dublin city centre but still made it there on time. Watching Bruce interact with Patti was a highlight this time, as was the country feel about the show: Bruce in bootlace tie and the fairground stage setting at the start.

A great show which has been overlooked and underrated in Bruce/Irish history. Great encores.

Nigel Flynn, Ballymoney

I really got into Bruce in 1979 (*Darkness* being still my favourite album).

At university "our song" was "The River" and Kieran Goss (a well-known artist in Ireland) even sang it for me at my 21st birthday party.

The first song played at our wedding was "I Want To Marry You" followed by "The River". Every house we have lived in has had Bruce as the first music to be played.

**Maggie Flynn, Ballymoney
on a Springsteen obsession**

I have been to over 20 Springsteen shows including every one in Ireland except for Slane. Unfortunately I was just a bit too young for that one.

My greatest memory from the shows was when I laid my eyes on Bruce for the first time in July 1988. Picture the scene: the band entering the stage one by one, each member joining into the intro of "Tunnel Of Love" before Bruce appears with "Hello Ireland, are you ready to ride?", and they break into the opening of the song.

That for me was my first and most memorable memory.

**Stephen Devine
Belfast**

THE GIRL ON THE BUS

On a warm afternoon in late summer 1984, I was 13 years old helping (hindering!) my father knock down our old kitchen to make way for a new extension.

During a break from swinging our sledge-hammers, I heard a beat and a voice on an old transistor radio that captured my imagination like nothing before or since – the song: "Born In The USA".

I took the pocket money I got for helping dad, bought the album and so the journey began.

By the time Bruce made his way to Ireland for the first time in 1985, I was a complete convert – I'd devoured everything he'd released and was known for fighting the Bruce corner in school music arguments.

Try as I might, I couldn't get tickets for the Slane show (being only 14, I wasn't allowed to go anyway!) but I still have fond memories of the day – a stream of cars snaking though town, stuck in traffic jams, the sun beating down, people sitting on car bonnets, drinking warm beer (a la "Jungleland") and music blasting.

I got my chance in 1988 when the *Tunnel Of Love Express* rolled into the RDS. I'd just finished my Leaving Certificate and was about to embark on a college adventure. What better way to kick off adult life than your first concert – and what better concert to see than Bruce Springsteen and the E Street Band.

What a show it was, and it would have an impact on my life that I couldn't have imagined possible.

After the show two girls who couldn't find their bus home to Dundalk eventually talked their way onto the bus I was on.

I was vaguely acquainted with both from school and we all got talking about the concert, Bruce and what we were planning to do after school.

Two weeks later, while watching a local GAA match, I got a tap on the shoulder – one of the girls from the bus! She told me the other girl, Tricia, wanted a word with me at the gate. Tricia asked me to her school Debs' Ball – all as a result of our chance meeting after the concert.

Twenty years later, we're still going strong and even more infatuated with Mr Springsteen. We married in 1994 (having officially gotten engaged during an acoustic "Thunder Road" – our favourite song – at the previous year's *Human Touch/Lucky Town* RDS show).

Our only bug-bear over the years was that Tricia was at Slane and therefore always one show ahead of me. Tricia balanced things up in November 2006, packing me off to London to see the first Wembley Arena *Seeger Sessions* show (and the world premiere of "Long Walk Home").

Bruce in Dublin holds many special moments for us – meeting in 1988, getting engaged in 1993, heavily pregnant with our daughter during 1995's *Tom Joad* stop, being at the RDS during the *Reunion* tour in 1999 less than two weeks after our son was born by Caesarean section, experiencing the emotion and celebration of *The Rising* tour in 2003, the artistry of *Devils & Dust* in 2005, the fun of all those *Seeger Sessions* shows in 2006 and the resplendent 'magic' of three unbelievable nights in 2008.

In Barcelona in 2008 we brought the kids to their first Bruce shows. These incredible performances were made all the more special watching our young children, Aoife, 11, and Fergal, nine, singing, dancing, arm-waving and air-punching their way through their first Bruce shows on warm Spanish nights.

Anyway, that's the Mulholland family's Bruce story. I'll leave it to others more qualified to explain and analyse the strength of the connection felt between Ireland and Bruce.

All I know is Bruce's music is always there for me, regardless of moods and situations. I'm sure we all have 'go to' Bruce songs/albums to fit various occasions (what parent of a newly born baby hasn't played "Living Proof" or sung "If I Should Fall Behind" to a loved one, cried through "You're Missing" after the death of someone close, been inspired by "Badlands" or provoked by "Roulette"?).

Whenever Bruce calls us to arms with a new record and tour we'll be there.

So here's to Bruce, the E Street Band, the 'Other Band', the Seeger Sessions Band and the next album and tour!

Bruce, Go raibh mile maith agat and go n-eiri on bothar leat.

Thomas Mulholland, Dundalk

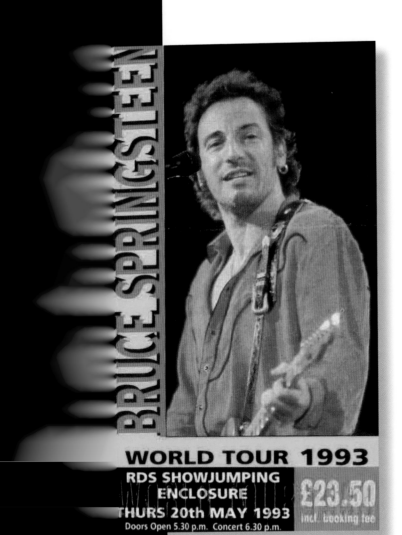

**RDS
Dublin**

20 May 1993

Crowd: 30,000

Tickets: IR£23.50-£26.50

plus special guest appearance at

**The National Stadium
Dublin**

19 May 1993

On May 1, 1993, the RTÉ magazine announced: "The Boss is Back."

"Thursday, May 20, sees Bruce Springsteen back in town at the RDS. He last played this venue in 1988 and in 1985 70,000 fans saw him in Slane," it stated.

It was a different boss *again*. This was not the fun in the sunshine, t-shirted Bruce of 1985, who explored his own growing maturity as an artist and man through not only his own songs but one from The Beach Boys, or of 1988, a man who as suspected had found love and marriage to be a more complicated beast than the Fender guitar.

The Boss had changed again – but so this time had the band he led.

In late 1989 Bruce had phoned around the members of E Street Band and said he was looking to work with other musicians. It was not clear to the band, the fans and maybe even to Bruce what he had planned.

In the end he went into the studio with Roy Bittan and some session musicians and came up with a bunch of songs which would form the album *Human Touch*. He then carried on recording – largely alone – and produced a tighter collection, *Lucky Town*.

It was decided to release both albums at the same time and on March 30, 1992 they hit the shelves together. The band Springsteen put together for the accompanying tour featured Lone Justice guitarist Shane Fontayne, bassist Tommy Sims and guitarist, percussionist and singer Crystal Taliefero out front; Zachary Alford on the drums; with Bobby King, Gia Ciambotti, Carol Dennis (whose secret marriage to Bob Dylan was dissolved during the tour), Cleo Kennedy and Angel Rogers making up a formidable line-up of backing singers.

The only familiar face was behind the keyboards, Roy Bittan, and while Patti made the odd appearance on the tour she did not come on stage in Dublin. Taliefero and R&B singer King had great stage presence with Taliefero making a fine female foil for Bruce and performing the show's only sax solo, on "Born To Run".

It was an entirely new mix of musicians, all African-American apart from Bittan and Ciambotti, and British-Asian Fontayne. Critics had been split on the new albums with *Human Touch* in particular coming in for heavy criticism for being patchy and weak.

Dave Marsh, who has chronicled Springsteen's life in a number of books and articles, states of the E Street break-up: "Apparently, Bruce hoped to accomplish things working with other musicians that he could not have done with the E Streeters. Whether he did remains debatable."

Only 10 weeks after their release Springsteen would jokingly search through the *Billboard* magazine chart on stage and screech: "Wait a minute, *Lucky Town* at a *hundred and ****ing five*!", before telling the crowd, "We're here for bigger reasons than those damn record sales!"

And live, of course, Springsteen would prove exactly that. But fans as well as critics were cautious, in particular about the new stage dynamic. No Clarence, no Miami Steve.

And the onstage revolution was mirrored off. Springsteen's divorce from Julianne had come through in 1989, and he and Patti had not only married but started a family. Son Evan was born in 1990 and a daughter Jessica followed in 1991. (They would have a third child, Sam, in 1994.)

Had marital bliss changed The Boss? How would what was essentially a band of session musicians – albeit very good ones – compare with the E Street Band? Well, the band had now been on the road for the best part of a year. The tour had started in Stockholm on June 15, 1992, but there had been no Irish dates on the first leg. Through late summer, autumn and winter the band wound its way through the United States and Canada before taking a three-month winter break.

The second European leg had started in Glasgow on March 31, 1993. The RDS would mark the 22nd show of this leg of a tour which would eventually officially end in Norway on June 1, 1993, after 107 shows.

The fans' concern about the new direction was revealed in slow ticket sales. Only two days before the show, the *Evening Herald* was reporting that tickets were still available. Brian Boyd, of the *Irish Times*, expressed concern that Bruce had gone "a bit Californian" but with "a back-catalogue like his you can afford the odd error of judgement." Springsteen arrived in Dublin by private jet on Tuesday, May 18, flying in from his previous show in Mannheim, Germany. (A few days earlier he had made headlines by leading Shane Fontayne, Bobby King, Tommy Sims and the Heidi Schneider Band in an "invasion" of a private and rather posh school ball taking place at his hotel in Munich. They rushed through "Lucille" and "Twist And Shout" while ball-gowned guests looked on in astonishment). At Dublin airport, Springsteen shook hands with fans and signed autographs with a "How ya all doing?" greeting.

He told reporters: "I don't know what I will be doing over the next few days in Ireland. We are here to have a good time. I certainly hope I will have a pint." Asked about previous trips to Ireland by the *Irish Independent*, he said: "We had a great time the last time we were here." When told that there were still standing tickets available, he said: "I don't know about the ticket sales. I just play for the people that come." He then jumped into a waiting maroon-coloured Plymouth Voyager and was driven off.

Despite the ticket sales there would still be tens of thousands at the RDS and Springsteen planned on warming up for the big show, first in front of a handful of folk and then a few hundred.

The singing started at St George's Health Club in South Great George Street, Dublin, on the Wednesday when he rehearsed a song in the changing rooms. Gym-goers listened in as he sang. "He's the only person who has ever been allowed to wear cowboy boots in the gym," club owner David Bain said at the time.

Springsteen was also spotted strolling around Temple Bar where he popped into the Bad Ass Café for lunch and later bought a pair of shoes. Then, that night, about 600 fans went to the National Stadium nightclub to see Texan rocker Joe Ely.

About 20 minutes from the end of the gig, there was a surprise. On wandered Bruce, dressed in denim jeans and a shirt. His face was framed with stubble and there was a new earring in his ear. As the *Evening Herald* put it on page 3 the following day: "YO! Who's that guy with Joe Ely?"

It reported: "Bruce Springsteen may have been born in the USA – but he's made Dublin his home. Rock fans could not believe their eyes last night when the working-class hero from New Jersey made a surprise appearance in a Dublin club."

Seeds
Adam Raised A Cain
This Hard Land
Better Days
Lucky Town
Atlantic City
57 Channels (And Nothin' On)
Badlands
Satan's Jewelled Crown
My Hometown
Leap Of Faith
Man's Job
Roll Of The Dice
Downbound Train
Because The Night
Brilliant Disguise
Human Touch
The River
Who'll Stop The Rain?
Souls Of The Departed
Born In The USA
Light Of Day
Settle For Love *(with Joe Ely)*
Glory Days
Thunder Road
Born To Run
My Beautiful Reward
Great Balls Of Fire
(with Jerry Lee lewis)
Whole Lotta Shakin' Goin' On
(with Jerry Lee Lewis)
Working On The Highway
Rockin' All Over The World
Bobby Jean
It's Alright

The newspaper added: "Sharing lead vocals, Springsteen delivered a tribute to Jerry Lee Lewis entitled: 'I wear my finger nails long so they click when they play the piano'."

Ely, who was promoting the album *Love And Danger*, was also joined by Bruce for "Dusty Old Road" and "Settle For Love".

Kevin Courtney in the *Irish Times* noted: "Joe Ely may not be a megastar, but he's got friends in high places, and one of them joined him on stage at the stadium last night, for a jam session to end all jam sessions.

"What began as a pretty ordinary Wednesday night gig turned into something special as Bruce Springsteen trotted on stage adding his own musical weight to Ely's own hard rocking country."

The venue was only half-full, Courtney noted, but "Springsteen's appearance brought the whole audience to its feet … and brought this show into the realm of legend."

After the show, it was reported, Bruce and Joe headed off with Dave Pemmefather, of MCA records, to La Tosca, a restaurant owned by Bono's brother Norman Hewson.

Bruce was staying at the Westbury Hotel which that week was becoming a little bit of New Jersey in Ireland: Jon Bon Jovi was staying at the same place in readiness for his show at The Point.

Colm Watson

Colm Watson

Grainne and Les Swan

Colm Watson

Grainne and Les Swan

The real show took place on Thursday, May 20, 1993, with Springsteen catching many of the 30,000 crowd by surprise as he wandered out on stage alone at 6.45pm. It was a bright rain-free summer evening and the new Bruce was wearing a familiar uniform: jeans and waistcoat, both in the regulation black.

He opened with "Seeds", "Adam Raised A Cain", with the band slowly coming in on "This Hard Land". By "Better Days" the new Springsteen band was in full swing with music which was – for better and for worse – all their own. "Lucky Town" followed with Bruce then telling the crowd, "Let's play that sun into the ground!"

"Atlantic City", "57 Channels (And Nothin' On)", "Badlands" and a new song for the tour, a delicate gospel number "Satan's Jewelled Crown", whose introduction gave a hint of what was to come: "This is an old country gospel song … One of my great heroes is here tonight, I'd like to do this for you, Jerry."

The set now began to introduce songs off *Human Touch*, interspersing them with old favourites: "My Hometown", "Leap Of Faith", "Man's Job", "Roll Of The Dice", "Downbound Train", "Because The Night", "Brilliant Disguise", "Human Touch" and "The River".

Springsteen then introduced a blisteringly political trio of songs which took the show to a new level. "Who'll Stop The Rain?" was introduced as a "prayer for Bosnia and Herzegovina", and that sentiment linked in perfectly with two of Springsteen's analyses of war and peace, "Souls Of The Departed" – with its descriptions of the "road to Basra" from the recently fought Gulf War – and "Born In The USA", prefaced by a Jimi Hendrix-style "Star Spangled Banner". The speaker stacks bristled.

And then "Light Of Day" closed the main set by bringing the house down. The song which started as a simple three-verse rocker had developed into a live tour de force featuring blistering guitar solos and a full-on Springsteen sermon.

"I drove thousands of miles just to get here tonight," he told the crowd halfway through the song, breathing heavily into the microphone. "I came here with a purposeful feeling. I came here tonight because I know you are downhearted, I know you are depressed, I know you're disappointed. I know there's 57 f*****g channels and nothing on … So I came here tonight to testify, I came here tonight to bear witness, I came here to testify. I can feel something. I can raise your spirit, I can raise your hope, I can bring back something. I can increase your *sexual* drive. I want to say I … [*drum beat*] I [*drum beats get faster*] I-I-I-I-I … I'M JUST A PRISONER … OF ROCK AND ROLL!"

And back into the song …

A ONE-OFF FROM THE BOSS

I never thought it was possible that you could meet your heroes. But when news came through that Bruce was arriving at three o'clock at Dublin airport I raced there with my four-year-old son Conor.

Alas I was too late (my time-keeping is legendary). After a fruitless visit to the Berkeley Court Hotel where I thought Bruce was staying it was back home, disappointed. (He was in the Westbury!) The concert was great, no great surprise there. I got talking to a security man at the concert who told me that Bruce was flying out the next day at two o'clock.

So the following day it was off to the airport again.

Despite funny looks from people, Conor and I waited for two hours outside the VIP section of Dublin airport.

Then a red Voyager people carrier pulled up outside. Bruce was inside drinking a bottle of Evian. I didn't know what to say. He came over to me and said, "That's a beautiful child you have there."

To which I responded: "He loves the song, "Pony Boy", Bruce." And then it happened.

Bruce sang "Pony Boy" to Conor. The full version. I was in awe. The calmness of the man. It was only about two minutes, but what a two minutes. I have met him on three other occasions over the past 15 years. The most memorable was Asbury Park for the Christmas shows in December 2003. The others were Manchester during the *Tom Joad* tour and also a rain-soaked November Sunday night at The Point entrance during the *Seeger Sessions* tour.

That night he sang "For You" for the rain-soaked fans he met outside. (That was two Germans and I.) Conor is now a Bruce fan. My second son Rory is an avid Bruce fan and has seen him five times now. My long-suffering wife is in denial. She maintains that she is not big into his music but has seen him in concert 27 times! She likens me to the father in that film, *My Big Fat Greek Wedding*. Whereas in the film he claims everything originates from the Greek for this or that, I allegedly have to bring everything back to Bruce!

Anton Martin, Dundalk

"UP YOURS! LOVE BRUCE SPRINGSTEEN"

We had learnt enough now to know that Bruce stayed in the Westbury off Grafton Street, so we booked in as well. But the night before we had tickets to see Joe Ely at the National Stadium (a boxing ring venue across the city).

We had tickets for the entire front row, as a few friends were into Joe and the Flatlanders Texas songwriter 'thang'. We didn't really expect Bruce to show up and we were just happy to be getting two good shows in a row. We had more tickets than we needed and I headed off to the Mont Clare Hotel where I knew a few Bruce heads were staying. I offered everyone in the bar face-value front row tickets and no-one wanted them. They kicked themselves later I heard! So back by taxi to the National Stadium and standing outside offering tickets to anyone who wanted them. ⬇

Terry Thorp

There then followed an 11-song encore to end all encores. Firstly, Springsteen repaid the previous night's honour by inviting Ely up on stage for "Settle For Love". As Ely left the stage, Springsteen said: "He's got a record out now called *Love And Danger* – great record, go out and get it. Good rock and roll music."

The last few words provided the perfect curtain-raiser for what was to come, with the band whipping through three classics, "Glory Days", "Thunder Road" and "Born To Run", before bringing it down for one of the better songs off the new albums, "My Beautiful Reward".

During "Glory Days", there was the usual messing around – "I want to see some wild Irish people out there … Put your hands in the air … Make it like you don't care … Show the person next to you your underwear" – and giggling, and the band introductions.

And before "Thunder Road" Springsteen thanked everyone for coming out to the show. "I would like to thank all my Irish fans for your support over the years. We've been making records and travelling around a long time. I want you to know this far down the road it means a lot to me. I love ya all. This is for my old fans out there …"

But even the old fans would not have seen what came next.

"We got a real special treat tonight," Springsteen announced. "One of my great heroes and inspirations is here with us tonight.

No takers and I was starting to get desperate that the show was due to start. Maggie and I were standing outside as a few latecomers arrived for the show. A Toyota Previa van pulled up onto the kerb right outside the front door but behind me and I took little notice until I could see by Maggie's face that it was someone special inside.

I turned round as Bruce, Shane Fontayne, and Terry Magovern stepped out. I couldn't speak. There I was touting tickets and my hero since 1976 was standing in front of me. I think I even offered him the tickets but still no words came out.

Maggie at least managed to shout his name causing him to stop and smile but before she could approach him he was ushered inside by Terry. We then forgot all about selling the spares and went to find our friends having drinks in the bar. Initially they didn't believe us when we told them who had arrived, but when we walked into the hall to take our seats we had to walk past the entrances to the dressing rooms.

At one of the entrances stood the driver of the Previa. Maggie recognized him and realizing that Bruce would be in the close vicinity looked down the stairs towards the dressing room. There stood Bruce, Shane and Terry.

Maggie shouted down the stairs, "Any chance of an autograph Bruce?" and he nodded and gestured to send something down to be signed. Maggie produced her ticket from the Sheffield show and sent a pen down with the driver. Bruce looked at the ticket, smiled and nodded up saying, "Did you enjoy the show?"

"Brilliant!" replied Maggie. "Can't wait for tomorrow night!"

The driver then brought the signed ticket back up and gave it to Maggie. I then shouted down that we had front row seats for tonight going spare if Bruce and Shane wanted them. They both laughed and nodded and waved to me – I had my first real connection with Bruce – and he now knew that we were fans who were prepared to travel to see him.

I now had got my first autograph (which was later found by my toddler son aged about three who thought he should add his autograph as well, in a silver pen).

We finally took our seats and Joe did a great show. The stage was about waist high and there were no barriers between us in the front row and the edge of the stage.

By the time Joe started his encores we were already on our feet and expecting Bruce at any time, maybe for one song. But when we heard the words, "I'd like to bring on a friend", we just rushed to the edge of the stage and watched Bruce and Shane walk on, take guitars and let rip. It was very rock and roll, and I watched the show from Bruce's feet, in fact I remember realising that I was drumming the beat with my hands on Bruce's biker boots, which I also remember had a hole in the toe! It was 15-plus minutes of sheer joy and I remember thinking at the time, that I would never have a gig experience to match this again in my life.

Bruce seemed very relaxed and played off against Joe Ely, using Joe's own guitar. ⬇

He is going to come up and grace our stage with a song – the great Jerry Lee Lewis!"

The Killer stepped out on to the stage and with a "Thank you – it is a great pleasure to be here with you ladies and gentlemen" led the band into "Great Balls Of Fire".

Afterwards Lewis fixed the audience with a wild look: "You don't know what a great honour and a great pleasure it is for this gentleman here to call me up on stage, God bless his heart. He's got one of the greatest bands and one of the most God-given talents I've ever heard in my life. If it wasn't for that I wouldn't be here. Believe that … Bruce you really knocked me out tonight. You were fantastic. Your back-up singers ... superb … and the sound man is rock 'n' roll …"

The thank-yous over, Lewis turned to the keyboard again and the band ripped into "Whole Lotta Shakin' Goin' On".

Bruce had looked blown away throughout and as Lewis hugged him he held on for a moment, the fan realising a dream. As Lewis left the stage, Springsteen gasped: "The great Jerry Lee Lewis! Damn, shit, we better go home now!"

The crowd screamed: "No!"

Bruce shrugged, "Whoooa, only because you insist. Damn, it don't get no better than that. I don't know what to do, I'm all frazzled up.

"Hmm, alright, let's try."

Terry Thorp

Springsteen's "Let's try" showed he was determined to keep the tempo, digging deep to match his childhood hero – carrying on the memorable encore with "Working On The Highway", "Rockin' All Over The World", "Bobby Jean" and bringing the band down for a smooth close harmony for "It's Alright". It was 10.30pm when the band left the stage with a wave.

Despite fans' fears, it was a memorable night – and not just because as Stuart Clark of *Hot Press* said, "Springsteen never, ever, ever plays a bad gig". The *Evening Herald* reported playfully: "Last night a living legend took centre-stage in the RDS. A post virtuoso musician, rock 'n' roll icon and inspirational force. "His name is Jerry Lee Lewis. It was Bruce Springsteen's gig but The Killer stole the show. And good guy that he is, Bruce didn't mind."

The newspaper noted that the new line-up, dealing in "more subtle arrangements, many verging on acoustic" lacked the weighty punch to "shake-up a huge outdoor audience".

"However if you really listened to Bruce last night you would have heard something sincere. Something moving and deep. Something which would have probably blown you away in a small outdoor venue."

It described an emotional catch in Springsteen's throat as he sang songs like "Atlantic City" and identified an "underlying spirituality … gospel if you like" to the new set.

When the show ended we just hung around the stage as the crowd left. A few other Bruce fans made themselves known to us but in all maybe only a dozen of us at the show were more into Bruce than Joe Ely.

After we were ushered out, again we tried to get back down the corridor to see Bruce and amazingly both Maggie and another friend Mary managed to get back inside. Maggie didn't get much further but a friendly bouncer allowed Mary to actually get into the dressing room to chat with Bruce and Joe. Mary ended up getting Bruce to sign another autograph with an unusual sentence in it: we had missed Mary and Martin's wedding in August 1992, going instead to the States to see Bruce and sending a telegram which read "The screen door slams, Mary's wedding dress waves". So Bruce signed for Mary: "I saw you first – up yours Nigel" and that was Mary's way of saying that we had missed her wedding and gone to see Bruce – but she was the first actually to talk to him and get an autograph.

After the Joe Ely gig we were all ushered out and back in the taxi to the Westbury. Feeling hopeful, we hung around the hotel lobby bar which was on the first floor, hoping to see Bruce come in. I assume he went out on the town with Joe Ely and we didn't see him, but while waiting, I recognised a short bloke in a long leather coat and big hair and remembered that Bon Jovi were playing Dublin around the same time.

So I shouted "Hi, Jon, com'ere!" and he did. I didn't even stand up but reached into my jacket and produced my receipt from the Berkley Carteret Hotel in Asbury Park: we had been over to Philly shows in August 1992).

That caught his attention and he looked at it and commented that I hadn't spent much. But he signed it and eventually we went to bed.

Next morning we went down to breakfast and sat at the next table to Jon Landau, who was at breakfast on his own and studying the papers. We both got up to leave at the same time, so I thought why not, I'll ask for an autograph, but he was away before I caught him.

Anyway outside the band was gathering up in the lobby to be taken to the RDS. It was easy to walk up and get autographs. I remember Crystal Taliefero was very chatty but Roy Bittan was a bit more detached and left to talk to one of the guys from Bon Jovi.

A crowd was gathering outside to wait on Bruce but as residents we were free to walk around in the lobby. We got all the band autographs on the back of a 'Greetings from Asbury Park' postcard.

Eventually Bruce came down in the lift with Terry, I pushed Maggie forward and again Terry stopped her but Bruce waved her over on her own after she shouted, "Hey, Bruce, will you sign a photo from last night?"

Maggie showed Bruce a photo from the night before. Bruce had started to sign the photo at the top when Maggie pointed out that the hand at the bottom of the photo was hers. Bruce then signed over Maggie's hand on the photo and I got them to pose for a photo. ⬇

"Yes, he's still peddling the redemptive powers of rock 'n' roll," reporter Katie Hannon concluded.

Dave Fanning wrote in the *Irish Times* that Springsteen was not weakened without the E Street Band, he was just different. "His detractors will tell you that if he was once the future and then the king of rock, he's now the past. His fans know better. These days the 21 million sales for *Born In The USA* are just a 10-year-old rock fact; the truth is that over the last seven years (since '87's *Tunnel Of Love*) his songs have become introspective and intimate dealing with the hard realities of love, marriage and adult life rather than with the myths and legend of blue-collar USA."

Fanning said that on stage Springsteen's music and performance mixed the hard realities of life and the fantasy of rock 'n' roll to "sometimes glorious effect".

Fanning described the duets with Jerry Lee Lewis as "fun filled" and "Ballsbridge-shattering", but noted that naturally some of the subtleties of the more recent music were lost in the outdoor arena.

"Much of his current repertoire is dark and introspective, mirroring self-doubt and personal problems that have followed him since he became a Grade A superstar," he wrote.

"Older, wiser, slower. Scaled down Springsteen is still relevant and still a star but there's no avoiding the fact that this show would have had 10 times the impact indoors in the dark, with no lighting but stage lights."

For Tony O'Brien, of the *Irish Independent*, Springsteen "delivered the goods in a way none of his contemporaries could." O'Brien said the RDS became a "mass of gyrating bodies" during the double-shot with the Killer. "What a night!"

Springsteen would later joke that when he tried to make happy records, such as *Human Touch*, which analysed the power of love, and *Lucky Town*, which looked at the glory of love and parenthood, they bombed.

But in the RDS in May 1993 on the so-called 'Other Band' tour – it had no official name – Springsteen "preached his heart out". Dave Marsh wrote: "It was his old message of true love and rock and roll, the same exhortation to make that leap of faith he'd always encouraged, the same parody of the jackleg preachers who ran the televised part of his midnight world, the same fervour to reach out and touch … just … one … other … soul, in order that his own might be saved."

After all, during the shows Springsteen joked he had finally given in and accepted a tour sponsor, "because tonight our sponsor is love".

No-one else got an autograph as that was as much as Terry was going to allow. Bruce then went out the back door and we returned to the lobby bar. We then realised we needed to get out to the RDS through the Dublin traffic, so we asked the concierge if he would call us a cab.

He said that there was a difficulty getting cabs because of the crowds heading out to the RDS show and would we mind sharing with two other hotel guests? We agreed and ended up travelling to the RDS with two of the guys from Bon Jovi.

It was a great show but not as good as the E Street Band. Joe Ely appeared as did Jerry Lee Lewis in ridiculous trousers. Bruce was over-awed by him.

Nigel and Maggie Flynn, Ballymoney

The 1993 show had some notable highlights: a version of "Who'll Stop The Rain?" dedicated to the people of Bosnia and Herzegovina and Bruce introducing a special guest whom the crowd thought was Jon Bon Jovi (who was playing Dublin at the same time) but turned out to be Jerry Lee Lewis. He was a little under the influence but did great versions of "Whole Lotta Shakin' Goin' On" and "Great Balls Of Fire". Bruce finished that night with "Rockin' All Over the World" and a stonking "Bobby Jean".

Stephen Devine, Belfast

We were sent a bootleg C-90 tape probably 28 years ago. Leonard Cohen one side and somebody called Bruce Springsteen on the other. It was from my sister who lived in London

and she was the trendsetter in the family. I played it constantly, couldn't get enough time to listen to Cohen. Something made me keep fast forwarding and rewinding the other side to catch the beautiful lyrics of "Sandy".

We missed Slane. We had no real understanding of what was to hit us. Then we saw the "Dancing In The Dark" video on *Top Of The Pops* and my wife found the other man in her life. We've each seen him about 25 times, not only every RDS show, but also London, Manchester and the Giants Stadium, New Jersey.

We've spent some serious money just to make it there at times. Mere amateurs compared to others however.

Each and every announcement of a tour, from first knowledge to attaining your position at the very front of the barrier, is an emotional roller-coaster of anxiety, anticipation and endurance, each one etching memories on our minds that can only be understood by true Bruce fans.

Bruce makes standing in a ticket/concert queue for 15 hours (hail, rain, snow or shine) the thing to do.

And I'm sure that you'd agree that you feel that you're more than a fan, but rather a member of a worldwide family.

It's nice to see the same faces in the queues time after time.

John and Carol Mahon
Lifford, County Donegal

My husband Les and I have been Bruce fans back since the late 70s when Les went off to the US on a soccer scholarship and shared dorm rooms with a bunch

of Jersey guys and the passion began. I joined him Stateside in 1980. Soon I was hooked too.

We're back in Ireland since 1984 and have seen Bruce every time he has come to Ireland. The recent shows have been extra special with Belfast, Dublin (three concerts), one with our 22-year-old daughter, Aoife, now a de facto Bruce fan; plus Düsseldorf with our 14-year-old Katie who insisted on queuing for the pit and had the time of her life a stone's throw from the stage. Our son Niall, 20, also saw Bruce with us in 2003 at the RDS.

I've bumped into Bruce on two other occasions, lucky me! First time was in May 1993, the night before he was due to play the RDS. A bunch of us decided to head on up to the Westbury where we knew he was staying. It was a warm balmy evening and about 12 of us hung out at the front. It was a really good natured group and we had a good time waiting.

At one stage Daniel Lanois arrived in a taxi and I think for a minute he thought we were there to greet him. He saw the funny side of it. I was about four months pregnant. When Bruce's car eventually arrived and did a quick u-turn to the back of the hotel, everyone took off at a gallop. Not being able to gallop while pregnant I was kind of trotting behind.

When I caught up Bruce was in the car with the door open, chatting and signing autographs, and I said, "Bruce, how could you do that to a pregnant woman?" Instantly he looked up and connected with me and asked me why I wasn't home in bed at this time? (It was probably about 2am). ➡

So we had a funny little banter back and forth and I told him that this was the third time I was pregnant when he was in town, and he laughed when I said my husband wanted to know when he was coming back again.

I was so ecstatic and everyone was getting autographs as he made his way to the back door.

Someone was asking for a photo which he declined and then he said, "Okay, just one, with the pregnant lady!"

With that he put his arm around me and someone took the photo and then he bent down and kissed my head ... 15 years later I still swoon!

What a sweet guy. Needless to say I had to find the guy who took the photo. Now it goes everywhere with me.

Well, there's a little bit more magic to this tale.

We were at the Thursday and Friday concerts in May 2008, both nights in the Pit.

We worked all day Saturday and I wanted to go on a Bruce search around the city that evening. Anyway with a concert to go on Sunday we decided a night at home attending to our 'neglected' kids might be more suitable. We had just finished dinner when the phone rang.

My nephew works in our local pub The Queens in Dalkey and he phoned to say he had just served a pint to Bruce Springsteen. It took us all of about three minutes to get there.

Now you got to look cool in this place and that was very hard with our absolute hero sitting a couple of tables away with Bono and his wife Ali.

Anyway we waited until he was ready to leave and then walked over to greet him. It was funny because Bono came towards us first and I kind of just stepped out of his way and he winked over at Les as if to say, "I'm not flavour of the month here".

Bruce was as gracious as ever and when I produced my 15-year-old photo for him to sign he got a kick out of it.

Les got to shake his hand and then asked could we get a photo.

I knew they were in a hurry as Ali said so but he stood and once again he put his arm around me. I couldn't believe this was happening again.

In 2003 we'd spent a week around Freehold and Point Pleasant and visited the Stone Pony, Elm Street, his old school, Colts Neck, etc, and didn't get to see Bruce. Where should we meet him but in 'my hometown'!

The sad part to this was that some guy approached my husband and said he would take the picture, and he missed me out of the picture completely, except for my ear! It's a good picture of Bruce though.

Very coincidentally when we were in the queue for the pit the next day we met up with the very nice guy who had taken the photo at the Westbury. I recognized him straight away and he the same.

He looked at me and said, "You have a 14-year-old kid and I have a picture of you and Bruce on my wall". It was funny. He was with some of the people who were also there that night and we had a good time reminiscing.

It's always so great to talk with people who love Bruce as much as we do. What can you say about Bruce?

He's the best. His music has inspired me, lifted me up, and made me dance around my kitchen. It has spoken to me heart and soul.

He's a good man, morally, ethically, politically, and, as all female fans agree, gorgeous. May we have many more good times to share "further on up the road".

Grainne and Les Swan
Dalkey, Co Dublin

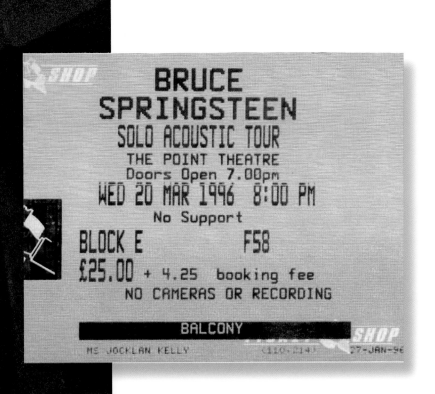

King's Hall
Belfast

19 March 1996

Crowd: 4,000

Tickets: £26.50 tickets

The Point
Dublin

20 March 1996

Crowd: 4,000

Tickets: IR£25

plus special guest appearance

The Mean Fiddler
Dublin

17 March 1996

Human Touch and *Lucky Town* had seen Springsteen having to deal with a mixed critical reaction to his music virtually for the first time.

The 'Other Band' had been an experiment which had resulted in some good shows but did not leave fans hankering for more of the same.

They wanted the E Street Band back.

A *Greatest Hits* album – apparently rushed out to fill a contractual gap when Springsteen decided to ditch a new album almost at the point of its release – hinted at an E Street reunion.

But Springsteen had other things on his mind. On November 21, 1995, he released *The Ghost Of Tom Joad*, a sparse collection of songs and his most nakedly political record to date. The album had a solo acoustic feel, although the singer was accompanied by a band on half of the 12 songs.

The album's characters largely belonged to an economic underclass. Most were either refugees or disenfranchised Americans.

The inspiration was cinematic and journalistic: John Ford's *The Grapes Of Wrath* – as opposed to John Steinbeck's – and newspaper reports of life on the Mexican border towns.

How would Springsteen tour on the back of an album whose tunes were often simple and stark, the vocal whispered? The night the album hit the stores he appeared at a theatre in New Jersey to launch the tour. He was alone and performed the 21-song set on an acoustic guitar.

The show set the tone for the tour, with Bruce – sometimes with humour but not always – stressing the importance of listening to the songs. "I got a couple of requests before I go on," he said early on. As many of the songs were "composed with a lot of silence", he explained, he'd prefer people didn't clap or even sing along. "That'll keep me from having to come out in the crowd and slap a few people around and ruin my nice-guy image." Someone whistled. "It goes for whistling too, pal," came the retort from the dark stage.

Other artists might have alienated their audiences by forcing them to sit down and listen to songs about Vietnamese immigrants, hobos intent on vengeful murder and Mexican teenagers forced to prostitute themselves to rich Americans for the price of sneakers and drugs.

And certainly Springsteen was doing it the hard way – for both himself and his fans. As Dave Marsh noted: "He could have gotten more love, bigger applause and probably higher ticket prices if he'd sung more old stuff, not just because it was old but also because it made fewer demands on the listener's conscience (and often, patience)."

However, in Ireland the album and accompanying tour was greeted with great anticipation.

The John Steinbeck-inspired, storytelling style, although often bleak, struck a chord. Irish fans knew that a true storyteller was worth a little patience and deserved to be heard. There was plenty in the songs for Irish audiences to identify with. After all if the stories were wound back a few generations the characters might well have been Irish rather than Mexican.

The title track offered the album's philosophy in a nutshell, outlining *The Grapes Of Wrath*'s Tom Joad manifesto for life, to fight for the poor and desperate, to highlight injustice. And the rest of the album probed even deeper. "Sinaloa Cowboys" followed Mexican brothers Miguel and Louis as they come to the States to find they can earn more cooking methamphetamine for local criminals than by doing honest but back-breaking work in the orchards. But it is a dangerous life and Louis is killed. The brothers learn a hard lesson. So too, equally tragically, does the young boy, Spider, in "Balboa Park", whose escape from the red light district of Tijuana takes him only to the drug-riddled streets of San Diego where rich men seek out young male prostitutes.

As this is Springsteen, he turns his focus to the other guys too, those doing their job on "The Line", including policeman Carl whose sympathy with the victims of the border's vicious circle of desperation, danger and crime, leads him to fall for a young refugee woman and to lose his job.

Each song provides a dreadful backdrop to the song of hope, "Across The Border" in which a man plans an escape into the US for him and his "corazón". This is the immigrant wanting his own piece of the American Dream, but the listener knows that has not been the experience of the others who have gone before.

True acceptance and redemption appear only on "Galveston Bay", in the potentially most violent confrontation of the album between Billy Sutter and Vietnamese refugee Le Bin Son who fish in the Gulf of Mexico. When the bars fill with "talk of America for Americans", Le is forced to kill two people in self-defence.

Billy plans to ambush and stab Le, but instead takes his boat into the bay and casts out his nets. Water, a redemptive source elsewhere in Springsteen's work, this time symbolizes not only the cleansing of the bitterness that almost ate Billy up but also the work and good living which redeems him.

Tom Joad's lyric sheet reads like it was put together by Raymond Carver during a day in a newspaper office in southern California. And as well as supporting one of Springsteen's most narrative-led albums to date, the live tour would feature plenty of in-between-song narration too, long stories, sometimes pensive, sometimes strange, and homilies on tolerance and racism.

The Irish dates were announced in January 1996, with Bruce not only coming to Dublin but to Belfast for the first time. The Dublin show would be the first of many at The Point theatre, while the Belfast show would be the first – and so far only show – at the King's Hall. The *Irish News* warned: "Demand is expected to be high for Springsteen's first-ever visit to the north but the all-seater show will hold only 4,000 and ticket sales will be restricted to four per customer."

Ahead of the full Dublin show, the *Evening Herald* warned fans about what was becoming known as Bruce's "Shut The F**k Up" policy. "If you are at The Point, be well behaved," it said. "There'll be no dancing in the dark and certainly no hollering out for favourite Boss tracks."

It said The Point had been adapted to accommodate the new mood. "It will be theatre style with tickets limited to 4,000, half what it normally holds."

The shows were arranged for Belfast on March 19 and Dublin, on the following night, March 20.

But arriving in Ireland ahead of both shows Bruce had a surprise in store for fans, with a special St Patrick's Day appearance.

Once again, the show was one from Joe Ely who was ending his tour with a night at the Mean Fiddler.

The Ghost Of Tom Joad
Adam Raised A Cain
Straight Time
Highway 29
Darkness On The Edge Of Town
Murder Incorporated
Nebraska
The Wish
It's The Little Things That Count
Brothers Under The Bridge
Born In The USA
Dry Lightning
Reason To Believe
Youngstown
Sinaloa Cowboys
The Line
Balboa Park
Across The Border
Bobby Jean
This Hard Land
Streets Of Philadelphia
Galveston Bay
The Promised Land

The Point, Dublin
included
Johnny 99
Mansion On The Hill
Spare Parts

Evening Herald writer George Byrne later described spying Springsteen in a dark corner of the club. "Punters coming back from the toilets were initially surprised to see him standing at the stairs beside the bar but once they realised it was him they never bothered him beyond nodding in recognition and the odd handshake," he recalled. "He had a minder with him all right but he was standing well back and obviously reckoned that he was going to have an easy night of things."

Until that was, the fans could allow themselves to go wild as Springsteen walked on to join the Texan rocker on a set consisting mainly of Ely numbers – "All Just To Get To You", "I Keep My Fingernails Long" and "Settle For Love" – a Woody Guthrie track "Blowin' Down The Road", and a couple of rock 'n' roll classics "Oh Boy" and "Long Tall Sally". The next day Bruce was driven up to Belfast for a sight-seeing tour. "The Boss refused the offer of a Jaguar for his drive around the streets and instead opted to be driven in a tour van," the *Belfast Telegraph* reported. "He wants to see the City Hall where Bill Clinton switched on the Christmas tree lights, the Shankill, the Falls and Stormont."
His tour of the city was something he later discussed with UTV journalist and fan Ivan Little. In his autobiography *Little By Little* the UTV man wrote that in his time he had interviewed a host of

celebrities including Bob Dylan and Diana Ross but that "nothing will equal the euphoria I felt as I stood on the stage of the King's Hall in Belfast interviewing the Boss".

I RAN TOO HARD
I PLAyed too Rough
I GAve my Love
Not Near Enough
I Bled too R-ed
I CRIED Too BLue
I Beat my Fist
AGAINST the Moon
All Just to Get to you

"O BOY"
ALL my LIFE I Been
a-waitin'
Tonight There'll be no
hesitatin'
OH Boy when you're
That you were meant with me

via Nigel and Maggie Flynn

After sitting in on the sound-check, and asking Springsteen's co-manager Barbara Carr if it would be okay to ask for Bruce's autograph (she was surprised as no-one had actually sought permission before), Little got his chance to speak to Bruce. "He spoke for about six or seven minutes, discussing his solo acoustic tour, his visits to the Shankill and the Falls

earlier that day, and his knowledge of Irish traditional music," wrote Little, who had first seen Springsteen at Slane. Ivan left "walking on air" – and with the autograph.
The show which followed, the *Belfast Telegraph* reported, was one which "virtually no other superstar could have got away with. No back-up band. No onstage antics. Almost no hits. Just that voice, a couple of 'geetars' and harmonica."
With his goatee beard and thinning hair, the "greatest living rock 'n' roller finally made it to Northern Ireland" for a "breathtaking show".
In 11 years Springsteen had travelled as far as he could have from the t-shirted sunshine of Slane. He stepped out onto the King's Hall stage in front of long black drapes and opened with "The Ghost Of Tom Joad".
The show which followed lasted two hours and 20 minutes and included two encores. Not a long show by Springsteen standards but this was Bruce totally alone.
It was not exactly folk; it was the rock star master of the highway making a detour, creating as charged an atmosphere by his subdued, sometimes brooding, and always quietly-intense demeanour, as he did when mustering the E Street Band for another big number.
"The man they once called the future of rock is now a huge slice of its past but

Bruce refuses to rest on his laurels or hardy annuals," said the *Belfast Telegraph*.

Although Springsteen was on his own with just his guitar and the lonesome wail of his harmonica, these were still Springsteen songs. They were still stories of faith and loss, of redemption and murder, of hope; and they took the audience by the collar and demanded attention.

Springsteen played 10 songs off *The Ghost Of Tom Joad* that night – everything but "My Best Was Never Good Enough" and "The New Timer".

That album then was the spine on which the show was built but it was complemented superbly with songs going back 20 years and others recently composed: "Adam Raised A Cain", "Darkness On The Edge Of Town" and the night's closer "The Promised Land" from *Darkness ...* ; "Nebraska", "Reason To Believe", the blues version of "Born In The USA" and "Bobby Jean"; "Murder Incorporated", "The Wish" (a song which tells the story of how *it* all started: when his mother took out a loan from a finance company to buy Bruce his first guitar); the hotel room seduction of "It's The Little Things That Count", an album out-take "Brothers Under The Bridge", "This Hard Land", one of dozens of songs originally recorded for *Born In The USA*, and "Streets Of Philadelphia", Springsteen's Oscar winner .

HIDING IN A CAR PARK

Like a few other Bruce fans we had seen the listings and knew that Joe Ely was performing the night before Bruce in a small intimate venue, the Mean Fiddler, so we had our tickets bought and hopes were high. We arrived early and were first inside the venue when the doors opened, taking our spot at stage front and centre. A long wait was rewarded by a great set from Joe. Word filtered through that Bruce had watched some of Joe's early set from beside the mixing desk. Bruce came on for the encore and played a blinder. Joe was up for it and the rest of the band was just in awe. There was a real sense of Bruce enjoying playing rock 'n'roll live again after all the *Tom Joad* acoustic. We thought it was just special. Walking off stage we gave Joe pictures of the last show (1993) in a folder. We never saw it again! At the end of the gig I lifted the handwritten set list and saw the words of "Oh Boy" written by Joe for Bruce to sing.

After the gig a few of us managed to get to a door back stage where Bruce would have to walk through to get out.

Eventually Bruce came out and just stopped long enough to get patted on the back and say hello, but I gave him a handwritten note offering him a lift up to Belfast and asking him to play "This Hard Land" in Belfast and to dedicate it to our peace process.

He took it and as he walked out with Terry beside him I saw him read it and put it in his back jeans pocket. Even though I didn't get a name mention I have always known, that when he mentioned "This one's for peace" before "This Hard Land" in Belfast a few nights later, that maybe my little note had something to do with that ... Anyway back to the Westbury, where weirdly we were staying with Bruce and Oasis in the same hotel. Next morning we were waiting in the first floor lobby, as were a few other people, hoping Bruce would go out that way. Once again we had a photo from the Joe Ely gig the night before to get signed.

Maggie was keeping her eye on Bruce's driver. When she saw him leave the lobby – she turned to me and said that we had better go downstairs to see where the car was waiting. We checked out the front and back doors but there was no sign of the Previa – only hundreds of fans waiting for a glimpse of Bruce.

"The car park," Maggie whispered to me, so as not to draw too much attention.

I told Maggie to go down on her own, again to not draw too much attention, and she made her way to the door but was stopped by security, until she pointed out that as a resident they couldn't stop her and that she only wanted to get her brush from the car. So down the stairs she went until she heard an engine running. Eventually the lift opened and Bruce and Terry appeared and so did Maggie.

She said to Bruce, "Will you sign a couple of photos please Bruce?" and he replied, "What? Hiding in a car park?"

To which Maggie answered, "You know Bruce that whenever you're in Ireland I'll always be hiding round the corner somewhere!" Bruce laughed and Maggie presented him with another photo of him and Joe Ely which she asked him to sign 'To Nigel' for me. ➡

(Bruce was to fly straight back from Ireland to the United States to take part in another Oscar ceremony; this time the song was "Dead Man Walking" and this time he did not win).

The *Belfast Telegraph* concluded: "It was no celebration. It was the stuff of looking in other people's souls. Challenging and depressing. But not without a little humour."

"I had a load of self-knowledge when I was 23," Springsteen told his audience. "Since then I've become a stranger to myself."

Springsteen chatted about his young family, about how the kids were plugged into the grace that adults constantly try to rediscover through movies and novels, and about being in Belfast. He left wishing "all peaceful lives".

After the King's Hall show Springsteen told Nigel Gould of the *Belfast Telegraph*: "It has been a very valuable experience for me – one that I will never ever forget. I just don't know why we didn't come here before now."

With his boots and socks off, relaxing backstage, Bruce was exhilarated by the welcome he had received in the small venue.

"I've had a wonderful time and I want you to tell the people of Northern Ireland how much I appreciate the support they gave me. I'd heard the crowds here were really loud and appreciative – they certainly were that.

"The people are without doubt among the friendliest I've ever encountered."

Maggie Flynn

Greg Lewis

Belfast Telegraph

Maggie Flynn

He added: "I want to … I hope to come back here one day. I went on a tour of Belfast – saw the sights – and it's something I will always remember.

"It was very intense I felt, but I was never frightened.

"My experience here might one day end up in a couple of songs, who knows?"

Outside the dressing room were Bono and the Edge, who had both sat in the front row of the show. Bono, hunched in a brown leather jacket, said: "Springsteen's acoustic music was unbelievable. I was enthralled."

The same newspaper's Eddie McIlwaine reported that after the show the three stars headed to Joe Webb's TL2 restaurant on the Stranmillis Road for a bite to eat and a chat.

"They just wanted a quick meal and a natter before heading back to Dublin," said Joe Webb later. "I was happy to oblige."

The Boss and his guests tucked into steak and chicken and salad and sipped a few glasses of Budweiser.

Springsteen was heard telling the U2 pair about his trip around Belfast.

Bruce also became a star-attraction to another celebrity too, jump jockey Enda Bolger who was celebrating a big win at Cheltenham by going to see his idol in Belfast.

After the show he was delighted to bump into Bruce. "I even name the horses I train after Springsteen," he told the newspapers. "I have 57 Channels and a Thunder Road in my string."

After snacking with Bono and the Edge, Bruce was driven back to Dublin to prepare for the following night's show at The Point.

The Dublin show differed little from Belfast, with Springsteen dropping "Murder Incorporated" and "Nebraska" in favour of "Johnny 99" and "Mansion On The Hill", and "Reason To Believe" for "Spare Parts".

"The Wish" got a special introduction as an old song he had written but not sung "for about nine years" for an "embarrassing reason, you see it's a song about my mother". Bruce added: "You can get away with quite a bit in rock and roll music (but) singing about your mother, no."

During one of the night's many guitar changes, Bruce introduced Kevin Buell, "my guitar technician, financial advisor, guru, yoga teacher, personal trainer, sexual counsellor (and) fellow New Jerseyan."

Springsteen dedicated "Sinaloa Cowboys" to a "mysterious friend" he met while touring the desert of Arizona on a motorbike. The Mexican stranger had told him about the loss of his brother in an accident.

"There was something in his voice that always stayed with me," Springsteen told the Dublin audience. "We sat for about an hour and talked about his brother." Springsteen described the fear of losing a family member, the sense of needing to protect them at all costs.

She then showed him a photo of him and her together saying, "And here's a photo of you and me". Bruce replied, "Yeah, there we are", and she asked him to sign it which he did.

Then Maggie asked Bruce if she could have a kiss. Bruce grinned, and she puckered up and so did he.

When she came back upstairs to tell me this all, I had to get a first kiss after Bruce ... sad but true. The *Tom Joad* concert in The Point was eerie. The lighting and acoustics of the old building gave it an eerie feeling I thought. So we all headed up to Belfast, us and Bruce, but he didn't take up my offer of a lift.

By the time we got to see Bruce in Belfast I had seen a few *Tom Joad* tour shows and knew the structure of the set list. We had good seats to the front and side of the stage in tiered seating. Halfway through the set a few extra seats were brought out and placed beside us. In the darkness few people noticed but I recognised Big Danny Gallagher from Asbury Park (then living in Dublin) and beside him, two other guys who on closer inspection turned out to be Bono and the Edge from U2.

We decided to give them their space and let them enjoy the show but when we knew the show was over Maggie reached over with our Bruce ticket stub and asked Bono for an autograph. They scurried away just afterwards. Not a bad show but more special as a first for Belfast and the usual respectful crowd. But when he had introduced "This Hard Land" it had made my night.

Nigel and Maggie Flynn, Ballymoney

I worked for Sony in Northern Ireland for 18 years as a PR officer.

In advance of his Slane gig, Sony decided to offer a promotion to record dealers. Buy 10 catalogue Springsteen albums and receive a picture disc of *Born In The USA* free. It was mental and one of the best campaigns ever undertaken.

I met Bruce on the *Tom Joad* tour in Belfast March 19, 1996. I handled the media interviews. He did a TV interview with Ivan Little from UTV on the stage after sound check in the King's Hall. This was his first visit to the North and first interview for the region. After the show I took Nigel Gould from the *Belfast Telegraph* back stage to meet Bruce. Barbara Carr arranged this.

We waited for 10 minutes in a cubicle next to his dressing room and were able to hear the conversation with the people he had in before us.

We heard him bid farewell to the two people by saying, "See you soon, lads, I have to meet the guy from the record company." Then out came Bono and the Edge to make way for Nigel and myself. We spoke to Bruce for 10 minutes without anyone else in the room. I asked about Clarence and what he was up to, Nigel spoke about the others. Bruce apologised that he was unable to offer us a drink as the lads before finished the bottle. He held up an empty Jack Daniel's bottle.

He posed for pictures and gave me the set-list for that night's show.

Brian Jordan
Belfast

"So I was writing a song on the Central California drug trade, they have Mexican gangs that come up into the Central Valley and hire migrant workers to work in these drug labs, they're the ones that usually get blown up or busted by the DEA. It's a song about two brothers and I was hearing my friend's voice in my head."

He introduced the story of violated innocence of "Balboa Park" with his own humorous recollections of having to indulge friends when they told him stories about their children's achievements. Now, he said laughing nervously, he got his own back by visiting those same friends with his own family and by getting to "bore thousands speaking about my own kids".

Before "Across The Border" Springsteen described first seeing John Ford's *The Grapes Of Wrath* and realising this was what he wanted to do: "You always hope that you'll be able to do work that'll mean something".

And before "Galveston Bay", "We were up in Belfast last night ... very powerful. This is a song about small decisions that change the world. (It's) based on some incidents that happened in the Gulf Coast of Texas in the mid-80s. At the end of the Vietnam War there were a lot of Vietnamese refugees that came into the Gulf Coast and there was a lot of tension. They went into the fishing industry and there was a lot of tension and a big deal of violence between the Vietnamese fishermen and the Texas fishermen."

For the *Evening Herald* the show provided "without frills thrills".

Its reviewer Tony O'Brien said Springsteen's "remarkable tour de force" held a "4,000-strong audience spellbound with just the aid of an acoustic guitar, harmonica, his trademark gravel-throated voice and some great songs".

He added: "There was no big-time stage show, flashing lights, pyrotechnics or tricks. Just one man alone with his music.

"But what a man. This was a very different Bruce from the triumphal Boss who raged across Slane and RDS stages roaring out his songs with the aid of the E Street Band. Here everything was stripped to the bone." Springsteen's stripped down solo tour went on for more than a year. It meandered through Japan and Australia, the US and a second leg of Europe, but in every way it was a journey through adulthood.

By its close he was already re-evaluating his relationship with his blood brothers of his rock 'n' roll youth. How would it be if they came back together now?

Why is Bruce so big in Ireland? Ireland has always been somewhere people had to get out of, due to economics or something else. So many of Bruce's songs are about breaking away, "Born To Run", "Thunder Road", "The Promise", etc, etc, so I think thematically the music fits with some of the Irish psyche.

But the main reason, I think, is the literary aspect to Bruce's songs.

The obvious affinity we have for storytelling in Ireland means Bruce's music is so attractive.

It's funny that Bruce acknowledges that he felt a special connection was made during *The Ghost Of Tom Joad* tour. I don't think that's a surprise. The acoustic nature of the show made people listen to the words, to the story. Previously I think many went to Springsteen with a passing knowledge of the music, coming out wondering why "Dancing In The Dark" or "Born In The USA" wasn't played.

I think the acoustic tours prompted people to listen to the new and old music and hear the stories behind the songs.

The result? A better educated audience at the larger concerts and decent sales in the Irish market.

Eddie Barron, Liverpool

About three songs before "Youngstown" was played I shouted out a request for it, and Bruce thought he was being heckled. I managed to get a bootleg of the gig and my voice is very audible on it.

**Jocelyn Kelly
Dublin**

Being my first visit to Belfast (like Bruce), I remember being nervous, seeing armoured cars on the streets, and the patrol towers on the border as we took the train in from the south. I guess that's my dominant memory of the show, the sense that both Bruce and I were strangers in town, and I'm sure we both felt the uneasiness of a recent, tentative peace that enabled us to be there. A curious combined sense of humility and privilege, too.

That whole period was a bizarre few days, as just two days before I'd been in Dublin on a tip-off that Bruce would play on St Patrick's night with Joe Ely and his band at the Mean Fiddler ... and of course as we know now he did. Only the second time ever I'd seen a club/guest appearance by Bruce (the first was a Stone Pony show in 1982).

Even when I saw Terry Magovern it hardly seemed real after all the speculation, so it wasn't until the man himself walked on to thunderous applause that it started to sink in. He looked so different too, since we'd been used to the troubadour look of the previous *Joad* shows: he had his hair brushed forward, not slicked back ... and he was carrying an electric guitar for the first time that year.

Talk about goosebumps!

A superb set of encores with Joe and co, and then it took a couple of hours to walk back to our base in the outskirts of Dublin, with barely enough time for a cup of tea before it was time to leave for the airport and fly home at dawn to London.

A surreal moment followed at work that morning, when I tried to explain to non-

Bruce-fan colleagues that, yes, I'd flown to Ireland for the weekend and, yes, I was flying back to Ireland again two days later for the two 'proper' shows in Belfast and Dublin! Not sure I ever lived that down ...

Dan French, Hertfordshire, England

The Point show was the only concert I couldn't get a ticket for as they sold out in ten minutes so you can imagine my disappointment but such is my love and dedication to Bruce I knew I had to go.

My mate, who I converted, and myself went to put our faith in the touts and what a result. We not only got tickets but got sitting three rows from the front.

The Boss didn't let us down as he played for over three hours, just himself on an acoustic guitar and harmonica. It was a magic night and when he came to the front of the stage to shake hands with the fans in the front row I seized the chance and went up and waited until he came to where I was standing and, like a child waiting for Santa to come, it was a dream come true when he shook my hand and all I could do was say to him, "Thanks, man, I love ya."

I think that night ranks with the highest of my Bruce experiences as I never thought I would get the chance to meet my hero.

John Flannery, Ballymote, Co Sligo

I met Bruce during the Tom Joad tour in 1996 in Belfast. I had a couple of hours free in between lectures at college and I decided to go to the venue to see what was going on. I was stopped by security who thought I was with BT and let me into the venue. ⬇

I was stopped again inside the venue, but I asked (politely) if I could see the stage and equipment being set up. Unusually, they agreed as long as I didn't get in the way.

Backstage I met Kevin Buell tuning Bruce's guitars. I asked him if I could watch the soundcheck and he told me to speak to the stage manager.

Kevin pointed him out to me and I asked. He told me that this wouldn't be a problem but to come back at 5pm and tell security I was expected. 5pm came round and I was allowed in. After a few minutes Bruce appeared on stage casually strumming his guitar. He proceeded to go through the setlist for the show while I was sitting on the top step on the stage. The stage manager asked me if I was enjoying the performance and asked if I was going to the show later, which of course I was. He told me to wait around for a few minutes after the soundcheck as he wanted to see me. Bruce finished the soundcheck, went to the other side of the stage and did an interview with UTV. When he was finished Bruce walked over towards me at the side of the stage.

All I could say was to ask for an autograph and tell him how much of a fan I was. He graciously thanked me for my support and wished me a great show that evening and made his way up the corridor. The stage manager came back to me and asked for my tickets to the show. To my surprise he produced alternative tickets and my girlfriend and I enjoyed a fantastic evening second row centre from the front.

Paul McCann, Keady, Co Armagh

Arriving early at the Point, my wife and I took our seats. Way, way back, up in the balcony and about as far away from the stage as it was possible to be.

Empty seats all around us, a glum look on my face. This wasn't going to be great. We sit silently. A bloke, dressed in black, comes in from the stairs behind our head, looks around and shakes his head. "Man, these aren't good seats are they?" he says.

Eimear, my wife, is nearer and talks to him. I'm still sulking a bit.

He asks, "Are you big Bruce fans?"

Eimear, being very honest, says, "Well my husband is, has been for years." (Since 1979 as it happens.)

Man says, "Would you like front row seats?" We say, "Yes, please!" but figure there's gotta be a catch so we warily exchange our ticket stubs with him for fresh Row A tickets. He's gotta be joking but sure we'll see what happens. We take the tickets and head off down the stairs, and approach the first security check - through it no bother and the second and then are shown to our seats in THE FRONT ROW, for the up-close and personal Tom Joad tour. Unbelievable. You should have seen the smile on my face.

At the end of the show when making our way out we saw our mysterious benefactor backstage and later found out he was The Man in Black, Bruce's personal Santa Claus.

Stephen Ryan, Blackrock, Dublin

Terry Thorp

RDS
Dublin

25 May 1999

Crowd: 30,000

Tickets: IR£28.50

As the 1990s drew to a close Bruce Springsteen marked 25 years as a recording artist. It seemed an appropriate time to take stock of all that had gone before and to see how that might inform the future.

After completing the *Tom Joad* tour he made a number of guest appearances at charity and award shows, and in November 1997 invited some folk musicians to his farm to record a tribute song to Pete Seeger (the full significance of which would not become clear for virtually another decade).

Most significantly at the time, Springsteen issued *Tracks*, a collection of 66 unreleased songs going right back to his audition recordings for CBS. Most, of course, had been recorded with the E Street Band and in March 1999 word leaked out about secret band rehearsals which were taking place in Asbury Park.

Tracks was no new album, though, and some wondered if it marked a big enough progression to provide the creative and narrative drive needed for a new tour.

Even Bruce expert Dave Marsh was "as nervous as a spurned lover about to meet his darling once again." He asked: "What if they weren't as great as I remembered? What if this turned out to be another run-of-the-mill rock-band reunion, guys going through the motions to cash in or try to recapture a little of the old glory?"

Perhaps some of the answers were provided at the Waldorf Astoria in New York on March 15, 1999, when Bruce was inducted into the Rock 'n' Roll Hall of Fame by Bono, who recalled first hearing Springsteen's music in Dublin in 1974. "Bruce Springsteen was comin' on, saving music from the phonies, saving lyrics from the folkies, saving leather jackets from the Fonz … In Dublin, Ireland, I knew what he was talking about. Here was a dude who carried himself like Brando, and Dylan, and Elvis. If John Steinbeck could sing, if Van Morrison could ride a Harley-Davidson ... He was the first whiff of Scorsese, the first hint of Patti Smith, Elvis Costello and the Clash."

Bruce responded, first with a quick aside: "Remember: You always want an Irishman to give your induction speech ... I knew I always liked you, Bono."

Springsteen's thank-yous started with the Italian side, his mother Adele, and then with the Irish side, his father, Doug, with whom he had such a difficult relationship and who had recently passed away. "I've got to thank him because what would I conceivably have written about without him? I mean, you can imagine that if everything had gone great between us, we would have had a disaster. I would have written just happy songs and I tried it in the early 90s and it didn't work; the public didn't like it! He never said much about my music, except that his favourite songs were the ones about him. And that was enough, you know!"

But the main thank-yous were for the band members, past and soon-again-to-be present. For Nils Lofgren, "the most overqualified second guitarist in show business. He plays 10 times better than me and he still wanders over to hear my solos when I play. I guess he's checking to see if I'm getting any better."

For Danny Federici, "the most instinctive and natural musician I ever met and the only member of the band who can reduce me to a shouting mess", and Garry Tallent, "my lovely friend, bass player, rock 'n' roll aficionado, whose quiet and dignity graced my band and my life", and Roy Bittan, whose "playing formed the signature sound of some of my greatest records" and whose "emotional generosity and his deep personal support mean a great, great deal to me".

For Max Weinberg who "found a place where Bernard Purdie, Buddy Rich and Keith Moon intersected and he made it his own", for Patti Scialfa who "busted the boys' club, big time", and, of course, for Clarence Clemons, "a source of myth and light and enormous strength for me on stage".

He spoke of standing next to Clarence on stage of feeling a special presence: "He has filled my heart so many nights - so many nights - and I love it when he wraps me in those arms at the end of the night. That night we first stood together, I looked over at C and it looked like his head reached into the clouds. And I felt like a mere mortal scurrying upon the earth, you know. But he always lifted me up. Way, way, way up. Together we told a story of the possibilities of friendship, a story older than the ones that I was writing and a story I could never have told without him at my side."

He spoke in similar terms of his old friend Steve Van Zandt. "He's a lifetime rock 'n' roll friendship. We did it all, you know. Great songwriter, producer, great guitarist. We haven't played together in 15 years, and if it's up to me, that won't ever happen again. I love you, Steve."

With passion like that, what else was the reunion of the E Street Band going to be other than a marvellous re-birth and re-dedication of the spirit that had suffused that band of musicians since they had first come together?

Bono's speech for Bruce had hinted at Bruce's impact on Irish music.

U2 had paid tribute to Springsteen before. The Edge has said Springsteen's concert at Wembley Arena in 1981 changed U2's approach to live shows. "I was a fan at that point, but seeing him live is a whole other thing. We certainly borrowed from Bruce in terms of trying to reach out to the guy at the very back of the room.

As a musician and a songwriter he changed the game." And in 1985 Bono described to *Hot Press* his own ambitions to mature as a songwriter: "Most of the writing I've done - five years of it - has been more prose than song. I feel I must begin to come to terms with being a songwriter and actually start communicating on the first level as well as just on the third level. Springsteen is an expert at communicating on the first level."

In the same year, the Dublin band held its first gig at Dublin's Croke Park and played "My Hometown" as a homecoming tribute. They have also shared the stage with Bruce on a number of occasions.

Six years after Springsteen's Rock 'n' Roll Hall of Fame moment, Bruce returned the compliment when he inducted U2 into the roll of honour. "One of the best and most endearingly naked messianic complexes in rock 'n' roll," he said in tribute to Bono. "It takes one to know one."

The connections do not end with U2 either. Thin Lizzy's "The Boys Are Back In Town" owes its spirit to the romance of "Born To Run" and parts of its melody to "Kitty's Back" (in town) from *The Wild, The Innocent And The E Street Shuffle*.

Similarly, Springsteen's imagery struck a chord with The Boomtown Rats who also drove some of their biggest hits – "Rat Trap", in particular – with a soaring sax rising straight up from E Street.

My Love Will Not Let You Down
Prove It All Night
Two Hearts
Darlington County
Mansion On The Hill
Youngstown
The River
Murder Incorporated
Badlands
Out In The Street
Tenth Avenue Freeze-Out
Red Headed Woman
Working On The Highway
The Promised Land
The Ghost Of Tom Joad
Born In The USA
Jungleland
Light Of Day
Cadillac Ranch
Hungry Heart
Born To Run
Thunder Road
If I Should Fall Behind
Land Of Hope And Dreams

CHAPTER FIVE REUNION

Springsteen, in turn, has always been keen on Van Morrison, citing his influence back before he had even started the E Street Band.

The Bruce Springsteen and the E Street Band *Reunion* tour kicked off at the Palau Sant Jordi in Barcelona on April 9, 1999, and did not reach the United States until July. As Dave Marsh notes: "Bruce had been for the last several tours a bigger act overseas than at home."

The Irish show was to be the 19th of the tour and was planned for the RDS, Dublin, on May 25, 1999.

In the arts section of *The Irish Times* Harry Browne asked whether the new tour was just following the path of a "rock dinosaur" (Springsteen was now 49 – a dinosaur in rock years).

Bringing the E Street Band back had to be "let's face it … a bit of a throwback". They had "played hundreds of gigs that left audiences gasping for superlatives" but for the past decade Springsteen "has been trying new sounds, different moods – for the attention, it must be said, of a dwindling audience".

However, Browne, who first heard Springsteen on the radio when he was a teenager in the late 1970s, went on to write a passionate and enlightening analysis of Bruce, concluding that when the band kicked off at the RDS: "I'll be the guy pushing my way to the stage to scream out the names of the musicians in a Jersey/Dublin accent".

all photos Chris Carry

The reason was simple. The ties were too strong to break, no matter what the band was doing this time: reunion or dedication.

"The songs and stories have changed over the years but running through Springsteen's work is a strain that has taken me and other listeners from adolescence to – well, maybe, it's helped keep us there. *Homo Springsteenicus* is the flawed hero of an essentially spiritual struggle, for respect, for peace, for forgiveness, for redemption, for love.

"In so many of the songs there's a desperate quasi-religious sense that getting your own head and heart together - preferably in the company of someone else - is sanctified work, even when you've got to crawl through some dirt to do it. The fact that completing the task seems to be impossible just lends the effort more credibility."

All that, said Browne, explains why lonely music fans paw over Springsteen lyrics as they try to make sense of their lives.

"What's rather incredible is what tens of thousands of people in the RDS arena and surrounding neighbourhoods will rediscover tonight: in concert Springsteen takes a deeply personal and pained collection of songs and turns them into one of the loudest most exuberant parties you've ever seen."

So why should the sceptical still care – or start to care – about Springsteen?

"Well, the songs. All the clichés about Springsteen being the (presumptuous) chronicler of grease-stained working-class life or the (heavy-handed) romantic balladeer of beautiful losers – they're wrong. Damn, even a rudimentary listen to his lyrics will tell you that, for Springsteen, the way you walk is more important than what you drive."

Browne added: "At his best … he embodies, in passionate, precise words and powerful, mood-soaked melodies the contradictions we all know about. The lies we tell to find the truth. The hurt we cause in the name of love. The solitude we embrace in search of companionship. The dreams we abandon, so we can dream again."

Previewing the show in the *Irish Independent*, George Byrne felt that by blending the grand and the intimate, the youthful rock 'n' roll with songs about some of the joys of family life, the new show could prove a true, full band sequel to what had gone before – right back to the sunshine of Meath 14 years earlier.

"That he could work a crowd like few other artists on the planet was confirmed in the summer of 1985 when over 70,000 people packed into the grounds of Slane Castle on a gloriously sunny day for a three-hour plus show which was one of the highlights of the decade," wrote Byrne.

"I am a true blue fan of Bruce. I became an instant fan at his appearance in the RDS on May 25, 1999. He just walked out and the place went crazy. It was the best ever gig."

George Humphries, Dublin

I am French and I have been living in Ireland for the past 18 years. Although I am not Irish I have made my life and my home in this country and I never looked back.

I remember buying the *Live 1975 -1985* box-set in the 80s. I liked the music but at the time I couldn't speak any English so I didn't really understand the songs and their meaning. I never got the chance to go to a concert in those days, and I very much regret it. My life took me to Africa, where music was the last thing on my mind. Then a few years after moving to Ireland, a friend of mine gave me the CD *The Ghost Of Tom Joad* and I loved it, I could understand English and this was a whole new experience for me.

One day that same friend invited me to see a concert in the RDS in 1999 … I was never the same after that. The power of the music, the intensity and the energy on stage was phenomenal, I had never seen anything like that. I went back home, being aware that I had witnessed the music that was going to change my life. I did my "homework" and gradually bought all the CDs and read all the books I could find. This music became the soundtrack of my life, helping me through the tough times.

Dominique Jumelle, Quin, Co Clare

Bruce was staying at the Merrion so off we went to wait on the comings and goings of the band. This time Maggie said I should get the photos as she had had her moments of glory. So all day one at a time we "picked off" the band. Danny walking out pushing a pram, Garry Tallent walking out with singer Steve Forbert, Clarence lifting me off my feet as he pulled me in a big hug for a photo, Steve and his horrible snakeskin shoes, the Mighty Max - the perfect gentleman, Nils worried about the camera flash in his eyes, so keeping his sunglasses on and Roy small and so polite.

Eventually as the crowd grew, out came the boyo with security and I was pushed to the side but we had managed to get an autograph of every one of the E Street Band on the cover of a *Born To Run* CD. (Guess what, it's framed!)

My favourite meet that day was Patti. She was very gracious and seemed embarrassed to be approached but was very attractive.

There was a story that not only did Bruce's mum watch the show from side stage but earlier that day she and Bruce had gone out to do some research into the family history.

Best show memories would be "Red Headed Woman" for all the Irish girls.

Nigel and Maggie Flynn
Ballymoney

"After that album and tour things were never quite the same commercially for Bruce Springsteen – and you got the impression he preferred it that way …
"And now Bruce has decided to reunite with the E Street Band after a ten-year gap on a tour which – so far – has touched on every aspect of his musical career. Happily married to singer Patti Scialfa and with children to raise, Bruce Springsteen approaches his 50th birthday at ease with himself and still utterly in love with rock 'n' roll – which was what brought him here in the first place."

Having landed in Dublin, and taken time to visit friend and racehorse trainer Enda Bolger in County Limerick (the *Evening Herald* reported Bolger had been helping Bruce choose some horses for his farm), Bruce was ready for his first show with the E Street Band in Ireland since 1988.

A sound check at the RDS featured four songs they would play that night – "My Love Will Not Let You Down", "Prove It All Night", "Red Headed Woman" and an acoustic version of "Born In The USA" – and an old Elvis gospel number "Working On The Building", performed for a group of men who were, of course, working on a building opposite.

Despite the recent release of *Tracks* only "My Love Will Not Let You Down", the night's opener, came from that box set. The band then turned the clock back 15 years by ripping into "Prove It All Night", "Two Hearts" and "Darlington

Terry Thorp

County" before breathing new life into two tracks from a couple of Bruce's "solo" projects, "Mansion On The Hill" and "Youngstown".

Dave Marsh said that it was at this point in his own first *Reunion* concert that he *got it*. "The band did exactly what it had always done – better … The E Street Band had grown."

Clarence Clemons framed "The River" with a beautiful, extended bluesy intro and an outro accompanied by Bruce's own lingering falsetto which wrung every ounce of pathos out of the song. As the final chords hung in the air, the band continued a set which absolutely rocked: "Murder Incorporated", "Badlands", "Out In The Street", "Tenth Avenue Freeze-Out", "Red Headed Woman", "Working On The Highway" and "The Promised Land".

He slowed for "The Ghost Of Tom Joad" (dedicated to Boston civil rights worker and Springsteen fan Lenny Zakim) before draining the last out of the night's main set with "Born In The USA", "Jungleland" and "Light Of Day".

The encore was to be a blistering one. "Cadillac Ranch" and "Hungry Heart" turned up the party; "Born To Run" and "Thunder Road" tipped the nod to the "old" fans; then a new arrangement of the ballad "If I Should Fall Behind" and a new song "Land Of Hope And Dreams", the hymn to tolerance, companionship and understanding which was to end every show of the tour.

It all started in 1987 when school pal Donal Lillis gave me a 90-minute cassette, his 'Best of Bruce' at the time. The cassette eventually snapped from playing "Born To Run" over and over again. By that time I had treated myself to the *Live 1975-1985* box set on vinyl and was hooked. A small ad in the then *Cork Examiner* the following year announced my first Bruce show – RDS, Dublin, July 7, 1988. Funnily enough my first ever Bruce queue was to get a ticket for the bus to Dublin for that gig. I remember it as being a long and wonderful show. Many highlights included "Tunnel Of Love", "Adam Raised A Cain", "Spare Parts", "Chimes Of Freedom", "Paradise By The C" and what an encore!

Little did Donal and I know that our first E Street Band show would be our last for more than 10 years. Over the next 10 years or so there was a constant theme of sleeping on floors, in cars, never having any savings.

The 1992/93 tour with the 'Other Band' doesn't stand out as being a great tour in the history books but I still remember the May 20, 1993, RDS show as being a great night. The surprise of "This Hard Land", my first ever "Badlands" and "Thunder Road". I was in the pit that night, Donal was in the stands, that wouldn't happen again for 15 years. The lack of internet in those days meant that there were a lot more surprises in the set-list but it also had its disadvantages. As Donal collected me at Dublin airport on March 19, 1996 after a St Patrick's weekend in Glasgow he informed that Bruce was just coming on stage in The King's Hall in Belfast at around the same time, bummer! March 20, 1996 was a great night. My first of many Bruce shows in The Point. Great acoustic versions of so many classics, "Adam Raised A Cain", "Darkness …", "Born In The USA". Great new songs like "The Wish" and "It's The Little Things That Count".

What fantastic years 1998 and 1999 were. *Tracks*, the reunification of The E Street Band, the return of Steve Van Zandt to the band, killer classic set lists …

I was back in college in 1999 and didn't have a lot of spare cash but I still managed five Reunion tour shows. Four stellar nights in Earls Court and then back to the RDS. "My Love Will Not Let You Down", full band "Born To Run", "Prove It All Night", "The Promised Land".

We almost missed the start of the RDS show thanks to the non-arrival of a DART train and only arrived in time thanks to a fast taxi driver. We did miss the sound check unfortunately which included the only ever performance of "Working On The Building" played for some construction workers working across the road.

Kieran Lonergan, Mitchelstown, Cork

"DON'T MEET YOUR HEROES"
'Twas the day after the night before … May 1999. Bruce had just played the RDS on the *Reunion* tour. I live in North Meath so it was a late night getting home, getting up again at 6am to head back to work in Dublin the following day. I was wrecked after putting every available ounce of energy (like we do) into singing and 'dancing' at the show. ⬇

There were plenty of nods to the Irish crowd throughout and, in particular, to Bruce's own Irish roots.

Adele Springsteen, watching her son on his first tour since his Irish-American father's death, was there at the side of the stage. In the middle of "Tenth Avenue Freeze-Out" came the band introductions, Springsteen striding the stage describing the "many avenues" down which he had walked. Halfway through, about to arrive at the saucy introduction of his wife, he caught sight of his mother's beaming smile: "… And then I walked on like I was in a dream, and in that dream I swear I was in Ireland and I thought I saw my mama … Freud, where are you, baby, when I need you!?"

But it was on "Light Of Day" that Springsteen the mock preacher resurfaced with a vengeance.

"Well, I'm glad to be here in your lovely city tonight. What I want to know is, are there any O'Farrells out there? Are there any McNicholases out there? Are there any O'Hagans out there? Cos if you are, you're my relatives … on my daddy's side."

A pause.

"But I'm not here tonight to visit relatives, to see the sights of your beautiful city or kiss up to the audience by telling them about my lineage …

"I'm not here tonight to drink that fine Guinness I know that's waiting for me down at the bar somewhere … or maybe I am here tonight for that a little bit … "But that's not all I'm here tonight for. We're here tonight with a purpose. That's right, we've come to bring a message … and it's been a long journey. We've come a long way to deliver this message for you. I've been to [singing] Alabama, California, Minnesota, Oklahoma, Louisiana, Bogalusa, East Paducah, Reno, Chicago, Fargo, Buffalo, Toronto, Winslow, Arizona, Wichita, Tulsa, Ottawa to see you ma, Black Rock, Little Rock, Hackensack, Hennessy, Tennessee, Dublin and back …

"But everywhere I've gone, I've found people that are lost, I've seen people filled with confusion, I've seen people lost in the wilderness, I've seen people downhearted [drum beat], dis-spirited [drum beat], dispossessed [drum beat], analyzed [drum beat], downsized [drum beat], stigmatised [drum beat], factionalised [drum beat], fractionalised [drum beat], retropsychedelicized!

"And I'm here tonight to let you know that if your soul has bad credit, it's good here. And I want you to know that if your heart is running on empty, then pull on up to the pumps, we're selling high-test supreme. If your spirit's bankrupt, we're here to lift that debt up off you just a little bit and help set you free.

"I want to [fast again] re-educate you, I want to regenerate you, I want to reconfiscate you, rededicate you, I want to, I want to reliberate you, I want to, I want to, I want to take you to high ground. Holler if you hear me! [cheers] "I want to fill you with the power, the promise, the power, the promise, the power, the promise, the power, the promise, the power, the promise, the power, the promise, the majesty, the mystery, the ministry of rock and roll!

"Now, I know you got your worries. You're worried about the Y2K problem. My stocks up, my bonds are down, mortality is rearing its ugly head.

"I know you know the Good Book says 'Louie, Louie', Chapter 1, Verse 1, 'Louie, Louie, oh-oh, we've all got to go', but I can't, I can't, I can't, I cannot, I cannot, I cannot promise you life everlasting … but I can promise you life … right now!"

It was a promise that, as usual, he kept. Before his final song Bruce gave his usual thanks "for coming down to the show tonight".

He added: "We've had a lot of memorable times here in Ireland. It's something to come back this long after we started to find this kind of a reception. We appreciate all the years of support for our music, and these are kind of a special series of concerts for us, sort of a rebirth, rededication of our band, our commitment to serve you, and so in that spirit we want to leave you with a new song called "Land Of Hope And Dreams"."

Aidan Twomey's review of the show in the next day's *Irish Times* reminded readers of the pre-show fear about artists going back over old ground: "Even though there was plenty of juice left in the E Street Band when Bruce prematurely disbanded them in 1989 conventional pop wisdom would suggest that they belong in the past, that to dredge them up again would be the lazy reaction of a man basking in box-sets and greatest hits packages."

The concert blew that myth clean across Ballsbridge. "How refreshing then that last night's concert was a tour de force which confirmed (the band) as one of the most awesome combos in pop." Twomey's review confirmed that this was not the usual re-tread of all tracks, the true spirit was undimmed.

"Springsteen's songs, although melodically simple, are grenades which can be exploded at will, releasing stories and emotions as pungent as anything since Dylan. This is achieved without gimmicks and, while there is a showmanship (like the guitars-together bonhomie and the milking of his Irish roots), there is also a complete lack of pomposity, which makes these honest, powerful songs what they are."

The *Reunion* tour ended with 10 nights at Madison Square Garden with Bruce riding the storm over another new song "American Skin (41 Shots)", about the shooting dead of an unarmed African man named Amadou Diallo by New York City Police.

I got into work and noticing an invite on my desk to a trade show back at the RDS I decided I was too fragile for sitting looking at a PC all day so, after chatting with some of my team about the concert (my enthusiasm and anticipation for the gig made some of them go out and buy tickets too!), and after letting rush hour go by, I headed back into the city centre to make my way back towards the RDS Exhibition Hall.

I found myself sitting at the traffic lights at Holles Street and Merrion Square. As I sat there waiting for the green light I wondered to myself, 'Hmm? If I was Bruce where would I stay in Dublin?' The first two hotels that came to mind were the Westbury and the Merrion. As I was right on Merrion Square I decided what the heck, I'd go and park and mosey up to the hotel to see if anything was happening. Nothing ventured, nothing gained, etc.

As it just so happened I had a bunch of CD booklets in the boot of my car. I don't know why I was carrying these around with me, but I'd had a dream that I'd bumped into Roy Bittan in St Stephen's Green park, so, inexplicably really, I put CD booklets of Stevie Nicks, Bowie, Meat Loaf and Dire Straits - albums that Roy had played on - in my car the week before the gig. For good measure I also had the CD booklet from *Born To Run* and *Tracks* as well. Just in case.

I stood around on my own, feeling more than a bit self-conscious that at 36 years old I was in effect 'stalking', and that a grown man should have known better.

After about 15 minutes Roy Bittan walked up to the hotel (he'd been down Grafton Street shopping). To say I couldn't believe it would be ever-so-much a slight understatement. He stopped when he saw me (maybe fearing for his safety) but when he saw the CD booklets he said, "Hey! You've got all my stuff there, that is so cool." He autographed everything I had.

I also knew he was originally from Rockaway in New York. I lived in Rockaway for 18 months in the 1980s so I mentioned this to him. He asked whereabouts in Rockaway. I said, "Belle Harbour." He said, "Hey! I'm from Belle Harbour!" He asked, "What street?" I said, "126 St."

He said, "*No way*! I was *born* on 126th Street." It turned out we had neighbours in common.

Great chat with Roy, such a nice bloke. I rang my wife and was barely able to verbalise my excitement at what had happened down the phone. At this stage I thought if I hung around a bit more and got to meet Nils Lofgren I'd be a very, very happy boy. I was a Nils fan back in the mid 70s before I'd joined the Bruce brother-sisterhood. *The Old Grey Whistle Test* had brought me to both of them.

I was still the only person outside the hotel. Eventually an official-looking American chap came out and was standing on the path. I politely asked was he with the tour and expressed sympathy with the schedule that had them heading immediately to Belgium for the next show. We started chatting. ⬇

The band had been revitalised and rededicated, alright, blending the darker shades of Springsteen's music with the essential elements of the house party. "American Skin (41 Shots)" illustrated Springsteen's need to keep himself and his music absolutely relevant and engaged.

Wider forces would ensure that was one demand which Bruce would have to remain firmly focussed on next time out.

After a few minutes and, I guess, figuring I wasn't a threat to anybody, he said to me, "If you go into the hotel, hang a left at reception, go through the doors, you may meet someone that you'd like to speak to." Gulp!

So I went into the hotel, followed the directions, and found myself in what seemed a private breakfast room. Patti Scialfa was in there with (I assume) the other tour wives, significant others, etc. As they were still eating breakfast I quickly started to apologise for wandering in.

Patti immediately told me it was fine, I said, nope, sorry ladies I didn't mean to interrupt etc. Patti insisted I came over to her. She asked my name (her voice was shot and sounded very sore) and what I'd thought of the show, etc, and she insisted on autographing some stuff for me.

She couldn't have been more lovely. Thanking her and the other ladies, profusely, with more apologies I headed back out onto the street.

When I had calmed down a bit, I noticed another chap, in a suit, loitering with what looked like no intent at all. However, I sensed the presence of another Bruce fan. So we got chatting about Bruce, music, etc, and another 20 minutes flew past.

He had a disposable Fuji camera, but no pen. He worked in *The Financial Times* (next door to the Merrion) and decided he was popping back to get a pen, as all I had with me was a ballpoint I'd found in my car. So off he went.

I turned back to face down the street, smiling away to myself like a loon. As I turned back to face the hotel, big Terry Magovern, God bless him, walked past me giving me the once-over. He looked me up and down and opened the door of a wine-coloured MPV that was sitting at the kerb. He seemed satisfied that he could take me if I got antsy, so he left me alone.

As I looked back at the hotel Bruce Springsteen was walking down the steps, on his own, heading for the car. As he stepped onto the path he looked at me, probably familiar with the deer-in-the-headlights look on my face, looked at the CD stuff in my hands, came over to me, smiled and said, in post-show rasp, "Hey, whatcha got there?"

I looked down at my hands, was able to stick out a hand which he shook, then thrust both hands out to him while making a kind of gurgling, mumbling, humming, noise which was supposed to be words.

For the love of God, I was 36 years old, but my knees started to shake uncontrollably – twenty-plus years of fandom kicking in. The living breathing man that is Bruce Springsteen was standing in front of me. Not the icon in the videos or on the album covers. A bloke. Real. Looking me in the eye. He needed a shave. I gurgle-mumbled something else completely unintelligible, there may have been drool involved, as Bruce took the stuff from my hands along with my pen.

He started to autograph my *Tracks* booklet. He stopped, looked at the pen and said, "We gotta get ya a better pen." Bruce Springsteen, rock star, moved to the MPV then proceeded to hunt around the car,

finally producing a Sharpie marker from the glove box. "Ah, that's better," he said, as he re-signed *Tracks* and then *Born To Run*.

I was able to verbalise something along the lines of, "Bruce, thank you for the music, it's meant so much to many of us ... God bless you ..." Maybe it was a lame thing to say. Some of you may have wondered what you'd say to Bruce if you met him: "Hey Boss, I had a hard time growing up, I took great solace in your words", or "Thanks for making me feel part of something", or something else pithy, original and bursting with deep meaning that covered all the bases.

When it actually happens, you feel as if your tongue is 10 sizes too big for your head, and it all goes out the window. He smiled at me and said, "Thank you, that's nice of ya to say." I think he got it.

In the background I was vaguely aware of my fellow Bruce fan frantically legging it back down the street, with his camera in his hand. He screamed to a halt beside us (Terry took two steps nearer to Bruce) and asked Bruce if he could have a photograph taken with him. "Sure, no problem, my friend," he answered.

I immediately offered to take the picture, delighted for the guy with his arm across the back of Bruce Springsteen (Rock Star). When I said it was done, Bruce pinched his eyes and looked real quizzical at me. "Don't *you* want one?" Holy Crap! I hadn't even thought about it!

I said, "Hell *yes*!" (Well, it may have come out as another gurgle-mumble).

Sure enough I was given a big man-hug from The Boss. Jesus, he squeezes really tight! I'd never hugged a man before that,

or since I might add, but he's ruined me for any other bloke out there.

Picture taken, Bruce said, "See ya guys, I'm off to the gym. Take it easy."

We both said 'thank you' about ten times each as he climbed into the car and was driven away. Exit stage left, Mr Bruce Springsteen. He was probably wondering why the fans who stalked his hotel did so in a suit and in a shirt and tie, and where the heck were the Irish women? If it was me, I know who I'd rather be hugging.

Myself and The Suited One (Patrick, I think) made our way to the 24-hour photo shop on Baggot Street, laughing our heads off at our good fortune and we arranged to meet there the following day at 11am.

The next two hours after that were a total blur. Time stood still. I drove back to work in Blanchardstown. Don't remember it. At all. Drove about 10 miles in Dublin traffic. No recall.

I went in to the two folks sitting beside me, and wasn't able to speak. I just put the autographs in front of them. They looked at me wide-eyed. I think I was eventually able to say, in a whisper, "I just met Bruce". One of them, Mary, (how appropriate) burst into tears. (Mary knew how much that must have meant to me).

I met The Suited One (God bless you, sir, wherever you are) at the agreed time the following day to pick up the photos.

They say don't meet your heroes. I did, and Bruce is still a Class A Hero. I've been blessed to be at 29 shows since Slane.

I've *never* been let down. Not once. Ever.

Chris Carry
Kells, County Meath

BRUCE: THE MAN FROM MULLINGAR
"I'm not here tonight to kiss up to the audience by telling them about my lineage…"

If your name is Garrity, Farrell, McNicholas, Sullivan, O'Hagan or McCann then the chances are you are related to Bruce.

His paternal lineage is made up of generation after generation of Irishmen and women and there is little doubt his ancestors hailed from all four provinces of Ireland.

While he regards his paternal grandmother Alice as Irish she was actually born in New Jersey. It was, in fact, his great great grandparents Ann Garrity and Patrick Farrell who made the trip across the Atlantic, met and fell in love, and began the family line that would produce the Boss. They had their American Dream but could they ever imagine how long it would be before it really came true? (They were married in 1875, 100 years before Springsteen recorded his break-through album, *Born To Run*.)

Ann Garrity was born in the 1830s and while official Irish birth records from that time do not exist it appears from parish documents that the family hailed from Co Westmeath, most probably near the town of Mullingar.

When Ann was growing up, families of Garritys were to be found in Co Cavan, Co Kildare, Co Longford, Co Mayo, Co Galway and Co Dublin but the Garrity strongholds were in Co Westmeath and Meath. So, when Bruce made his first appearance on stage in Slane in Co Meath in 1985, without even knowing it he was pretty much returning home!

Around 130 years before that famous gig, his great great grandmother Ann left Irish shores for the Promised Land. She was one of around two million Irish citizens to flee the country between 1845 and 1855, as the Great Famine ravaged the island and its people. One million people died, while others like the young Ann risked a terrifying Atlantic crossing in search of a better life.

Ann's relatives went too. Her sister Elizabeth lived in New York but Ann, arriving in 1852, chose to find a home among the strong Irish community of Freehold, New Jersey. Living in Freehold, Ann quickly carved out a life for herself as a wife and mother. She married John Fitzgibbons (sometimes Fitzgibbon), a house-painter. He was also an Irish immigrant.

By 1870 the couple had six children – Catherine, Mary, John, James, Annie and Emma. Ann kept house and raised the family while John was the bread winner. But tragedy struck the young mother and her children on March 23, 1872, when John committed suicide – an act which at the time would have brought shame on the Catholic family. With no income of her own, she had little time to grieve.

She needed another husband to support her and her family. She was remarried by 1875 to another Irishman named Patrick Farrell.

Ann and Patrick were Bruce's great great grandparents. Patrick was a shoemaker and by 1880 Ann was bringing home some much needed extra cash by working as a washerwoman. It appears that Patrick had also been married previously and had possibly lived in Canada before crossing the border in the early 1870s. When he and Ann set up home together they had 10 children between them.

Shortly after Ann and Patrick were married, the couple had twin girls Amelia and Jennie. Jennie is Springsteen's great grandmother. The family were now living in Randolph Street in Freehold, the same street the young Bruce would call home some 70 years later.

But 22 years after her first husband killed himself Ann's family life was shattered when Patrick died of kidney disease after falling ill three weeks before. His requiem mass was held at the St Rose of Lima Church on the corner of McLean Street and Randolph Street and his body was buried in the nearby cemetery.

Cemetery records reveal that Patrick Farrell died on February 1, 1894, in Freehold, New Jersey, from Bright's Disease. His official death certificate states that he was aged 60 when he died. Three years later the church would be the focus of a happy occasion for the family when on St Patrick's Day, 1897, 19-year-old Jennie married labourer John McNicholas, aged 21.

Rev Frederick Kivelitz, who officiated at the ceremony, had been appointed the parish's first pastor in 1871. The parish was just four years old when a one-storey church school opened on Randolph Street with 60 children and one teacher. The following year a second floor was added to serve as a convent.

In 1878 the Sisters of Francis began a ministry, which in the 1950s and early 1960s would see them tangling with a young and terrified Bruce (and on one occasion would see one nun stuffing little Springsteen into a waste paper basket as that was "where he belonged").

John McNicholas grew up in Baltimore, but he would not have been able to escape his Irish heritage. His father Richard and mother Annie Sullivan were both born in Ireland, and had also almost certainly emigrated during the famine. Jennie and John had three children including Bruce's grandmother, Alice, but it appears that within a few years Jennie was widowed.

In the early 1900s Jennie and her three daughters were living in the Farrell family home in Randolph Street. And Alice would live with her grandmother Ann for the next 20 years. It was during this childhood that Alice would develop the strong Catholic faith and Irish wit which years later would have such an influence in shaping her grandson Bruce Springsteen.

It was through Alice that Bruce got something else: his surname. Alice married a local Freehold boy named Fred Springsteen. Fred's father Anthony was of Dutch descent but his mother Martha provides yet another Irish branch to the Springsteen family tree: her parents, John O'Hagan and Sarah McCann, were both born in Ireland.

Anthony and Martha had married in 1899 in Monmouth, New Jersey. Anthony was a farmer in Upper Freehold in the early years of their married life. By 1930 he was living in Standpiper Road in Freehold and was working as a carpenter in the construction industry.

He headed a household which at that time included his wife Martha, son Fred, daughter-in-law Alice and his grandson Douglas Frederick Springsteen. Douglas married Adele Ann Zerilli and Bruce Frederick Springsteen was born in Monmouth Memorial Hospital on September 23, 1949.

The family were living at number 87 Randolph Street in Freehold - just as three generations of the family had done before. And in keeping with that family tradition of securing your Irish roots for the next generation, Bruce's second wife had true Irish credentials.

Patti Scialfa only has to go back one generation to find her Irish roots. Her mum Vivian Patricia Morris left Belfast for America with her parents when she was five years old. The family had lived in Haddington Gardens off the Cregagh Road in the east of the city.

Patti's grandfather was a songwriter called Jerome Morris who had written for music hall stars such as Marie Lloyd. His best known song was "A Little Of What You Fancy Does You Good".

Talking about Jerome Morris in an interview in the *Belfast Telegraph* in 2004, Patti said: "My grandfather was Irish and a songwriter, and some of that must have rubbed off on me. When I was small he would sit me at the piano all day playing and writing songs. He was very creative and with a ribald sense of humour, very saucy. He used to tell me stories about Oscar Wilde and I didn't understand them, but it was just the way he told them.

"He was very open and full of joy, he was very musical and kind of bohemian in a way. He was hysterical – he loved his drink and he always kept a cigarette dangling out of his mouth, he never used the ashtray. I guess he was a very typical Irishman."

Justin Evans

31 May 2003

Crowd: 40,000

Tickets: 65-75 euro

TV3 * DOWNTOWN RADIO * 2FM

RDS MAIN ARENA

BRUCE SPRINGSTEEN
& THE E STREET BAND

GATES 5:30PM   NO SUPPORT

SAT 31-MAY-03 7:30PM SHARP

BLOCK E

ROW   E   SEAT   46

ANGLESEA STAND

IRISH INDEPENDENT
EVENING HERALD
75.00   (INC BKG FEE)

1-19366

16-NOV-02
ZDI799
40203

In the summer of 2001 Springsteen made a number of fun cameos on stage in the bars of New Jersey. The run ended in Sea Bright, near his home, on September 3 with Bruce blasting out "Jersey Girl" at a club called Donovan's Reef. Just over a week later four aircraft were hijacked over the United States, two of which were flown into the World Trade Center in New York. Almost three thousand people were killed that day. Back in Sea Bright a short while later a fan famously shouted at Springsteen: "We need you – *now*!"

Springsteen had always been truthful about his country. He had always loved it, but not unconditionally. "Blind faith," he had always said, "can get you killed." Now, in its time of trouble, it was that truth, that faith in the essence of his country, that understanding that it was the people who were the nation, which the country looked to.

He played *America: A Tribute To Heroes*, the national telethon which aired ten days after the attacks, and the Alliance of Neighbours shows for victims in the area where he lived. A few years previously he had read intently the stories of people on the Mexican border and played them through the prism of *The Grapes Of Wrath* to create *The Ghost Of Tom Joad*. The stories he was listening to now were very different and came from people across his own Monmouth County where many relatives of the

all photos Paul and Michelle Lavery

victims of the September 11 attacks lived. By Christmas 2001 he was writing, but the songs this time round were not dense narratives but lyrically light impressions of the sunny morning on which New York's landscape and so many lives had changed forever.

By July 2002, the E Street Band were back rehearsing for a new tour – now with Soozie Tyrell, who had appeared on the *Tom Joad* record, drafted in on the violin – and on July 30 the new album, *The Rising*, was released. It was, Dave Marsh notes, "received as the first major artistic statement about 9/11. Not the first major rock work; the first important work of any kind".

But *The Rising* was a measured response. Its lyrics were rarely specific and even reached out beyond the understanding of Springsteen's own small-town America to the actions of a suicide bomber. That song, "Paradise", appeared to suggest that the kinds of heavenly rewards offered by the religions followed by both a grieving widow in the United States and a bomber in the Middle East were "empty", not genuine spirituality, not what we should be searching for. (Tackling unsettling material in a brave way, the song provoked a predictable backlash and was slated by one critic who declared: "You could find no more direct example of the wickedness of liberal multiculturalism and moral equivalence.")

As world events moved on, Springsteen used the live shows – which started in August 2002 in the United States – to explore his own philosophy which, despite the horrors inflicted on his country on September 11, remained centred firmly on truth and the rights of all human kind to freedom and dignity. "We're in the midst of a rollback of civil rights," he told an audience in Washington state. "I think it's a good time to sort of keep your eyes open. Civil rights are a reaffirmation of our strength as a nation, of laws, due process. Usually, you don't think about it until it's a little too late."

The band played a short tour of Europe before Christmas and went back on the road in the United States in February 2003. Soon after, with events in the Gulf looking more and more like a US-led invasion of Iraq, "War" sometimes opened the set and an acoustic "Born In The USA" underlined the point quietly and eloquently.

Concerts in Australia and New Zealand briefly interrupted the US and Canadian shows and then, in May, Springsteen headed for Europe.

The Dublin show would be the 13th concert of the tour leg and was listed for May 31, 2003.

May 31 was the Bank Holiday Weekend. Eighteen years to the weekend after Slane, Springsteen was back in Ireland and staying with Patti in the Merrion Hotel in Dublin.

And so, of course, after a period of miserable weather, the sun shone, warming the thousands who wandered up to the RDS for the evening's rising. There was a massive sense of expectation outside the RDS. Tickets had gone on sale the previous November and had sold out quickly.

Springsteen hit the stage at 7.20pm. He was early and alone, and he nailed his bluesy acoustic version of "Born In The USA". Dressed all in black, hunched over the acoustic guitar and a study in concentration, he held the crowd spellbound.

As on many nights of the tour the band then kicked into two of the central songs off the new record, "The Rising" and "Lonesome Day", before keeping up the pace for "Candy's Room", "My Love Will Not Let You Down" and the full band version of "Atlantic City" with its heavy sense of foreboding and desperation.

Now, he spoke for the first time. "Good day to you," he said, his face huge on the screens each side of the stage. "It's great to be back in Dublin. Thanks for coming out and I hope you enjoy yourselves tonight - we plan to kill ourselves making it so!"

He then revealed that the bleakness of "Atlantic City" had concentrated the mood for a reason. "Actually, I need a little bit of quiet for these next two songs, thanks."

Born In The USA
The Rising
Lonesome Day
Candy's Room
My Love Will Not Let You Down
Atlantic City
Empty Sky
You're Missing
Waitin' On A Sunny Day
The Promised Land
Worlds Apart
Badlands
Out In The Street
Mary's Place
Meeting Across The River
Jungleland
Into The Fire
Thunder Road
Kitty's Back
Ramrod
Born To Run
Seven Nights To Rock
Glory Days
My City Of Ruins
Land Of Hope And Dreams
Dancing In The Dark

Two of the songs dealing most directly with the shock and the loss of September 11 followed, a haunting version of "Empty Sky" with Patti Scialfa on close harmony and "You're Missing". Springsteen's voice crackled with emotion and the crowd fell silent, lumps remaining firmly in the throat until well after the last chord had faded.

Springsteen then quickly switched the mood and smiled, "So you want to sing a little, huh?" and Soozie Tyrell's violin rang out the intro to "Waitin' On A Sunny Day". To crown the sing-a-long which followed, Springsteen charged from one end of the stage to the other, took a jump and slid along on his knees, the arms of the fans against the front barrier reaching out to touch him as he passed by.

"The Promised Land" was given a freshness by linking into "Worlds Apart", Springsteen's prayer for peace framed within a love affair between a soldier (American?) and a young woman (from Afghanistan?).

The song features the most blistering guitar solos on *The Rising* and as it gave way to "Badlands" and "Out In The Street" the show had officially become Dublin's biggest house party, a fact Springsteen acknowledged as he introduced the next big number, "Mary's Place".

"Are you ready for a house party now? Dublin-style by way of New Jersey? Let's see, I think some people are ready but some people are not.

Greg Lewis

Michelle Lavery

John Tondeur

Michelle Lavery

I think if we are going to have a house party, three conditions must be met - actually we will add a fourth one here in Dublin.

"One, you've got to have a Guinness. Two, the music has to be righteous. Three, the music *must* be *righteous* … "And, four, [*looking right round across each stand*] for f**k's sake you've got to get up off your *arse*. You got to get up off the Irish ass now.

"It is time to come up for the Irish ass rising. You can do it! I know you can!" He caught sight of a few stragglers. "Come on, we are much older than you are!"

The fooling on "Mary's Place" included Springsteen's introductions to the "greatest little house band in all the land".

Firstly, Roy Bittan who was now lauded as "a graduate of the Bruce College – which I see has done very well in Dublin – and, ladies and gentleman, a Nobel has been overlooked somewhere" and "the illegitimate son of Jerry Lee Lewis and Little Richard!"

There was "Sister" Soozie Tyrell and – in honour of Miami Steve's elevation to star of TV's *The Sopranos* – "On the guitar we got Silvio, Silvio, wherefore art thou? Keeper of all that is righteous on E Street, little Stevie Van Zandt".

Garry W Tallent, "the Tennessee Terror" was "the man that brings the thunder from down under" and "Mighty" Max Weinberg (now Conan O'Brien's band leader on US TV), was "the man that brings the power hour after hour, night after night, minister of the big beat, secretary of syncopation and star of late night television".

Pointing, head bowed like a preacher, Springsteen continued: "We got the secretary of heart and spirit, one of the greatest guitarists in rock 'n' roll, brother Nils Lofgren" and "on the organ, keeper of all that is mysterious and secretive on E Street, brother Dan Federici".

Introducing his own wife had by now become a familiar set piece: Springsteen acting all goofy and cod romantic; Patti smiling but looking embarrassed. "We got the first lady of love on guitar and vocals … My honey-baby-sweetie-child, Miss Patti Scialfa," he said, following up with a little of Marvin Gaye's "Let's Get It On".

"And last but not least, to the far side of the stage, the man himself, emperor of all-Ireland, minister of soul, secretary of the brotherhood, ladies and gentlemen I know you wish you could be like him but you cannot! Because under the sun there is only one Clarence 'Big Man' Clemons.

"That's right. That's the heart-stopping, pants-dropping, house-rocking, Earth-shaking, booty-quaking, Viagra-taking, love-making, *legendary* E Street Band!" The crowd cheered and Bruce immediately leaned on the microphone for a long "Sssshhh!"

The music came right down before Bruce carried on with the song.

I have been a huge fan of Bruce from around 1999 when I was 18, starting with the studio albums and books and wondering how in the hell I was ever going to see this band, how do I get my hands on some of these legendary bootlegs and why couldn't I have been around in the 70s and 80s to see some of the now famous shows?

Anyway from 1999 until 2002 I slowly but surely Bruce-ified my girlfriend (now my wife) Emma and when *The Rising* tour came around we felt this may be the only chance we'd ever get to see Bruce and the E Street Band. So with credit card in hand, on the telephone as in those days our internet connection was snail-like, we failed miserably at getting tickets to the Wembley show in October 2002.

Shortly after the summer 2003 leg was announced and Dublin was there on May 31. After much panicking about getting tickets, driving through Dublin six months after I just passed my driving test, we sat in the very last row of the RDS arena thinking how far away we were and that we may be in for a disappointment ... how wrong we were.

This was the first concert we had been to on such a large scale and the whole event was awe inspiring. The stage was huge, nestled in amongst the tree tops and church spire just beside the venue. The top of the stage could be seen from outside the grounds of the RDS.

The greatest thing about Springsteen as a performer is his ability to make a show in a 30,000-plus venue feel like he's playing in your local bar or better still your living room. Even if you are in the back row he somehow manages to reach out and make you feel a part of what's happening. The main highlights for me at this show were many: "Born In The USA" acoustic to open, Bruce's voice so powerful, totally filling every corner of the RDS; the "Candy's Room"-"My Love Will Not Let You Down"-"Atlantic City" three-pack - a powerhouse of screeching guitars and pounding drums; and hearing "Thunder Road" in all its beautiful glory.

I was amazed at the connection Bruce made with us (all 30,000 of us). There was so much passion in his playing and singing; the quiet songs were touching and moving (the whole place gently singing "My City Of Ruins" until the 'Come on, rise up!' part which was sung with intensity. Of course, we got the sliding across the stage, standing on piano, hanging from mic stand and messing around with Steve and Clarence *shtick* that is classic Bruce. After this we were both hooked.

Ciaran Gallagher, Belfast

I was lucky enough to meet Bruce in the Merrion Hotel lobby in 2003. By sheer fluke we had bumped into Max and Roy in the street and had a chat with them. We went into a bar opposite the hotel and had a few beers with a few friends, but there was no sign of Bruce.

We gave up and headed round the corner but, on a visit to the loo, I thought I'd just stick my head round the corner to see if he was around. I saw him on the steps of the Merrion talking to a couple of fans. ⬇

'Forget "Mary's Place",' said a banner in the crowd, 'And come back to mine!' But no-one who heard the energy of that song, with Springsteen, aged 53, at times hanging upside down on his microphone stand, was going to forget the song that night.

The next section of the show told a remarkable story. First, Springsteen brought the mood right down, telling the story of the two cheap hoods of "Meeting Across The River" (a live rarity) and melded the story into the tale of the Magic Rat, "Jungleland", so that first tinkling piano, then soaring sax and jangling guitar rang out across the city.

"Into the Fire" continued *The Rising*'s tribute to courage, before a back-to-back, double-shot of classics, "Thunder Road" and "Kitty's Back".

The encores began as a roadhouse knees-up, kicking in with "Ramrod" ending with some goofing for the big screen from Bruce and Steve.

"Steve?"

"Yeah, baby."

"I do believe it's quittin' time."

"Oh, yes."

"It is getting very late," said Bruce. "I got to go over there and get some fish and chips before Burdock's closes, baby."

The band played on.

"I have got to go back to the hotel and have one of those big black beers that make you feel like you weigh 500lbs. It is quittin' time, baby."

"*Nooo!!*" came the cry from the crowd.

Michelle Lavery

Michelle Lavery

John Tondeur

John Tondeur

"Oh, yes, I'm telling you."

More shouts from the crowd.

"Steve," said Bruce, acting all confused, "if it ain't quittin' time what I want to know is, what time is it?"

The band stopped and the crowd shouts, overjoyed to be a part of the charade.

Steve struggled to speak: "The damn sun is *still up*. It's boss time!"

A ten-minute version of "Ramrod" finally ended with a "Thank you, Professor O' Roy O' Bittan, Mr and Mrs Dublin", but as the band kicks into "Born To Run" they hit a wrong key and Springsteen, laughing, waves his hand to get them re-started. "This is how it should go."

Moon Mullican's "Seven Nights To Rock" was a new one on many of the crowd but it *rocked* so hard that the crowd continued to bawl out now when Springsteen asked, "Is the sun down yet?"

Then into a wild and joyous version of "Glory Days" with Bruce pretending to be on his last legs.

"Steve! Is the sun … ?"

This time the crowd interrupted the question: "*Noooo!*"

"Oh, f**k it!" came the call from the stage and the Fender sprang into life again.

After "Glory Days", a moment of reflection at the start of the second encore with Bruce coming out alone to the piano. "I want to thank everybody for coming out to the show tonight. We had a great time. We also want to thank you for your years of loyalty and support. Me and the E Street Band appreciate it. Thank you. We will try and continue to serve you well."

And then "My City Of Ruins", a song originally composed for Asbury Park but now given new life as a hymn to New York City, and, with the band back at his side, "Land Of Hope And Dreams".

Many artists might have left on the latter, a song which metaphorically puts its arms around everyone, but Springsteen had never been one to stop until *everyone* has corns on their feet. "Let's dance everybody!"

"Dancing In The Dark", a pop song which describes a man determined to tear himself out of his loneliness, drained the last ounce of energy out of the crowd.

It was, as the title of the bootleg of the night suggests, "the longest night" of a very long tour.

The reviews tried hard to describe to people who were not there just what they had missed.

Tony Clayton-Lea, in the *Irish Times*, wrote: "Sometimes all you need to hear to realise that the old fashioned and important values of rock music (redemption, exultation and the internal conflicts between what is intrinsically right and wrong) still mean something is a few chords and the plain truth.

I ran like mad as he disappeared into the building and just managed to call out, "Bruce!" as he went in. He stopped, turned round and I just said, "Can I just shake your hand please and say thanks for all the joy you've given us?"

He was charming and we talked for a couple of minutes.

After four pints of Guinness, I'm afraid I can't remember too much detail but I know we talked about the old Van Morrison song, "Gloria". I said it would be great to play it in Ireland and he said it would but it was a long time since they played it and probably wouldn't be up to scratch.

Next afternoon outside the RDS we were listening to the sound-check. A familiar song was played. "What's that?" I said to the bloke next to me.

"Sounds like "Gloria"," he said.

Well, the band never finished the song and it wasn't played at the gig. Was it "Gloria" and did he play it because I asked him? I suppose I'll never know.

What's worse is the only photographic evidence of this story is a photo of the back of Bruce's head as he disappeared into the Merrion.

I'd had my two minutes with him and I was happy and didn't think I could ask for more. I've got a friend who's a massive Bruce fan but doesn't want to meet him in case he lets him down. Well, he doesn't. Top man!

John Tondeur
Grimsby, England

On the day of a concert, queuing all day with all the fans that are from the same planet as me (Planet Bruce!), there is a very strong connection between us. We are all coming from different backgrounds, but we have all in common a passion for this music.

We start queuing very early in the morning, and we share stories, we worry about the inevitable rush when the gates open, and whether we will manage to reach the barrier quickly enough to be at the very front row.

The atmosphere is electric, the tension mounts, and if we are lucky enough to hear the sound-check it gives us the reassurance that we need to keep on waiting, and that we are exactly where we want to be.

I have met a lot of fans, and we keep in touch through emails between tours … and share Bruce news.

Some of the fans I have met have been to over 80 shows, and from concert to concert there are a lot of familiar faces.

Dominique Jumelle, Quin, Co Clare

The weather was perfect and although the concert wasn't supposed to start until 8pm, at 7.30pm Bruce came out on stage himself and started to sing.

What a night! The concert was absolutely fantastic – the atmosphere was electric and the music will forever be unforgettable in my mind. Bruce Springsteen is without doubt the best live act ever. I think Bruce is so popular in Ireland because he came here when none of the big international acts would play here. ⬇

"When bluster and bombast are stripped away – when you've got a singer with a guitar or a piano and a song that says something real and honest in a straightforward manner – you've got something truly special and valid."

Springsteen concerts, he noted, have "their own history: epic, mythic, never unwieldy, never experimental in the arty sense of the word, never short-changing".

This was the rock star reaching out to the audience. "The fact is there are few of his kind around these days, too few artists that straddle the interface between community and communication".

Clayton-Lea noted that one of the strengths of the Springsteen shows was the contrasts of the music, from "pulsating rock tunes" such as "Badlands" and "Born To Run" which "have all the propulsive qualities stadium rock cries out for" to mournful songs such as "Empty Sky" and "Atlantic City" which "might be the antithesis of stadium rock but … work in a way that defies genre convention". And at the stage-show's centre there was always Springsteen himself. "He mugs theatrically, dances very badly and emotes in a way only someone who really means it can. It is surely no mistake to note that as he grows older his face is attaining Mount Rushmore character and definition.

all photos Justin Evans

"Likewise his status as a rock 'n' roll icon and a man who truly is tougher and much more tender than the rest."

Mary Anne Kenny, of *Sorted Magazine*, described an artist who, although he had been playing live since a teenager, was still enjoying every moment. "No fancy pyrotechnics, no flashing lights. No self-indulgent fanfare or even an opening act to warm up the crowd. Just trademark denims and an acoustic guitar," she wrote, describing his arrival at work. As he left after the three-and-a-half hour show, she concluded, "The sun had long gone down on the RDS and Springsteen's working day was finally over. He clocked off to the cheers of 40,000 tired but happy fans, after once again proving that this blue-collar worker is still, undisputedly, The Boss."

George Byrne noted in the *Evening Herald* that not only had Springsteen become "the first mainstream artist to put the 9/11 tragedy into a thoroughly human context", he also "still rocks like a demon".

Byrne wrote: "There are artists who, when faced with a devoted audience, all buzzing on sunshine and whatever they're having themselves, could coast their way through the most perfunctory performance but from the solo acoustic version of "Born In The USA" which opened the set it was clear that Springsteen wasn't about to let the good mood of the night lead to any lethargy from his side of the stage."

Irish people have a real love of good music and we love Bruce so much because his lyrics are brilliant and every song tells a story.

Bruce loves to come to Ireland as he knows how much we appreciate and enjoy his music and I'd say his Irish audience is definitely the best in the world!

Oona Conlo
Crossmaglen, County Armagh

I was six months pregnant at the time and reluctantly swapped my GA tickets for seats. Luckily, we got great seats directly across from the stage. The stage went the length of the venue as opposed to the width so the seats were so close.

I brought Brian, my husband, with me on this occasion and yet again - another fan was born. From the opening chords of the acoustic "Born In The USA" to the rocking chords of "Dancing In The Dark" which ended the show, we were both in awe of this great musician and his amazing E Street Band.

This was my first time hearing the "What time is it, Stevie?"; "It's Bossssss Time!"

Tracy Hegarty
Limerick

Bruce made a reference to a girl carrying a sign all round Europe with "Kitty's Back" on it and played it. It was a real highlight to hear.

Jocelyn Kelly
Dublin

We had decided to take our kids to their first show and so we had seats some way from the stage, but the greatest highlight - possibly my best ever Bruce experience - was when as the sun started to go down behind the stage at the RDS and Bruce kicked off "Jungleland" (my favourite song) and my daughter snuggled up saying, "That's your favourite song, isn't it dad?"

It doesn't get any better.

The kids had been listening to "Seven Nights To Rock" all week before the gig and so when Bruce sang this they jumped up and danced in the aisles much to the amazement of the crowd who wondered how these kids knew a song that they didn't.

Nigel and Maggie Flynn
Ballymoney

"YOU'RE TALKING TO *THE* BOSS!"

One Friday afternoon Bruce and his entourage called into the shop for some fish and chips, as usual when he is playing in Ireland.

There were a couple of local girls also in the queue who recognised who he was, and they asked me was it really Bruce Springsteen! When I informed them it was indeed him, he obliged them by letting them take some photos and signing autographs as he normally does.

One of the girls took out their mobile phone and called her boss, who was a *huge* fan and was going to his show that very night, to tell him that Bruce was in Leo Burdock's. ⬇

The following few hours "sped by in a gig that was an affirmation of faith in the power of music and reminded me why and just how much I love rock 'n' roll. I can't really ask much more than that of anyone. Thank you, Bruce."

Byrne's colleague Ken Sweeney highlighted the band too. "For teamwork you could not fault it," he noted. "And maybe that was why Brian Kerr took the Irish team to watch from the sidelines."

The international soccer players were not the only well-known faces in the crowd. The VIP area also included The Cranberries' singer Dolores O'Riordan and broadcaster Gerry Ryan.

Promoter Peter Aiken was delighted. "One of the greatest shows we've ever put on in Ireland and we've been doing this 40 years," he said.

Earlier in the week Dublin had hosted Paul McCartney but Miriam Lord of the *Irish Independent* noted that Springsteen was "streets ahead of the opposition".

"Not only did he have the crowd eating out of his hand; he milked them to such effect that by the end of the night the hordes could have been sold into intervention," Lord noted. "What a guy. What a performance."

Her colleague Niamh Hooper said Springsteen "played every chord and sang every note like his life depended on it."

She added: "Quite simply there are good gigs, there are great gigs and there are Bruce Springsteen gigs."

Obviously the boss did not believe her as he asked her to put Bruce on the phone. Bruce took the phone off her and asked who was on the other end, and the man told him his name and asked who he was talking to, and Bruce replied, "You're talking to *The* Boss!".

They had a short conversation.

Bruce got his fish and chips, left the lads a tip as usual and left the shop.

About five minutes later the man he had been talking to on the phone, burst through the door in a sweat, huffing and puffing, as he had ran from the job looking to catch a glimpse of Bruce. He was disappointed that he had missed his chance to meet him face to face.

Darren Salmon, manager of Leo Burdock's, Christchurch, Dublin

Since I first saw Bruce live during *The Rising* tour in 2003 at the RDS I have never looked back.

My husband and I queue all night at different places to make sure we're in with a better chance of tickets and we always follow the fans' roll-call system for pit queuing on the day of the concert. During the *Seeger Sessions* tour of 2006 I met Bruce outside his hotel in Dublin. Truth be told, I had waited five hours - I didn't want to let the opportunity of meeting him pass me by.

He came out quite gingerly and was more than accommodating to the people who were there. He was extremely polite, gracious and willing to please. He seemed happy to hold a conversation and chatted away and, when our camera wouldn't work, he waited patiently holding me from behind until it was fixed. I even managed to get a kiss on the cheek.

During this time I simply thanked him for everything and he received the compliments very humbly.

I have some great pictures of the day I met Bruce and in typical form the one with him and I is shockingly awful. I like to call it the worst but best picture of my life! So what – I have the memories and they can never be taken away.

I've always believed in the saying that 'life is not measured by the number of breaths we take, but by the moments that take our breath away'. Mine was certainly taken away that day, in just a few minutes.

Time passes quickly in life, especially as we get older and things come and go in split seconds, but should I live to be 100 years old I will never forget the few minutes I spent on that street in Dublin with Bruce Springsteen.

And I would do it all again in a heartbeat. I would wait twice as long to grab a few seconds to say, 'thank you'. That's it, just a 'thank you' for being a constant source of strength and support in my life.

For me it seems that every aspect of my life has Bruce in it.

I was getting married six weeks after this and when I went on my hen weekend to Liverpool all the girls turned up in Bruce t-shirts, while I wore a top with the picture of Bruce and I on the front. The back read, "I'm with the Boss".

We had a Bruce-themed wedding where we named all our tables after Bruce songs, had Bruce played in the chapel during our ceremony and had a dedicated two hours of only Bruce music for the party.

Having been at all the concerts in Dublin in 2008 my husband and I travelled to the Emirates Stadium, London, for the Saturday night show. During 'Mary's Place' Bruce leaned down, held my hand and sang. That definitely made the trip worthwhile.

Call it crazy, but we even have a 'Bruce room' in our home. My husband is an avid painter and has painted me several Bruce canvases. These are on the walls that are also adorned with our Bruce memorabilia. I recently got a Bruce tattoo which reads, 'Badlands – live it everyday'. It's not on show and never will be but the strength and confidence and inner peace it brings me simply knowing it's there is truly remarkable.

After the love of my family, Bruce Springsteen's music is my greatest earthly blessing, my richest treasure. I could survive without it, but I just don't want to. It gives me strength, contentment and empowerment. Bruce Springsteen is my religion and I believe in the faith that can save me … I could talk at great length about what exactly Bruce Springsteen and his music mean to me, however I can honestly say, and am not ashamed to, that Bruce Springsteen has changed, perhaps even saved, my life.

Michelle Lavery
Craigavon, Co Armagh

DIARY OF A GLORIOUS OBSESSION

1983: Start of obsession, year of the Leaving Certificate, discovered *The River*. "How can you possibly study with that awful noise?"
Went back through the other albums. This guy has an awful lot to say to a confused 17-year-old.

1985: Slane: hazy memories now, second-year student in UCD, scouting around Dublin in the wee, wee hours for a *Born In The USA* poster which would just look so good on my wall. Day of the concert hammering to Slane after an Economics exam. Don't remember much from the show, how can anyone play at that pace for that long?

1988: Bramall Lane, Sheffield. Missed the Dublin show because of a prior commitment involving an Interail ticket and a brother. Arrived back in London and the cousin announces he has come by two tickets for Sheffield (thanks, Sean, forever in your debt!) Five-hour drive north in a yellow Nova. What a show – *Tunnel Of Love*, was there ever a better album about breaking up? Near to the front – there's definitely something going on between Bruce and that backing singer ...

1993: Dublin, a show with the new band. Persuade the second brother to come for the first time – "Ah, but you should see the E Street Band". Jerry Lee Lewis joins Bruce on stage. Still have t-shirt from this show, let's just say that nowadays it emphasises my shape …

1999: May 1999 sees the band back together. Went to this show with my two younger brothers, Paraic and Fergal. Best memory of that show – the acapella version of 'If I Should Fall Behind' – absolutely gorgeous. Now have a two-year-old who can play air saxophone, note perfect, to "Janey Don't You Lose Heart". Must set her off on the right track (wife calls it indoctrination).

2003: *The Rising*, again attended with two younger brothers having now persuaded them that there is nobody else to see live. Really strong start to this show, "Doesn't mess about, does he?", brother 1 to brother 2.
Afterwards we nipped around to Burdock's thinking it would make one of the all time great pics – Springsteen and three O'Dwyers. No sign.
Second daughter now knows all the words to "Trapped"; wife thinks it has gone beyond an obsession.

2005: What a moment at The Point when the heavens start to open during "The Hitter". Possibly "Jesus Was An Only Son" could be the all time favourite. The description of kids as "a franchise on the future" pulls on the heartstrings. Must get Sarah to a show the next time around, wonder is seven too young!

2006: The *Seeger Sessions*, this is where it gets a bit difficult. Diagnosed with a large tumour on the spine at start of year, and not sure if I'll be around for the wains, never mind to sing very badly at the top of my lungs at a Springsteen show or punch the air through "Badlands". Really want to see them grow up.
Operation over, rehabilitation complete; missed the SSB first time around. Caught them in November, twice in Dublin once in Belfast. Dublin in November was with Fergal, Rory, two friends from Carn and brother number three.
Large lump in throat when he comes on stage, really didn't think I'd make it.
Brilliant show, it ain't the E Street Band, but what a bunch of musicians.

2007: The Odyssey Arena, the best version of "The River", ever. Standing just behind the pit with a couple of Christy Moore fans from Nottingham.
As usual you're awestruck at how he wrings every last drop out of himself on stage. Makes the heart pound, there will never be anybody else.

2008: RDS, three shows, my daughter Sarah comes to the Thursday night with Paraic and Ferg (the two younger brothers) – now this is special.
Thursday night is good, but Sunday night, a show to die for.
Highlights of the three shows: "Rosalita", "Trapped", "Atlantic City", "Mary's Place" (because Sarah knows all the words), "Prove It All Night" and "Growin' Up".
Made it into the pit all three nights. Sarah enjoyed it, I think (she's ten, teenage years approaching, feedback slightly limited), hopefully she's on the right road.
You see Springsteen matters – most don't get it – "Where's he gone this time?"
This guy was the soundtrack to everything, teenage years, soft-infested summers, weddings, daughters, bad times, good times. From skinny, confused 17-year-old to balding, (only slightly) overweight 42-year-old accompanied by one New Jersey genius. Why? Because he never goes through the motions, because he always leaves nothing behind, because he consistently will take a chance musically, because he cares, because he doesn't do commercials, because even now he still thinks he can be better, because friendship still matters to him, because he means it, because he's the best.

Philip O'Dwyer, Buncrana, County Donegal

BORN TO DANCE
(to be sung to the music of "The River" - with sincere apologies to the man himself)

Come ye all and hear my story of how I was in a mess
I had an arthritic hip joint which gave way in the RDS,
It was decades of Springsteen worship
That brought me to my knees, 2003,
It was "Point Blank" for me
As I was ferried off to casualty.

Chorus:
That night I went down with a whimper
As my hip socket took a dive
Oh-oh down with a whimper I dived-aha-ha,
Down with a whimper
"At a Bruce gig," I cried Oh-oh,
"Down at a Bruce gig", I cried-aha-ha.

I danced back in the seventies
when I knew I was "Born To Run"
My steps were changed forever
by the music of the chosen one
Through my trials and tribulations,
Bruce was my constant friend
From *Nebraska* and out through the *Tunnel Of Love*
His words of wisdom would transcend.

Chorus:
That night I went down with a whimper
As my hip socket took a dive
Oh-oh down with a whimper I dived-aha-ha,
Down with a whimper
"At a Bruce gig," I cried Oh-oh,

As I was wheeled in to the theatre
To be carved up with the surgeon's knife,
I was armed with my copy of *The Rising*
which I guarded with my life,
As the saws and hammers battered, well,
I was in "Paradise" with the Boss, the band and morphine,
Well, hell, it felt alright.

So I was ready for the *Seeger Sessions*
with my two artificial hips,
I danced with the Saints and Jesse,
Till I thought my scars would rip,
And even when I tried to sit this music filled my heart and soul,
My hips they danced independently
 with the spirits of the West's Dustbowl.

Chorus:
That night I went down with a whimper
As my hip socket took a dive
Oh-oh down with a whimper I dived-aha-ha,
Down with a whimper
"At a Bruce gig," I cried Oh-oh,
"Down at a Bruce gig", I cried-aha-ha.

So calling all you Springsteen fans
who reside on the Emerald Isle
Plan well for your arthritic futures
and listen up for a while,
When we face old age and the Zimmer frame
and think our *Magic*'s gone,
Bruce will still be there to light our flare We will still be "Born To Run".

Chorus:
That night I went down with a whimper
As my hip socket took a dive
Oh-oh down with a whimper I dived-aha-ha,
Down with a whimper
"At a Bruce gig," I cried Oh-oh,
"Down at a Bruce gig", I cried-aha-ha.

Maria Brick, County Kerry

Justin Evans

BRUCE SPRINGSTEEN
SOLO AND ACOUSTIC
THE POINT THEATRE
HOW 8PM SHARP (NO SUPPORT)
UE 24-MAY-05 DOORS 6:30PM
LOCK A

ROW   N   SEAT   40

2411130880970

GROUND FLOOR

NO CAMERAS, RECORDERS,
OR LASER POINTERS

00   (INC BKG FEE)

14-APR-05
0EI237
08630 X 1

24 May 2005

Crowd: 7,000

Tickets: 85 euro

In October 2004 Springsteen embarked on the 'Vote For Change' tour organised by moveon.org in an attempt to get US electors out to vote against George Bush.

"I always believed that it was good for the artist to remain distant from the seat of power, to retain your independent voice … but the stakes in this one are just too high," he told *Backstreets* magazine. "I felt like, given what I've written about, the things that I've wanted our band to stand for over the years, it's just too big a battle to lay out of."

After playing shows with artists such as REM and John Fogerty, Springsteen went on to play solo shows for Democrat candidate John Kerry right up until the eve of the election.

"Nobody's got all the answers to all of America's problems," he told a crowd in the critical election state of Ohio. But a John Kerry victory would mark "the beginning of the work that we need to do ourselves to create a humane American society".

Despite his efforts, Kerry – a weak candidate – lost. As Dave Marsh reported: "When Bruce Springsteen woke up the next morning, the lawn of his Rumson, New Jersey, home had been covered with 'Bush for President' signs."

Bruce returned in April 2005 with *Devils & Dust*, a cross between the stark, solo Springsteen and the full band Boss.

Although closer in spirit to 'acoustic Bruce' the music on the new album was less bleak than his earlier (partly) acoustic offerings (*Nebraska* and *The Ghost Of Tom Joad*), with arrangements filled out by violins, horns and an organ. However, the themes of despair and isolation remained.

Unsurprisingly, as his hands were still burning from his dip into party politics, the album was framed by the usual questions about America and personal commitments and integrity.

The album was built around a title track sung from the point of view of an American soldier who not only does not know if what he is fighting for is right, he does not know if he can trust those who put the gun in his hand in the first place.

Elsewhere, characters occupied landscapes in which parents and guiding hands have died ("Black Cowboys", in which a black child obsessed with cowboys steals his mother's boyfriend's cash and takes a train to Oklahoma, and "Silver Palomino", a painful exploration of a child's grief) or where their own desperate attempts at love had proved empty (the sexually explicit and heart-breaking "Reno").

Songs like "Long Time Comin'" had been written almost a decade earlier and slotted in to provide lighter moments recalling Springsteen's "happier" songs of the early 90s.

But "Matamoros Banks", in many ways the album's bleakest and most beautiful song, also dated back to the mid-90s and offered no comfort. The song is the sequel to *Tom Joad*'s "Across The Border" and revealed that the hopes that the Mexican immigrant had had on the former song of awakening to an American Dream had been cruelly dashed. With a narrative working backwards, the song starts with the character lying dead in the waters of the Rio Bravo, with eyes open to the stars. There are few more thought-provoking and heart-rending descriptions of death in song.

The *Irish News* made *Devils & Dust* the album of the week. Taking the stadium-storming Bruce as his starting point, the reviewer AP Maginness described the "complex story" at the heart of "Born In The USA". "The song may be a shout-out-loud anthem but it is also an intelligent and sensitive look at the nature of patriotism. It highlights the dichotomy of emotion and the ambivalence of passions that plague feelings of nationality … Herein lies the genius of The Boss, he is able to infuse a song with a sound that is democratic in its widespread appeal and at the same moment write a song with a powerful and challenging theme."

He noted, however, that the song "would perhaps have been more powerful had it had a stripped-down acoustic performance".

"The beauty of *Devils & Dust* comes from the fact that it harks back to the themes of ambivalence found in *Nebraska* and also *The Ghost Of Tom Joad* as well as mimicking – to some degree – their stark nature," added Maginness. But: "Again, like "Born In The USA", Springsteen is questioning the world around him."

The characters on the album, wrote Neil McCormick of the *Irish Independent*, are "bewildered and bereft, honourable ordinary men and women clinging to fading ideals".

As the *Irish Times* said of *Devils & Dust*: "It's an album which needs time and attention to work its spells, things which have gone astray in an industry where the best-selling single features a frog from a mobile phone ringtone."

Peter Murphy, of *Hot Press*, wrote: "What *Devils & Dust* is, is Bruce making a literate roots rock record without having to worry about where old friends like Clarence and Little Steven fit in. If anything, it sounds like the kind of record you'd expect from perennial New Bruces like Steve Earle or Joe Ely or Kathleen Edwards, heartland wood-stained tunes where sawing fiddles and lap steels rub comfortably against the boss-man's Fender, all delivered by a team of players as efficient as they are un-showy." He described the songs as "closely observed country noir vignettes, the testimonies of losers reaching a detente with the fates and promising to do better".

He added: "This is where Bruce is at these days – a place of decency and disappointment, squalor and spirituality, nobody making any harsh judgements. The country of Jim Thompson as well as John Steinbeck. Or as Cormac McCarthy puts it in his forthcoming novel, no country for old men."

Perhaps mindful of the sparseness of some of the tunes on *Devils & Dust*, Springsteen had chosen to use an array of backing musicians on many of the songs in the studio; but now he was going out on the road, he felt the live show was something he wanted to do on his own.

The tour started in Detroit and after only 14 shows headed for Europe.

Two decades on from Slane, Springsteen's Irish show again would be the first on the European leg of the tour. The date was set for May 24, 2005, at The Point in Dublin.

The US shows revealed that Springsteen was using the solo format – him, a piano and pump organ, some guitars and a harmonica, on a sparsely-lit stage – to turn a microscope on the themes which had obsessed his work. America's wars and election decisions would be looked at, of course, but so would creationism; Catholicism would get a review (especially in Ireland), and Jesus too; so would love and lovers in all their glory and especially in all their failings.

My Beautiful Reward
Reason To Believe
Devils & Dust
Lonesome Day
Long Time Comin'
Silver Palomino
The River
Real World
Part Man Part Monkey
All The Way Home
Nebraska
Reno
Racing In The Street
The Rising
Further On (Up The Road)
Jesus Was An Only Son
Leah
The Hitter
Matamoros Banks
Ramrod
I'm On Fire
Land Of Hope And Dreams
The Promised Land
Dream Baby Dream

Springsteen, almost uniquely among major artists, had also managed to make parenthood a theme of his work and his live shows, without ever becoming naff or mawkishly sentimental.

Bruce's one-night-only acoustic set in Dublin would be in complete contrast to the E Street Band performances two summers previously – and interestingly, would differ from Springsteen's previous solo performances during 1996's *Tom Joad* tour.

Springsteen's manner on stage would be warmer and more open. He still insisted on silence but he himself could not stop talking.

In an interview a year later with David McCullagh of RTÉ, Springsteen explained why *Devils & Dust* required silence from the fans. "To get the characters out in that music you really need the quiet, because really a lot of the stuff on *Devils & Dust* I'm writing from the interior of someone's head, you're not hearing what they're saying, you're hearing what they're thinking. There's a certain level of reflectiveness, and those songs live in the silences in between the lines and in between the beats."

Getting tickets for the show was a challenge. The lucky few who walked up to The Point that night were handed small brown leaflets from Aiken Promotions telling them they were attending a "solo acoustic performance, set in a theatre style arrangement".

BRUCE SPRINGSTEEN
DEVILS & DUST

Welcome to the The Point Theatre

We would like all of our guests to have a great experience at tonight's performance!

* Tonight's show is a solo acoustic performance, set in a theatre style arrangement.

* There will be no intermission.

* All guests must be seated by the start of the first song.

* There will be no seating during each song.

* Curtains and doors to the lobby will remain closed during the entire performance.

* All concession stands will close 10 minutes prior to the start of the show and will remain closed for the duration of the show.

* No cameras, video, or recording devices are permitted.

* Please turn off all mobile phones and pagers during tonight's performance.

Thank You for coming and enjoy the show!

AIKENPROMOTIONS

There would be no intermission or coming back to seats during songs, and all mobiles should be turned off. "Thank you for coming and enjoy the show."

What followed was a remarkable two-and-a-half hour show which while leaning heavily on the new album also breathed new life into some familiar tracks from his past – "The River" and "Nebraska" – and some less familiar live numbers, "Real World" and "Part Man Part Monkey".

Springsteen's keenness to communicate and describe what he was trying to do was obvious: following a blistering opening section in almost complete darkness – the spotlight coming up on the third song – Springsteen provided spoken introductions for virtually every song which followed.

Coming out to sit first at the pump organ/harmonium, Springsteen opened with "My Beautiful Reward", one of the warmest and on the face of it sweetest ballads off *Lucky Town*, which he turned into a slightly disconcerting hymn. This was a show during which you would not take your eyes off Bruce. By just the second track he had the audience held spellbound. Hairs raised on necks as he belted out a blood-curdling "Reason To Believe", with vocals and harmonica distorted through a bullet mic and with Springsteen stamping out the beat with a board under his right foot. This truly was a manic street preacher.

While I loved the *Devils & Dust* album I felt slightly disappointed that there was no E Street Band this time. With it being a smaller venue than the RDS (The Point) the panic was definitely on to get tickets and some severe queuing outside Virgin in Royal Avenue, Belfast, was required.

I queued from about 6am, had some very stiff legs, met some very nice fans and acquired two decent tickets - 8th row, we'll actually be able to see his face this time! So on May 24, 2005, my wife Emma and I made what has now become a pilgrimage to see the Boss in Dublin.

On entering The Point the mood was set by the stage, beautifully dressed in long drapes with gorgeous blue and red up-lighting.

Finally walking on stage late, we saw Bruce up close for the first time. My immediate impression was, 'I know him, I feel like I have seen him this close before', and although I hadn't I presume this is related to his ability to connect and almost speak/sing direct to you, in concert or on CD.

My reservations about not having the E Street Band disappeared with the standing ovation given to Bruce before he had even picked up a guitar.

I've seen Bruce eight times in total - from the back of arenas, front row in the pit, sitting and standing - and this was maybe the most intense, personal and exciting performance I've ever seen from any performer anywhere.

The Point became a cathedral and something spiritual and indescribable hung over the place that night.

Bruce Springsteen was possessed, this one man on stage with just a guitar and harmonica was at times summoning up the feel, sound and presence of a whole orchestra.

Ciaran Gallagher, Belfast

A magical night. We moved heaven and earth to get tickets and it lived up to my expectations. The crowd really got what Bruce was trying to do and lots of shushing went on! I remember hearing rain hitting the roof of The Point because the audience was so quiet, hanging on Bruce's every word.

The house lights went up for some of the encores and Bruce started to play "Ramrod". I couldn't sit still any longer and stood in my seat to dance, it was great.

I felt I made contact with him that night, as I am sure that everyone else did as well.

Jocelyn Kelly, Dublin

It seems to be like Clint Eastwood says in *Million Dollar Baby*: the world is full of Irish people or of people who would have been Irish.

You can see them buying a green t-shirt at the airport, or showing the shamrock tattooed on their wrists, or you can hear them moaning because the Guinness they are drinking is not as good as the one they had in Dublin.

We are not an exception. In May 2005 we landed in Dublin longing to see a new place and an 'old friend': it was to be our first Bruce show together, more or less a year after we met (because of him). ⬇

He turned to the guitar then for "Devils & Dust" and "Lonesome Day", before stopping to say, "Thank you, my friends."

He smiled: "If you can spare me some of those mini-camera shots I will stand here at the end of the night and you can shoot away."

Fiddling absent-mindly with the guitar, he introduced the next track.

"Long Time Comin'" is a song about having kids. You know, you kinda go through the three stages.

"When they're little, you are kind of that benevolent hand of God in their lives …

"Then they get a little older (and) you are kind of that tolerable idiot.

"I am worried about the next step … *f**king idiot*. I hate to say it but I can feel it coming.

"So, when you get 'em, they come along and you think you are not going to make any mistakes that your parents made and all that stuff but, of course, you will.

"I had a fight with my boy the other night. The next thing I hear coming out of his room was [*strums loudly on his guitar*]. What was I going to say? 'Turn it down!' It ain't going to work."

The audience laughed. Springsteen had already turned the cold grey space of The Point into the intimate setting of a local bar where friends sat to listen to the local hero play a few songs and tell a few tales.

"Anyway, here's to second chances."

Lorenza Pravato

After the celebratory "Long Time Comin'", Springsteen introduced one of the new songs about loss.

"I've spent a few years around horses," he said. "I can't say that I can ride them but they are kind of these very big spirits. A good horse kind of takes care of everything.

"This was a song about … a boy loses his mom and he imbues her spirit in this horse that comes out of the mountains at night. I do this for my friend Emily …"

After "Silver Palomino", Springsteen put down the guitar and the lights went down for a moment. When the spotlight returned Springsteen was at the piano.

"When I started out I didn't write many love songs," he said, with his nervous, self-conscious laugh. "The first three, four, five, six records did not have many love songs on.

"I had a kind of confusing upbringing. My mother was Italian. My father was half-Irish. You see, that is why I am a manic depressive right there. That's a hell of a combination.

"In the house in the morning my mom always had the radio on and it was a time when there was all these beautiful doo-wop songs on the radio. It was a generation of men who were trying to sing and sound like women. And there were all these beautiful voices.

"And occasionally in the States they have these TV shows where they would try to get them altogether again and they are like 60 or 70 years old and they would open up their mouths and out would come these voices that are filled with youth and still retain that classic 1950s horniness. They are beautiful singers, beautiful singers.

"So in the morning this is what was coming across the radio.

"My dad had a different approach. His idea was that all love songs were a government conspiracy and propaganda to get you married so you would have to pay more taxes.

"I figured that out in about 35 years [*more laughs*]. While I was figuring it out I think I wrote some hidden love songs and I think this was one of them."

He played "The River", without doubt a great love song but one which placed love in a very different setting to the one envisaged by the crooners on Adele Springsteen's radio: a world of unemployment, disillusionment and economic depression.

Then, staying at the piano, another view of love; this time not dashed by hardship, but mature and honest in the face of it: "This is a song I wrote in the early 90s … It kind of got away from me on the record. We did not get a good version. It was a good song. [*A laugh*] This was when I was feeling the love and showing the love …"

The song was "Real World", a reworking of a song which got overlooked amid the criticism of *Human Touch*.

It's useless to explain how Ireland puts a spell on you, and how we were immediately enchanted by Dublin.
Okay, we said, let's play the tourist. In a few hours we were standing at the hotel door to see if he came out. It wasn't our fault that that's where the tour took us - we turned up there by chance. We turned a corner and - dash! - there they were: a few fans were waiting, calm and relaxed. So we started waiting. And we waited. And we waited. And then we waited some more.
And he appeared at the top of the stairs; he simply appeared in his leather jacket, tanned and holding a camera.
He took some pictures of us.
I mean: *he* took some pictures of us - just as we were taking some pictures of him.
Bruce makes funny things happen inside of us. This was particularly true for that afternoon: steel-nerved Tsitalia got worked up and missed the moment in which always-saying-something-Larry lost her voice while touching Bruce.
So we have no picture of the moment in which Larry says, "Bruce", in a soft voice and put her finger on his left shoulder, as light as a falling leaf.
Tsitalia collected himself first and said, "Racing", before Bruce left.
That night Bruce played "Racing In The Street", and we'll never know whether he heard Tsitalia or whether it was pure coincidence. Probably the latter, but we love to believe he listened to us and played our song.

Lorenza "Larry" Pravato and Alessio "Tsitalia" Rozzi, Trieste, Italy

I think this is where Bruce realised that he had a special relationship with Dublin. He knew he was always popular in Ireland and that his records sold well here but now he knew that it was an audience that would listen to the kind of stuff he was playing on *Devils & Dust*.

Nigel and Maggie Flynn, Ballymoney

I first met Bruce in 2005. I mumbled something about how much I was influenced by him, to which he responded: "It's my pleasure". He signed an autograph and posed for a photograph. I was so excited about having my photo taken with him that I forgot all about the autograph until I came across it a few days later.
Later that night after the concert in The Point a couple of us were in the lobby in his hotel when in arrives Bruce. He kind of snuck in behind us and asked if we enjoyed the show. It was so embarrassing because we just froze. About a half hour later we heard him approaching the lobby again to be met by a young blonde girl in his path. She was obviously not a fan but had realized that he was a famous rock star. She went up to Bruce and asked him what his name was. We all thought she was being sarcastic but she was actually serious. It was hilarious. Bruce looked at her and said his name was Frank.
So then she asked for an autograph and he puts a marker to her hand and writes 'Frank' on it. I was in his company again in May 2008. Again he walked past me but as I'd met him before I left him alone. ⬇

The next introduction was made over a twanging guitar, echoing notes coming from the deep, deep South. "Evolution. Hot topic in the States right now," drawled Bruce. "In Kansas the school board just opened a session to decide how evolution is taught 80 years after the Scopes Monkey Trial. Now, the Scopes Monkey Trial is when they put a man on trial for teaching evolution. I believe at the end of the trial everybody agreed that monkeys had something to do with it which in no way takes anything from the Big Man. It just shows that he had a sense of humour. But monkeys don't vote and they don't make campaign contributions so we are currently living in the United States of Amnesia.

"And the President, he is just doing what he has to do so that he can do what he wants to do. A lot of folks do that. I don't want to feel like I am talking out of school here.

"But if they remade the movie *Inherit the Wind*, a movie about the Scopes Monkey Trial, they could not make it today ...

"Now *The Flintstones* - do you get *The Flintstones* over here?" The crowd shouted: "Yeah!"

Springsteen laughed: "That's one of our finest exports. That would be banned today. The whole Neanderthal setting and the homosexual undercurrents of the Barney-Fred relationship would rule the whole thing out.

all photos Madeleine Harbison / Alan Toner

That's kind of our temperature back there [*a chuckle*] so as Dorothy said about Kansas. There's no place like home.

"We've come a long way, and we're going back ..."

"Part Man Part Monkey" fitted perfectly into the night's setting and at the end after feeling reverb on the guitar ("The ghost of Jimi Hendrix is in the room somewhere") Springsteen went into one of the few light love songs of the night, "All The Way Home".

The mood then again quickly became more introspective ("Everybody knows what it feels like to be condemned.") for the Death Row confession, "Nebraska". Then a "love song about not being able to handle the real thing", the darkness of a night with a prostitute and the longing for a lost love in "Reno", a song so intimate it forces the listener to hold their breath and ends with one of the bitterest pay-offs any songwriter has committed to record.

Springsteen's back-catalogue is littered with dreamers. "This is another one of those hidden love songs," Springsteen laughed from the piano. "A while back I had two different endings. One ending was two guys and another ending was a guy and a girl. I don't even want to get into all that!

"But there were two people I asked about the ending. One was one of my oldest fans and she said, 'Man, you got to use the one with the girl.'

I figured she was just going for romance and the other person I asked was Steve Van Zandt. Now, I would have assumed Steve would have said the two guys, due to his great fear of women but he kind of surprised me and said, 'No, no, no, the one with the girl. That's what really happens, you know. You got your pals and then life changes ...' and so that's the one I went for. I think it was the right one ..." and the piano announced, "Racing In The Street".

Springsteen at the piano is a fascinating sight, because the image of him with his familiar Fender Esquire is so strong and Springsteen himself looks a little uncomfortable at the keys, giggling if he hits a wrong note, smiling broadly when he successfully completes a tricky instrumental section. As the beautiful outro faded to huge applause, Springsteen waved a hand and wandered straight back to the microphone. Striking hard at his acoustic guitar, he launched into "The Rising", then quickly into "Further On (Up The Road)".

Then, he was back at the keys for his story of Jesus, the mother's son, on his walk up Calvary Hill.

"I was brought up Catholic - I'm sure I don't have to tell you about that over here. I think I made it to about eighth grade in Catholic School and then I did everything I could to get out. And I figured that's it.

But I know he's got a soft spot for the Irish so I just casually said, "Keep it Irish, Bruce."
He replied: "It's a beautiful country, it's a beautiful place", and he asked if my ex-girlfriend, who was with me at the time, was Irish.
She said, "Yes", and he kissed her on her head. As down to earth as he is, any time I'm near him my nerves are all jumpin', actin' like a fool, ha!
Long live this man.

Declan Slattery, Dublin

A COMMUNITY INSPIRED BY BRUCE

The Salt & Pepper Lonely Hearts Club Band was formed in 1998. It is a band of singers and musicians made up of young people from Ashbourne, Co Meath, aged from 11 to 30. The band is directed by Josephine Reynolds and rehearsals take place at her home, which to all intents and purposes has become a 'youth club' in Ashbourne.

It is great to see such a wide variety of young people from national school, secondary school and college integrating together through music.

Many young people in this band have formed lifelong friendships and the true value of this band can be seen in the very fact that over the years this group has grown considerably in number. At the last count it had more than 50 members.

These young people have developed a real love for music and have channelled their energy and time through their musical talent into helping those less fortunate.

Back in December 2004, Jo (who is a huge Bruce fan) and the band organised 'A Night With The Boss', two shows in aid of the Irish Cancer Society.

They played two fabulous sets including "Atlantic City", "The River", "Streets Of Fire" and "Badlands".

Josephine Reynolds and the Salt & Pepper Lonely Hearts Club Band are not only an inspiration to the young people in Ashbourne, they have also raised a staggering €70,000 for charity.

by Bruce Springsteen fans of Ashbourne and supporters of the Salt & Pepper Lonely Hearts Club Band

Sometime around 2004 I got a call from Gordon McCann who we had met at the pre-show parties in London in 1999. A taxi driver mate of his had had Clarence Clemons in the car and had put him on the phone to Gordon. Later that evening Donal Lillis and I were on the way to Dublin. Gordon had been given a tip that Clarence was to make a surprise appearance that night with Don Baker in a small venue in Dublin. Don Baker was good but there was no sign of Clarence. After the gig ended Gordon hailed us a taxi and rushed us down the road to a club. He had a short chat with the door men who informed us that Clarence had played there earlier with two different bands but was now gone for something to eat. We naturally asked Gordon how he knew to come to this second club and he said, "Oh, this was my first tip." When we asked him who gave him the tip he informed us that it had been Clarence! ⬇

"But I realised once you are brought up Catholic, Jesus is your home boy, that's all there is to it. That's not going to change.

"So I am kind of in a funny situation. I guess I'm excommunicated cos I got divorced, so I think that's it. Is that it or not? [*The crowd told him it was, and he laughed*] You're screwed, right? So … oh, that takes a load off my shoulders!

"But you're always sort of still connected. All my relatives were big church goers. Where we grew up there was a little L-shaped street. We had about eight houses on this one street. The church was here, the convent was there, and the rectory was here, and after school I was usually here in the convent. "Occasionally I go back now to where I was tortured [*a laugh*] and it is one of those … what do you call it? The Swedish complex. I forget what it is called … But now I get free beer and they let me watch the baseball games - the wonderful benefits of fame and fortune right there!

"But, you know how they picked the pope a few weeks ago, that was kind of a big deal. It was sort of like watching a high end sports trade for a team you don't play for any more. I tried to get excited about that but who cares? I'm sorry.

"But I wrote this song. I wrote a lot about sons and mothers on this record. I was interested in the relationship between Jesus and Mary as Jesus being Mary's son, just her boy.

"I wrote this song sort of with the idea of looking into that because one of the things when you have a kid is there is nothing you won't do to protect them or keep them from harm. And this is called "Jesus Was An Only Son" …"

In between the verses of this gentle gospel ballad, Springsteen kept playing, but talked through his alternative version of the tale, revealing something of himself and hearing the audience mutter back, nod and laugh.

"The first thing that strikes you as a parent is that there is nothing in the world you would not do to keep your children safe. I remember it came as a shock to very self-involved musicians."

And later: "At the same time your kids have their own destiny … And the choices that they make and that we make are given weight and are given meaning by the things that we give up, and the parts of life we give up. When we chose something you give up something else but I always figured (Jesus) had to be thinking, 'Galilee is pretty nice this time of year … there's a little bar down there I could manage. Mary Magdalene could tend bar. We could do the preaching on the weekends … have some kids, watch the sun on their face'."

As Bruce picked up his guitar for the next song, someone wandered up to the front and left something on the stage. "Alright," said Bruce, "as long as it ain't ticking, I guess."

Moving on from Jesus, he turned to human frailties and started two songs which revealed the power we all have to be our own saviours and our own destroyers.

"We all carry the seeds of our own destruction. It is kind of a merry part of the human package and we do a dance with it our whole lives. But we also carry with us the seeds that make things grow, create things. This is a song about a guy just coming down on the right side of the equation.

"I wrote this song … I stole the title from a Roy Orbison song … It was about a pearl diver who dives to the bottom of the ocean, tries to get the pearl for the girl and, if you know the story, he gets stuck at the bottom …

"It was the kind of song that would be kind of kitschy with anybody else but Roy had a way of making that incredibly emotional.

"I got to meet him briefly before he died. I went to his house one afternoon and he told me he had another song about a windsurfer. 'Windsurfer? I don't know.' I didn't say this but I was thinking, 'That's not going to fly. You can write about surfing, that's big. You can write about the wind … but windsurfing, I don't know anyone who wants to hear that!' "It killed John Kerry in the election - the whole windsurfing thing was big in the States. For some reason that was it … The old trailers, the weapons of mass destruction, that's okay, but

windsurfing, no way. That's where the American people draw the line [*a lot of chuckling*].

"But, anyway, the record comes out with this big song about windsurfing on it. It's beautiful. Almost made me want to windsurf except I did not want to ruin my career. It's the kind of thing that can hurt you.

"Anyway, it just goes to show you gotta have faith. This is "Leah"."

From there, he introduced the song's "flipside" – "the seeds of your destruction".

"A song about a young guy who gets in trouble, goes off to New Orleans, becomes the champion … comes back home towards the end of his life and … this song's a conversation he has with his mother through a locked door. Freud's smiling somewhere …

"I kind of grew up in a house that was kind of touched both by fortune and the harsh hand of fate. And the only thing I learned is those things did not negate one another. That they define the perimeters of all my song-writing, those two poles. And all you can learn to do is learn to live with them both.

"This is "The Hitter"."

The next song featured characters defeated by the most cruel of circumstances, "Matamoros Banks".

"It is kind of the same story, the man making the same journey, trying to get across the wire into the United States, fuelled by the same hopes and love for

his family, trying to get something better. "In the States hundreds of people die each year trying to cross the border. They die in the deserts, in the mountains, in the backs of vans, in the rivers.

"And this is a song I wrote kind of backwards. It starts with the body at the bottom of the river, the journey across the desert to the banks of Matamoros which is a town across from Brownsville, Texas."

For the encore, Springsteen began to stride the stage, as the "theatre-goers" from the seats all began to venture up to the edge of the stage.

"Ramrod" saw people dancing in the aisles: "You are scaring me now."

Then, "I'm On Fire" provided the only chart hit of the night.

"We have got some friends with us tonight from Amnesty International," he said before "Land Of Hope And Dreams". "Amnesty International's focused on preventing and ending abuses of human rights, promoting freedom of conscience and expression, and fighting discrimination in all forms so, if you see them on the way out, give them a hand."

Following on, Springsteen took a moment to thank Dublin and "everybody for coming out to the show".

"I also wanna thank you for taking my music and this record into your hearts, I appreciate that a lot …" And referring to the huge demand for tickets, he added: "I know there's a lot of folks who wanted to come. I wish I could stay for ten days. Here's to you."

Springsteen patiently clawed every last pleasure out of his new working of "The Promised Land". It was played slow, Springsteen marking each strum of the guitar with a tap on the body of the instrument to beat out the rhythm.

Justin Evans

The haunting performance had everyone holding their breath, as Springsteen stripped down the stadium-pleasing favourite, usually backed by the might of the E Street Band, and turned it into a slow prayer for something good which focused entirely on the words.

The show had featured so many moments where the solo Springsteen had everyone hanging on his words. He now had one final trick for the Dublin crowd.

He stepped over to the pump organ and began a slow, swirling riff, before laying on top the circular repeated verses and chorus of "Dream Baby Dream". The effect was mesmerizing.

This version of a track from punk band Suicide had the crowd hooked for eight minutes right up until the moment Springsteen half-spoke, half-sang the line "I just want to see you smile" and, with the organ still playing on a loop (the night's only gimmick), slipped behind the curtain at the side of the stage with just a slight wave of the hand.

Colm O'Hare, of Hot Press, said of all the "dozen or so" Springsteen shows he had been to "this was without doubt the most memorable, and certainly the most emotionally intense".

He added: "Shorn of the formidable might of the E Street Band, the man-they-still-call-The-Boss arguably had to work harder than ever. That he pulled it off so successfully in the acoustically-unfriendly environs of The Point was a testament not only to his talent and experience but to his willingness to experiment."

For Brendan Crossan in the Irish News it was simply a "quite stunning performance". Despite being alone on

the stage for a 25-song set, wrote Crossan, Springsteen's "goose-bumped show was remarkably fluid".

"A genius was cut loose in The Point on Tuesday night. Who needs the Professor and Clarence of E Street fame when The Boss can do it all on his own?"

George Byrne, of the Evening Herald, said that 20 years on from his Irish debut Springsteen "is still the powerful headliner he always was". Byrne had entered The Point a worried man – "Forewarned with the knowledge from the US dates that a greatest hits show was out of the question, I was fearing the worst."

However, Springsteen "somehow managed to make that big boomy barn by the Liffey (ie, The Point) feel like the most intimate folk club one could possibly imagine".

Just after Springsteen left the stage, the mesmerizing sound of the pump organ still circling around inside Byrne's head, it "occurred to me that Bruce Springsteen had achieved something I wouldn't have believed possible earlier that evening – he made two-and-a-half hours of largely unfamiliar material fly by as if in an instant. There wasn't even a single shout for "Dancing In The Dark"."

Jim Carroll's review appeared in the Irish Times under the headline "Darkness and honesty on the edge of town".

"Many artists have tried to turn that God-forsaken train shed in the docklands into an intimate setting, yet few have so easily or willingly drawn their audience so far into the heart of their songs as the man from New Jersey. There are a lot of dreams in the world of Springsteen, but there are also a lot of hard times, and (in this show) you can sense the claustrophobic, quiet desperation which marks his finest songs."

He added: "What we're getting from Springsteen is honesty and integrity. Music only tends to do honesty and integrity these days if it comes as part of a marketing campaign. There are few acts in the big-league who haven't compromised themselves in one way or another as the commercial fat cats come calling. Springsteen's motives remain untainted and the only hawking he does tonight is for the Amnesty International stall in the foyer."

Springsteen covers songs sparingly. For Carroll the choice of Suicide's "Dream Baby Dream" to close an "extraordinary, enthralling show" was both inspired and inspiring.

"Despite all the bad times and the hard-luck stories which usually leave this cast of men and women lost and brokenhearted there is always room to dream of a better tomorrow in Springsteen's world."

Ireland was now very much part of Springsteen's world.

While he had played only one show there during the *Devils & Dust* tour, and while the tour rumbled on back into the States, only finally ending in November 2005, the music had pulled Springsteen even closer to the Irish audiences.

He remained current in Ireland in a way he perhaps did not elsewhere. He cropped up in unusual places – a band called Reloaded rewrote one of his famous songs as "Born In Tyrone" for that county's place in the All-Ireland final; Gaelic footballer Paul Finlay, of Monaghan, listed him as his favourite singer; and singer-songwriter Ben Reel revealed that *Devils & Dust* had been the last album he had bought and that Slane in 1985 had been the first concert he had attended.

The next project, while alienating fans, particularly in the United States, could have been tailor-made for the Irish fans.

**The Point
Dublin**

5 May 2006

Crowd: 8,000

Tickets: 75-85 euro

**The Point
Dublin**

17, 18 & 19 November 2006

Crowd: 24,000 over three nights

Tickets: 75-85 euro

**The Odyssey Arena
Belfast**

21 November 2006

Crowd: 10,000

Tickets: £40-£60

The end of a seven-month solo tour but where would Springsteen go next? Fans had loved the solo stuff – "a wonderful chapter" in Springsteen's long touring history – but thoughts turned to the E Street Band. Would they be ready to roll in 2006? The rumours started.

And, very quickly, came the news that there would be a new album. But this was a full block away from E Street. Springsteen had taken quite a different turn – again.

A clue to the future would be a distant echo from the past when in 1997 Springsteen had invited a group of musicians to his farm in New Jersey for a knees-up celebrating his 48th birthday. A few weeks later Springsteen had invited a handful of them back to help him record a song for a charity album being put together as a tribute to Pete Seeger. Now, it was confirmed, Springsteen had been working with an expanded version of this band to record *We Shall Overcome: The Seeger Sessions*, a whole album, exploring the heart of traditional American music.

The album was due for release in April 2006, by which time Springsteen was already rehearsing for live shows – the band now numbering 17, the largest Springsteen had ever put together.

The dynamic of the band meant that Springsteen was now more band leader than ever. The stage was packed with musicians; the banjo, the accordion,

fiddles and the brass section packing out every corner; and the male and female vocalists vying for a space near centre stage. Bruce was right in the middle, tucked into a waistcoat, acoustic guitar strapped high across his body. He strummed hard, he turned and conducted the musicians that surrounded him, he sang out his heart in the big songs and held back that rasping rock voice for the slower, spiritual numbers. He gave the horn section a nod as it took up the tune or shouted towards the piano, as he picked out new foils with whom to trade riffs and jokes. He was keen to share vocals, not only with Patti but with dapperly dressed Marc Anthony Thompson, who was at his side most of the time.

This was a world away from the solo Springsteen chatting in the dark but it was also a long way from the E Street Band. And whereas, with the 'Other Band' tour of 1992/93, Springsteen had attempted to create an alternative to the E Street Band, this was something entirely different.

And, while some fans just did not like it, it worked both in creating a wonderful and exciting show and allowing Bruce to express himself in some other way than with his trademark Fender. After all, folk music at its heart is about communicating with people, about telling their stories, and that was exactly what Springsteen had always

been about. "Though rich beyond imagination," wrote Joe Breen in the *Irish Times*, "he has been, like the subject of his tribute, an activist in causes that could be generally described as community-based, environmental, even, God-forbid, left-wing. So his decision to record a tribute album to one of the greatest living left-wing Americans should be no great surprise."

To Colm O'Hare, of *Hot Press*, the record might even be "quite possibly the least surprising album of Springsteen's entire career".

"(Springsteen) has always been a folk artist, in spirit if not in deed. Blue-collar credentials aside, he was once touted as the 'new Dylan' and signed to Columbia by the legendary John Hammond on the basis of a bunch of acoustic demos," wrote O'Hare, adding that many songs of Springsteen's first two albums – such as "Mary Queen Of Arkansas" and "Wild Billy's Circus Story" – were "decidedly folksy".

Springsteen had covered Woody Guthrie and Bob Dylan, added O'Hare, and "I'm On Fire" was a "folk song by any other name".

O'Hare described the Seeger tribute as "joyous, uplifting and exuberant stuff … Recorded over beer 'n' whiskey-soaked sessions on the Springsteen family farm in New Jersey with a cast of a dozen or so largely unknown musicians, it amounts to a knees-up par excellence with Bruce as bandleader and party-host directing the proceedings with a looseness and bonhomie that he's rarely shown on record. The results are sometimes spectacular and never less than compelling."

He said it was "a triumph which in time will be likened to The Band's *Basement Tapes*, Van Morrison's collaboration with the Chieftains on *Irish Heartbeat* and Billy Bragg's Wilco-assisted Woody Guthrie project *Mermaid Avenue*."

After rehearsal shows in Asbury Park, the band went to New Orleans to play the Jazz & Heritage Festival in a city ravaged by Hurricane Katrina. For some, *We Shall Overcome* became as much of a response to that disaster – and the US government's failure to help so many of its people – as *The Rising* was influenced by the events of September 11, 2001. "We had a chance to travel around New Orleans yesterday, from Lake View to the 9th Ward," Springsteen told the crowd. "I think I saw sights I never thought I'd see in an American city and the criminal ineptitude makes you feel furious. This is what happens when political cronyism cuts the very agencies that are supposed to serve American citizens in times of trial and hardship. This is what happens when people play political games with other people's lives."

5 May 2006

O Mary Don't You Weep
John Henry
Johnny 99
Old Dan Tucker
Eyes On The Prize
Jesse James
Adam Raised A Cain
Erie Canal
My Oklahoma Home
Mrs McGrath
How Can A Poor Man Stand Such
Times And Live
Jacob's Ladder
We Shall Overcome
Open All Night
Pay Me My Money Down
My City Of Ruins
Buffalo Gals
You Can Look
(But You Better Not Touch)
When The Saints Go Marching In

17 November 2006

also included
Atlantic City
Further On (Up The Road)
Growin' Up, If I Should Fall
Behind, Devils & Dust, Long Time
Comin', Blinded By The Light
This Little Light Of Mine
American Land

18 November 2006

also included
Bobby Jean, Highway Patrolman
The River, Shenandoah

19 November 2006

also included
The Ghost Of Tom Joad, For You
Jesus Was An Only Son

21 November 2006

also included
Mansion On The Hill

The speech introduced a Springsteen rewrite of "How Can A Poor Man Stand Such Times And Live", a song from the Great Depression updated for Katrina and dedicated to "President Bystander".

Neil McCormick, of the *Irish Independent*, noted that the album "might have seemed a complete departure except that, by reclaiming old protest songs, Springsteen was reasserting the innate political liberalism of that mythical America, built on principles of freedom and equality".

Backstreets said, despite early concerns, Springsteen had found a way to make folk music vital and current, with the live shows being huge fun. "Serving up a tasty gumbo of folk, Cajun, jazz, blues and gospel, the shows are delivering generous portions of raucous, dance-inducing sing-a-longs. Or shout-a-longs, as is often the case."

And Ireland was the place for a sing-a-long, as the tour would prove.

The tour proper was to start in Europe with a 10-show run – later expanded to include a special show for the BBC in London – and would open at The Point in Dublin on May 5, 2006.

Coming across the Atlantic on the *Seeger Sessions'* plane was a hold packed with all manner of horns, tambourines, a pedal-steel guitar, a washboard, a boogie-woogie piano, a tuba, a banjo …

Harry Scott

One look at the instruments played by Art Baron alone would tell any customs official the band was well in excess of its airline weight allowance.

Packing out the seats was the Sessions Band, slightly different from that which appeared on the record. As well as Scialfa and Thompson (both guitars and vocals), there were Sam Bardfeld and Soozie Tyrell (violins); Art Baron (sousaphone, trombone, mandolin, penny whistle, euphonium); Frank Bruno (acoustic guitar and field drum); Jeremy Chatzky (bass); Larry Eagle (drums, percussion); Clark Gayton (trombone, percussion); Charlie Giordano (accordion, piano, organ); Curtis King Jr (backing vocals, percussion); Greg Liszt (banjo); Lisa Lowell (backing vocals, percussion); Ed Manion (saxophone, percussion); Cindy Mizelle (backing vocals, percussion); Curt Ramm (trumpet, percussion); and Marty Rifkin (steel guitar, Dobro guitar, mandolin).

The New Orleans show had fans in Ireland buzzing. As the *Irish Times* noted it left Bruce with a "lot to live up to".

On his arrival in Ireland Springsteen explained the thinking behind the show to David McCullagh of RTÉ: "I think our main concern was to bring out the rawness and the raucousness of the original music, where the characters are all sort of wild and woolly.

JO'S PINT WITH BRUCE

I received a phone-call from my friend Josephine Buckley in Slane who was out of breath and couldn't get the words out quick enough.

Because she sounded so out of breath and incoherent at first I thought that there was something really wrong ... but, no, she was trying to tell me that she had *met Bruce in the flesh*.

Bruce, Patti and their children had just sat with her and her husband Ray and son Alan in her local, the small bar of the Conyngham Arms in Slane.

Of course, needless to say, I didn't believe her until she brought the photos into work the next day ... and, of course, I was absolutely raging that she didn't phone me when she was in the bar to tell me that Bruce was around! I would have rushed to Slane along with our great friend Marion, the biggest Bruce fan I know, to catch a glimpse of him or meet him.

Marion has a shrine to Bruce in our office in Ashbourne Community School, which we have recently updated with a *Working on a Dream* poster – so we and our students have a lovely view each day when we come to work.

And when we are feeling under the weather or need to be energised we just put Bruce on and the day just gets better and better.

Madeleine Harbison
Ashbourne, County Meath

A couple of days after the *Seeger Sessions* in 2006 word got out around Slane that Bruce Springsteen along with his wife Patti and family were in the local hotel, the Conyngham Arms.

Bruce Springsteen had been visiting Lord Henry Mountcharles in Slane Castle and dropped into the local hotel to have something to eat with his family.

Bruce and his family were very relaxed and casual and insisted on eating their food in the bar where the small group of locals and fans made them feel very welcome. He obliged by signing their concert tickets and posing for photos, a pint of Guinness in his hand.

Ray Buckley, Slane

THE FIFTH OF MAY

The *Seeger Sessions* first night in May 2006 was a golden gig.

I remember Bruce and the band coming onto the stage and it was really noticeable that they were very nervous. It was only their second performance, having played New Orleans Jazz Festival a few days earlier. The opening – "O Mary Don't You Weep" – had the audience joining in and it just got better and better from there on in. During "Mrs McGrath" a cheer went up when the date of May 5 was mentioned, Bruce looked a bit bewildered at that but I'm sure it clicked later on.

This is the sort of music that Irish people know really well, it's an invite to join a party and sing along and participate, have as much fun as the band.

Jocelyn Kelly, Dublin

"Some of it got lost in some translations, when people thought of folk music they tended to think of something that was mild in some way … When you go back to the roots of that stuff you find out how wild it was. It's wild music, so we tried to catch a bit of that."

And because of the sounds on the record, New Orleans by way of Louisiana by way of the Singing Pub in Donegal, Ireland, was the perfect place to launch the European tour.

"(There are) Celtic influences all over the place," Springsteen said. "That's where it came from. We're excited about coming here and starting in Dublin for that very reason … Celtic influences all through the night. That and a combination of a lot of southern American, New Orleans influences. It's just a complete melting pot of musical influences, so we're excited about playing here."

The *Seeger Sessions* had plenty to attract it to Irish fans. At its heart it celebrated a culture of story-telling and throwing a wild party. It had tales of immigrant experience and plenty of politics too ("We Shall Overcome" had been sung in the city of Derry as well as in Washington DC during the civil rights movement), although always delivered from behind great tunes.

"The *Seeger Sessions* is a joyful, thrilling collection of traditional Americana, recorded and performed in

Greg Lewis

Beate Rossbach

Greg Lewis

Madeleine Harbison

single takes, with no rehearsals or overdubs, in the spirit of the great American folk icon Pete Seeger (and strongly reminiscent of Dylan's legendary *Basement Tapes*," wrote Jane Graham in the *Belfast Telegraph*. "And though the songs themselves … are steeped in time and place, the link between Springsteen's version of the protest song "We Shall Overcome" and his current feelings about his home country is clear.

"Unlike Dylan, who long ago ducked out from political responsibility, Springsteen is strong and willing enough to carry the necessary weight on his shoulders. For this he should be celebrated and endlessly encouraged.

"He has become a giant amongst his contemporaries, more relevant today than he has perhaps ever been, with no signs of going soft on us or looking to pass on the baton."

In amongst the collection was "Mrs McGrath", a traditional Irish ballad from the early 1800s, around the time of the Battle of Waterloo and of the Peninsula Campaign of the Napoleonic Wars, in which a character returns to his mother after losing his legs in a battle. It was an anti-recruiting song which had most famously resurfaced around the time of the Easter Rising and World War One to become a favourite rebel song.

Strangely, the *Belfast Telegraph* reported, it had also had a "huge impact as an anti-war song in the unlikely setting of a green field at Glengormley" when Burl Ives had performed it at an open-air festival in the 1950s. Ives had said at the time: "The ballad makes an impact because of its use of wit to paint a tragedy and make the telling bearable."

A chandelier and banner hung above the stage on May 5, while orange and purple lights broke through the gloom. It was a simple set, the banner said only 'Bruce Springsteen and the Seeger Sessions Band'. But as the lights swirled across the piano and bass, and the waistcoats and hats of the musicians, the overall impression was of a wild frontier saloon bar getting ready for a dusty-booted scrap pitched somewhere between mountain-man knees-up and tub-thumping revival meeting. The whole project, after all, mixed blue-collar brashness with the spiritual highs of some of the most intense Gospel material.

Springsteen's set was based on what the band had played at New Orleans and was expanded to two-and-a-quarter hours with a bluegrass version of Springsteen's own "Adam Raised A Cain" and "Erie Canal".

Springsteen found the low number of his own compositions in the set to be liberating. He told David McCullagh of RTÉ: "The fact that (this music) didn't fit in with what I do was what I liked about it, it was outside everything else …

I have been a Bruce fan since 1984. I have seen Bruce live 15 times, my first show was July 4, 1985, at Wembley. The last 4 concerts I have been to have been in Ireland and are without doubt the most memorable of all the shows I have seen so far (apart from my first show).

My first trip to Ireland was to Dublin for the *Seeger* show, May 5, 2006. That night at The Point was amazing. The band were incredible, the crowd was wild.

It was the first time I had ever ventured close to the stage, into the pit. I was about 10 feet from Bruce and the band. I met a very nice couple from Northern Ireland who had driven down that day and were driving home that night. We blethered for an hour or two while we waited for the show to start.

This was only the second night of the *Seeger* tour and at one point Bruce turned to the band and said, "I told you when we came to Ireland the shit would hit the fan".

I remember too looking back up at the stands to the side and at the back and not a bum was in a seat. The place was bouncing.

When Bruce came back to Dublin for three more shows at the end of 2006 I took my 12-year-old daughter and we got seats to the side of the stage. For me the great joy of that night was taking my wee girl Morven to see someone I have been a fan of for the past 20-odd years. She got to meet some of the band after the show and had her picture taken with Art Baron.

Hugh Rapson, Aberdeen, Scotland

The *Seeger Sessions* at The Point was fantastic. This venue is an enclosed theatre, but still Bruce managed to sell out all three gigs in less than an hour.

"American Land" would have to be the one song that stands out. At first I thought it was an Irish song.

It had a real party swing to it and it seemed that everyone knew it. Just brilliant.

**George Humphries
Dublin**

I went to see him in Dublin during the *Seeger Sessions* tour for two reasons. I thought it made lots of sense to attend a show of the *Seeger Sessions* music style in Ireland as some of the roots of this music somehow can be found there. There's a big connection between this kind of music and Ireland. The other reason was that I wanted to finally visit Dublin. I had heard many great things about this city and was very interested to see it myself.

My first trip to Dublin in May 2006 fully paid off. I had loved the idea of a folk-based album from the first samples of the songs I'd heard on the internet. How joyous, sad, triumphant, happy was this music! Full of life! When Bruce opened with "O Mary Don't You Weep" it instantly took my breath away. There was a special richness in this kind of music with so many band members on stage. I hadn't seen Bruce having so much fun ever before or at least it seemed to me like that. What a joy! ⬇

It was connected, but it was outside everything I had created, so I was freed from what I had done, so you are freed from the 'hits', or not playing the 'hits', or just your own music, period. I play very few of my own songs so it was an opportunity to sort of free yourself from the burdens, the many blessings, but also the burdens of song-writing … I'm always trying to tailor my music towards my songs, but don't have to do that this time out, I just make the music that feels right. It was an opportunity to go back to the eclectic-ness I had on … particularly my second record [*The Wild, The Innocent And The E Street Shuffle*] where we used tubas and horns. There was jazz on it, there was circus music, street music, all kinds of things. (You) go back to those things and approach something almost purely musically … It's very liberating and fun to do."

"O Mary Don't You Weep" and "John Henry" were both points at which the violins of Soozie Tyrell and Sam Bardfield soared.

Then "Johnny 99", the first of only four Springsteen originals in the set, and the playful "Old Dan Tucker", which already had the crowd shouting out the lyrics as if it were a classic that had been in the Springsteen repertoire for 20 years.

Springsteen's presence at the centre of the musicians – despite the size of the troupe – remained huge. But new characters were emerging too:

Heidi Weber

Greg Lewis

Beate Rossbach

Ray Buckley

treacle-voiced Marc Anthony Thompson, his grin broad below his hat, and Greg Liszt, the banjo player who looked like he had hitched a ride down from the Appalachians on a mule train to come play in the band, were quickly becoming fan favourites.

The band moved into "Eyes On The Prize", "Jesse James" and then Springsteen's own, "Adam Raised A Cain", its Biblical imagery fitting seamlessly into the set. "Erie Canal" was slow and mournful, and "My Oklahoma Home" inspired a crowd singsong.

"Mrs McGrath" had been angry in 1815 (and 1916) and was angry now as Springsteen described how foreign wars live on blood and a mother's pain, and changed the subject of the song's wrath to the "king of America" to leave no-one in doubt of the topical message being delivered.

The crowd gave a particular cheer halfway through the song, as Springsteen sang the line about the cannonball which struck McGrath's son – on the "fifth of May", the day of the show.

Before the song Springsteen mentioned its Irish roots and described a phone call from a friend who admonished Bruce for his mispronunciation of the title name on the record. "Bruce, you dumb bastard, it's Mc*Gra*, not Mc*Grath*!"

Throughout the show Springsteen appeared to be enjoying himself immensely but his jaw was fixed for the next track and its newly relevant political message, "How Can A Poor Man Stand Such Times And Live".

"Jacob's Ladder" soared through the keys before a restrained version of "We Shall Overcome" saw the music purr and swell like the hearts of those in the protest movement the lines were written to inspire.

Springsteen's new version of "Open All Night" followed with the scat-fight between the male and female members of the band which would expand and develop throughout the tour, and then the sing-a-long of "Pay Me My Money Down", the beautiful "My City Of Ruins", the foot-stamping "Buffalo Gals" and a barn-storming new version of "You Can Look (But You Better Not Touch)".

Springsteen wanted to stimulate not only the song in the heart but also the thought in the brain, and closed with an interpretation of "When The Saints Go Marching In" which slowed down to such a pace that it hushed the crowd until the moment it ended to a burst of applause which echoed around The Point.

"He came to town with a very serious reputation and left with it enhanced," reported the *Irish Times*. "And by some distance."

How great that Springsteen went new ways, tried out another kind of music, experimented with styles and thus stayed relevant and so much alive as a musician and artist. The adaptation of these old songs was terrific with the vocal harmony section, the horns …

And when Bruce played some of his own songs such as "Johnny 99", "Adam Raised A Cain", "Open All Night" or the beautiful "My City Of Ruins" they were filled with a new different life. A completely other approach which only showed the more what a genius Springsteen is …! During those days in Dublin I also met Springsteen at the hotel. I had brought with me a picture I had taken of Bruce three years earlier in Munich. I really wanted it autographed by him. In addition to that I had written a letter to Bruce which included some personal things about me and my boyfriend at the time. We had met only because of Bruce. I wanted Bruce to know how happy I was that I had met my love at one of his shows and that he was kind of responsible and involved in our love story. I don't remember how long we waited. He finally came out and I felt very shy. I stood a few steps back and took some pictures of him. People were clustered around him and I couldn't get through. I also felt a bit stupid with his picture that I had to give him as my letter was on its back. I decided to give it to Terry (Magovern) who was always around him. I tried to explain that there was a letter on the back side as it seemed very strange to give Bruce a picture of himself … I don't know if Bruce ever read it or not.

Mirjam Kunz, Switzerland

2006 was a whirlwind for Emma and I. In January we decided to get married and planned the wedding for March. On our return from honeymoon my first task was to check the Backstreets website - a tour with the Seeger Sessions Band had been announced and was opening in The Point, Dublin, on May 5 - less than a year since the last Springsteen concert we had seen at the same venue.

On arriving at The Point car park around 10.30am we discovered a queue of around 40. We got in line. The weather was fine and we did the whole roll call, wristband thing. I stuck my camera down my left sock and ran when the doors opened to get a good spot. Emma made it to the barrier right in front of Bruce's mic and I was just behind because I almost lost my camera out of my sock.

The thing that stood out this time, due to the fact of being so close, was how hard Bruce plays and how much energy he puts in. From the opening lyrics of "O Mary Don't You Weep" on, each word seemed to travel through his slightly bent legs, up through his chest; his whole body tensed, the left hand tightly gripping the fret-board, right hand thrashing on the strings as if in an attempt to break each one by one. The sweat dripped from his face and elbows from the first song as he growled out song after song, some more than 100 years old, he made them sound fresher and more important than most contemporary songs.

We could hear him yell directions and count off songs off-mic, and it was amazing just seeing how he kept total control of such a huge band so effortlessly. ⬇

The "remarkably fluent" way in which the apparently ragged band of musicians came together breathed life into songs which were sometimes hundreds of years old. "These humble echoes of a distant past are renewed, Pogues-like, in a cauldron of sound enriched by many shades of American folk music from honky tonk piano to New Orleans brass, from Gospel choirs to Cajun accordion, from Irish ballads to Appalachian fiddles and banjo," wrote Joe Breen. "Yet the integrity of these songs remains, their purpose undiluted. This is not a rock 'n' roll show though certainly it rocks with a vengeance."

And despite the huge expectations of the show in Ireland, Joe Breen added, "I wager nobody among the packed audience left that hall … feeling short-changed after an awesome and exhilarating performance."

The following night, before going on to continue the tour in Manchester, some of the band headed up to O'Donoghue's pub and took part in a jam which was filmed and later formed part of a promotional video for "Pay Me My Money Down". Violinist Sam Bardfield remembered: "Soozie brought us to a place that she had known, I guess it was a famous place, the Dubliners had started there, and we had a little session and played with the band there – that was fun." Bruce and Patti visited the pub too, with Marty Rifkin, and enjoyed a leisurely drink.

All three signed the pub's visitor book, with Bruce noting: "Good pub! God bless."

Towards the end of May, the band flew back to the United States to continue the tour. Shows in America, though, were not the sell-out events promoters of a Springsteen gig would normally expect and, given the enthusiasm of European audiences, it was no surprise when a second European leg was quickly announced.

This time the band would start with seven shows in Italy and close in November with a total of four nights in Dublin and Belfast. The Belfast show would be only his second in Northern Ireland – following the King's Hall solo gig in March 1996.

It was praise indeed for the Irish audiences. Five shows altogether for the *Seeger Sessions* and the only three-night stand of the entire tour.

The tickets for the four new shows went on sale in June and sold out in phenomenal time.

There were to be three shows at The Point in Dublin, on November 17, 18 and 19. All three nights, the *Evening Herald* reported, were sold out in under an hour. "He's fairly popular over here," the newspaper quipped.

The *Belfast Telegraph* reported that 34,000 tickets for the winter shows were sold in just over 25 minutes at a rate of 1,360 tickets per minute. In the meantime Springsteen stayed in the news in Ireland when he and Patti bought a three-day event horse from Olympic rider Sasha Stewart, of Richhill, County Armagh.

Patti had been to see the horse near Dublin and Stewart had felt very sad to be selling him on. (Patti told her not to worry as What Now would have a "beautiful barn … and would go out in the field each day".) The family also bought a second horse from event rider Richard Irwin.

The Dublin shows were to be filmed for a *Live in Dublin* DVD/CD which would be released the following year. Fans attending The Point were warned that their "likeness" could end up being on film somewhere with Bruce – and to pretty much all that sounded like something they would welcome happening.

Bruce came in from the UK and again stayed at the Merrion in Dublin. The majority of the band were this time in the Westin Hotel and were regularly seen by fans exploring the city.

Springsteen did some exploring of his own, taking what Debbie McGoldrick of the *Irish Abroad* website described as a "trip down memory lane" when he visited Slane and popped into the Conyngham Arms Hotel with his wife. "He was very friendly and talked to the local people who were there," one member of staff told the website. "He was very down-to-earth and people came in to talk to him and get his autograph and he was quite happy with that. We wanted him to go into the restaurant where he could be more comfortable, but he said he was more than happy to sit and eat in the bar."

The heavy purple and red drapes which framed the stage at The Point were to provide a suitably unobtrusive backdrop to the three shows which were to burst across those three nights in November: it was the musicians who were to shine, creating the rainbows of colour with their music, and turning a well-honed jam into a heart-lifting spectacle.

The first show on November 17 opened with "Atlantic City" which, reworked from its original downbeat acoustic style, rumbled into The Point like a locomotive. Foot-tappers "John Henry" and "Old Dan Tucker" followed hard on its heels, with Springsteen's re-working of "Further On (Up The Road)" bringing the soulful voice of Marc Anthony Thompson to the fore.

The crowd then provided exuberant backing vocals on "Jesse James" and "O Mary Don't You Weep".

"Here's a song from one of my folk music albums", said Springsteen, introducing an old song of his own: "Growin' Up".

Patti had not played a show for around six weeks but she was back for Dublin, and her return brought not only a dash of elegance amid a ragged bunch of waistcoats and bootlace ties, but the return of a special musical moment.

We left this show totally exhausted hands aching from clapping, feet sore from stomping, throats sore from shouting 'BRUUUUUUCCCCEEEE' all night. We headed up to Belfast that night, shattered but exhilarated.

A few days after this show we discovered that our unborn child (our first) had actually been in attendance at The Point that night.

Ciaran Gallagher, Belfast

After seeing *Devils & Dust* at The Point, Dublin couldn't be anything but a special place for us.

We came back in 2006. Maybe when we grow old we won't be able to remember much any more, but believe us it will be hard to forget "Mrs McGrath" the way Bruce played it May 5.

Just a small note for those silly Italians who laughed at Larry when she threw an envelope on the stage: it wasn't a letter, it was an invitation to our wedding which was coming up.

Okay, we supposed that Bruce and Patti weren't going to come to our wedding, but if they only rang us up, just to say that they weren't!

Lorenza "Larry" Pravato and Alessio "Tsitalia" Rozzi, Trieste, Italy

Diary, Dublin, May 5, 2006
Tonight Bruce was the MC, the Musical Director, Clown Supreme.

It was gorgeous to see him and Patti and the whole band so happy and having so much fun. Bruce seems to be just loving this tour, the music, and the awesome, rapturous welcomes.

The crowd erupted into song at the first chords of "Old Dan Tucker" and sang along as if they had known the song forever.

The smiles in the crowd matched the wide grin on Bruce's face, as they were enthralled by this fabulous band and the wealth of evidence of Bruce's growth and ability to surprise and follow new directions.

We have witnessed an extraordinary feat of reinvention as Bruce has gone from E Street *Rising* to *Dust* to Ragtime in a very short three years.

This has been a work of pure genius, an amazing example of musical strength and depth, and we as fans are truly privileged be a part of his ongoing journey.

Karl Birthistle, Zurich, Switzerland (originally from Dublin and a veteran of more than 130 shows)

A PINT WITH BRUCE
May 2006: Our weekend in Dublin was one my friend Heidi, my husband Burki and I will always remember.

We queued up from about 5pm, and there were about 100 fans in front of us. We were among the first 150 fans who got red wristbands and we were let in first. The three of us ended up second row in front of the stage.

Bruce and the Seeger Session Band sure "blew" us away with their performance. For me, the highlight of the whole set was "When The Saints Go Marching In". ❧

Dublin II
11/18/06

1. OL Dan
2. John Henry
3. I⁻ 99
4. Eyes
5. Jessie
6. Oh Mercy
7. Bobby Jean
8. Free Behind
9. Oklahoma
10. Atlantic Philadelphia
11. M Grace

12. Poor Man
13. Jacob
14. Coyote/Adam
15. Jesus
16. Open
17. Pa 1
18. We Shall/Shenandoah
19. You Can
20. Saints
21. Thes
22. Amen

via Aisling Barron

130

It's absolutely moving and I had tears in my eyes. The splendid Irish crowd was a crowd to remember. Very enthusiastic, very respectful and quiet, if needed. I'll never forget, dancing and singing and clapping along.

When Bruce sang "Mrs McGrath" all the Irish around us sang along the refrain with Bruce at the top of their lungs: too-ri-oo-ri-oo-ri-aa, too-ri-aa. I was in Ireland! I felt it, and I loved every minute of it.

The day after …

At around 2pm we decided to go to Bruce's hotel. There were about 40 fans waiting in front of the hotel – and at about 4pm we just couldn't believe our eyes: there he was, Bruce Springsteen, next to us, stepping out of the front entrance. There was just Terry Magovern with Bruce, no additional security guy was in sight. It wasn't necessary, Bruce seemed to know that.

Bruce stayed for about 10-15 minutes, signing lots of autographs. I think everyone who wanted one got one. He was very relaxed and friendly.

Heidi, who stood in front of me, got a Bruce picture signed (that she'd taken in '96). After that my dear, dear friend stepped back letting me stand next to Bruce. Then it was my turn, I got my *We Shall Overcome* booklet signed. I told Bruce how much I enjoyed the show last night and thanked him for that. He told me he himself had fun too and he had enjoyed the evening and especially the crowd. I said that to my eyes an Irish audience is just kind of wonderful. He sure seemed to agree.

After about 10-15 minutes Bruce got into his car and drove away. Burki stood there with a big smile on his face. Heidi and I were beaming with joy. We hugged each other, we hugged some fellow Irish fans who were just as happy as we were. After saying good-bye to these guys we decided to go to a pub.

Burki and Heidi were yearning for some Guinness after all this Bruce stress, and I was very interested in a nice cup of Irish tea. A friendly Irish couple, Bruce fans too, told us about O'Donoghue's, just around the corner.

At about 7pm Heidi came back from the washrooms, telling me very matter-of-fact: "Beate, you have to come with me, there's Bruce sitting in the back room."

At first I didn't believe her. But I followed Heidi who had a very determined look on her face, and the two of us went to the back room. Heidi had taken her camera.

And there he was again, Bruce Springsteen sitting at a table with Patti and some other folks.

At first I stopped dead in my tracks, unable to move. I just stood there and watched as Heidi, with her nerves like steel, went up to Bruce. He beckoned her to come when he spotted her, allowing her to step next to his table. She asked him if it's okay to get a picture with him, but if he doesn't feel like it she'd leave at once. Bruce told her that's okay, they were just leaving anyway and he shook hands with Heidi.

Meanwhile I was able to move again and I went forward too, shaking Bruce's hand as well. Then Bruce stepped between the two of us, putting his arm around Heidi. I put my arm around Bruce as the security guy took the picture – and off we went with a big smile on our face, still not being able to believe our luck. We were absolutely dumbfounded.

Sometimes you're just lucky enough being at the right place at the right time – with the right guys.

Beate Rossbach, Munich, Germany

Seeing Bruce in Ireland was kind of a dream. Don't know why, maybe I've heard so many nice things about this country and the people. My friends and me went to The Point in the afternoon, standing in line and were the last ones who got wristbands for the pit. Ended up second row that night and saw a great show, surrounded by very nice Irish people. The next day we planned a city tour and wanted to go to Bruce's hotel. When Bruce came out everything was relaxed. Everybody got his autograph, photos were taken. It was just a fantastic experience. After Bruce went away, people were hugging each other, showing their autographs. Wonderful.

From Bruce's hotel to the maybe most famous pub in Dublin it wasn't far away so we decided to go there, to listen to some real Irish folk music that evening.

We sat down at the bar, had some Guinness and at some point a guy talked with the pub owner. All I heard was something like "Bruce … outside … beer." English is not my mother language and I thought I misheard something.

A little bit later we saw the waitress show the pub owner the guestbook. I saw Bruce's signature and told my friend Beate, have a look, Bruce wrote this. She didn't believe me. ⬇

Springsteen's new "Tennessee Waltz"-style arrangement of "If I Should Fall Behind" had him singing a heart-rending duet with his wife. The tune and mood the song created was infectious, with the crowd left singing out the melody long after the band had finished.

"Erie Canal" continued the thoughtful mood while "My Oklahoma Home" told its tale of tragedy with humour and a catchy chorus.

Although We Shall Overcome is a tribute to one of the great political singers, the politics on the album is discreet and understated. Springsteen turned it up in Dublin with a triple hitter, beginning with a song of his own.

"Well, we teetered back slightly from the brink of insanity in the States a week ago," he said, New Orleans on his mind. "But it was close, it was so close. I've lived through a few different presidents but I don't think I've ever seen anything like this guy [cheers]. It was Sinclair Lewis who wrote a book called 'It Could Happen Here', I'm not sure it didn't. The great Abraham Lincoln quote: 'You can fool some people all of the time, all the people some of the time but you can't fool all the people all of the time' ... but he should've added that if you fool enough of the people enough of the time ... [applause] Terrible ... terrible ... terrible, tragic mistakes, terrible, tragic mistakes ..." The anti-Iraq war "Devils & Dust" followed, with "Mrs McGrath"

developing the theme and "How Can A Poor Man Stand Such Times And Live" doubling up as both a condemnation of President Bush and a tribute to the "mother-city of American music, New Orleans".

Then, a laugh and a smile, "Alright, it's time for me to ask that age-old rock 'n' roll question, that I've come thousands of miles to find out the answer to. I've asked it before, I'll ask it again, but right now what I wanna know is ... are you alright?"

The wild joy of "Jacob's Ladder" followed. Then Bruce revealed the whole family had come along to Ireland this time. Introducing "Long Time Comin'", written back in the 1990s when his children were very young, and tonight dedicated to them, Bruce looked off stage right to search for them. "Where are they?" He shrugged. "Maybe they're in the pub, drinking their third pint of Guinness. I don't know. I might not be kidding, I don't know where they are, God bless 'em [chuckles]. Where are my young ones? [crowd applauds]."

Mom was there too, of course, and led the female voices in the tour's version of Springsteen's own "Open All Night", a song now unrecognizable from its original, sparse acoustic arrangement. Performed by the Sessions band it took on epic proportions with the male and female members facing off in a scat competition which brought the house down. Fan Karl Birthistle told

Backstreets: "(This) was probably the longest version of the tour, with scat upon duelling scat, clocking in at well over 12 minutes, and not a second too long. It was fabulous fun, and the whole band clearly loved the playful elements of the song."

"Pay Me My Money Down" kept up the pace with the crowd singing along at the end, as they had throughout the tour. And, as usual, the band wandered off stage towards the end of the song, leaving Art Baron on stage alone with his tuba. The usual routine had seen Bruce come back on stage to haul him off. But this time, Bruce left him play so long, that Art began looking round to see what was going on. He found that Bruce had not left the stage but was sitting on the stool at the organ with his feet up on the piano, apparently asleep. Eventually Bruce "awoke" and got Art off – but the crowd kept on singing so that Bruce decided to go back to sleep on the piano. To draw the whole thing to a close, Bruce eventually had to conduct the singing with a last "Pay me or go to jaaaaail ... pay me my money down" so that the band could get on with the encore. "It was very funny," fan Sally Parker reported to Backstreets.

Three Springsteen compositions in a row then followed. The soulful "My City Of Ruins", a recently entirely re-arranged "Blinded By The Light" (which sounded like it had been composed in Cuba) and "You Can Look (But You Better Not Touch)".

I told my friend that I have to go to the washroom. The pub has an outside area. I stood in the archway to this area and discovered Bruce and his band sitting at a table. I waved to him and ran back inside the pub, and told my friend Beate, "Bruce is outside". I grabbed my camera. Next thing I remember is that his bodyguard told me "no" while I was trying to get closer. I said I'd go if it was not okay.

Around this time the band members left. Bruce stood up from his chair and told me it was okay to come closer. He shook my hand. I told him that I was from Germany and asked if he would mind a photo.

In the meanwhile my friend Beate had joined us. Bruce agreed about the photo. But who would take it? I ended up arm in arm with Bruce, explaining to his bodyguard how my camera worked.

Heidi Weber
Hanau, Germany

The first show, right at the beginning of the tour: we thought we were getting special treatment. And then there was "Mrs McGrath", it was one of *our* songs after all. The show was a ceilidh and the band was fantastic for musicians still only getting to know each other.

November saw a great series of shows and the band had improved so much since May. As for the new song, "American Land", surely he had written it just for us! Now we knew for sure he had real Irish blood in him.

Nigel and Maggie Flynn
Ballymoney

With the help of family and friends, my husband John and I managed to get tickets for three *Seeger Session* concerts, two in Dublin and one in Belfast.

On May 5 we headed to The Point and were lucky to get to number 50 and 51 in the queue. Once we got our wrist bands we headed to the back gate hoping to meet Bruce. We queued for hours before we finally achieved our lifetime ambition of 21 years to meet the greatest man on earth. The gates opened and a minute later a black people carrier drove in and parked at the back door.

Bruce got out and walked over to us. I put out my hand and he came straight for it. John got a great close-up photo of Bruce reaching for my hand. I was so excited. It was a real handshake, not just a tap on the fingers from running across the stage. John also met him and said, "Welcome to Ireland, Bruce." There were only about 15 people waiting at the gate that day. Bruce shook hands with everybody. That was one of the best moments of our lives.

After that momentous occasion we headed back to the queue. At 7pm the doors opened and we all rushed in. We got centre stage, second row. As we waited on the concert to start we got talking to other fans beside us. There were fans from all over Europe and America, and they all had stories to tell.

Finally Bruce came on stage to an ecstatic audience. And to finish off a memorable weekend the concert was being recorded. We can see ourselves for a few seconds on the *Live In Dublin* DVD.

Tina Gill, Quigley's Point, County Donegal

When Bruce emerged with the Seeger Sessions Band I think he performed the most uplifting shows I had been to, up until that point. I had seen that tour at its infancy and then at full maturity in Belfast and Dublin and how much progression was made was fantastic. A real highlight of all the shows was "Pay Me My Money Down". I feel concerts are much better when the audience is involved and I do believe Bruce has great rapport with the Irish crowd. I guess it's down to the audience enthusiasm.

Stephen Devine, Belfast

I failed to get tickets for the May *Seeger Sessions* show in The Point but in November time, thanks to a fellow fan from Cork, I managed to get a standing ticket and managed to position myself very close to the stage.

I am a lover of the *Seeger Sessions* project and so I thoroughly enjoyed this show. My wife isn't really into Springsteen but she was a huge fan of the *Seeger* stuff and I was absolutely thrilled to score two very good seats for the third night of the *Sessions* tour in November. I was excited because she was attending her first Bruce show with me. It is very hard to describe the Springsteen experience to someone who has never been to one of his shows, so this was her chance to see one for herself. She described it as an experience of a lifetime and admitted that, without being there, she couldn't have conceived of the energy and joy that is part and parcel of a Springsteen performance.

Dan Kavanagh, Dublin

After the wild run of "You Can Look" Bruce spoke quietly into the microphone. "This is kind of the song that explains what our whole little experiment's been about up here and I wanna send this one out to you, thanking you for … this was the first place we played in Europe. You really set us off on a nice start, we've had a lovely adventure with all this music and all these wonderful musicians. This has been a learning experience and a real treat and I wanna thank you for taking a chance on us with all this stuff. We appreciate that a lot so, that said, I guess I'll send this one out to you."

Then they played their beautiful version of "When The Saints Come Marching In" with Thompson and Scialfa sharing vocals with their ringleader.

For the last two songs the sound of foot-stamping filled The Point. "We want you to rise from your seats now, please, and join us. We wanna send you home with a little love in your heart, a little light in your soul …"

"This Little Light Of Mine" was a recent addition to the show but it proved a brief and high-energy introduction to a new favourite, "American Land". This was a new Springsteen composition telling the story of the American immigrant experience, and while paying tribute to the immigrants who had made America, it was also a damning indictment of their treatment today. Its lyrics and theme were hewn from the same rock

that Pete Seeger had mined throughout his career, but its music made a folk band truly rock, from the thumping drumbeat that heralded its arrival to its wild play-out.

The second show on the Saturday (November 18) was just as lively, with the audience joining in with the night's opening number, "Old Dan Tucker" before Springsteen had even started to sing and making for a longer than usual intro. The crowd was most definitely there to party.

The set list which followed had changed slightly: "John Henry", "Johnny 99", the first of three songs from *Nebraska* that night, "Eyes On The Prize" (introduced as "a great American Civil Rights' song of the '60s"), "Jesse James" and "O Mary Don't You Weep".

Then "Bobby Jean", *Born In The USA*'s hymn to friendship now radically re-worked with a Bob Dylan "I Want You"-style tune. The friends Bruce had in mind this time were right out in front of him. "How are we in Dublin tonight?" he asked before the song, getting cheers back of course. "This is for my old friends out there. There's a lot of folks been following us around the whole tour. How are you living, that's what I wanna know? Does your family miss you? Do your co-workers wonder where you've gone? They must!"

"If I Should Fall Behind" brought Patti into the spotlight with Bruce and at the end as the crowd continued to sing out

the tune, Bruce turned to Patti with a look of joy. It was followed by "My Oklahoma Home", after which Bruce gave Marty Rifkin and his steel guitar playing a special mention. Then the first tour premiere of the night: the slow and sad "Highway Patrolman", a treat for older fans but some felt it held up the party a little.

The next section brought everyone back to life: "Mrs McGrath", "How Can a Poor Man Stand Such Times And Live", "Jacob's Ladder", "The River", "Open All Night" with "Pay Me My Money Down" bringing the main set to its usual joyous close. At its close the crowd kept singing until Bruce had to come back out, alone and improvise an accompaniment on the guitar and to finally bring the singing to a close. Bruce laughed: "Okay, I've just about had it with that!"

The encore began slowly with "Shenandoah", the performance making it the last of the original set of songs on *We Shall Overcome* to be performed on the tour. The song was dedicated to Elizabeth, an English fan who was badly injured by a car while waiting in line for a show in Rome, and her daughter Clare. "We're gonna do this for Elizabeth, wishing her a quick recovery, quick as possible, let her know that we're thinking about her. We send our prayers out to her. This is for Clare. Clare out there tonight somewhere? There she is, alright, this is for you and your mama."

This was my one and only trip to Ireland, with my wife to see the Seeger Sessions Band at The Point on a rainy Sunday night. One or two things stand out from the concert: Bruce telling those sitting to get their arses off their seats, someone beside me (obviously a Bruce novice) asking her friend why everyone was booing, and the spontaneous reel dancing during "American Land" - certainly a night to remember.

Chris Johnson, Bromley, England

It was Springsteen who again brought me back to Ireland in November.

I was in a very difficult phase of my life. I had been drawn into a depression that left me nothing but sad and without any energy at all. It was probably one of my worst times in life.

Anyway, we went to The Point on Saturday and tried to get tickets outside, but no one sold any except for a few scalpers who asked horrendous prices. They even didn't want to go down when the show started. When I heard the sound of the music coming out of the venue, I had to go away. Never had it happened to me that I couldn't get hold of a ticket. It was a huge disappointment!

At least we had our pit tickets for the last night of his stand in Dublin.

The weather was bad – windy and rainy. After the last roll call we stood for hours in the cold and rain.

Finally we were let in early. Bruce was still doing the sound check. We cheered loudly to let Bruce and his people know that we were listening and enjoying it.

Again, the show was full of energy and everyone expressed the pure joy to play music. My favourites were "For You" and "Blinded By The Light". I danced and jumped like mad.

Mirjam Kunz
Switzerland

My only personal encounter with Bruce happened in 2006, when he was coming in at The Point for the sound-check for the concert on November 17.

My daughter Marie and I were just walking past a side entrance. We noticed a handful of people waiting. They said that the band had arrived a few minutes earlier and that Bruce was coming any time.

So we decided to wait, and a few minutes after we saw a big SUV with tinted windows arriving, the gates opened and before the car went in we caught a glimpse of Bruce.

The gates closed and we were a bit disappointed, but then they re-opened and Bruce walked out to greet us.

It was such a great experience. He shook our hands, said hello to everyone, and, "Hi guys, how are you?"

Some people took pictures, we only managed to capture him on our mobile phone, and the photo is sort of blurry. But still we cherish this memory.

There is something magic about meeting Bruce, even for a few minutes, because of the energy emanating from him.

Dominique Jumelle
Quin, Co Clare

I have tried to make as many shows as possible in Dublin. The most memorable was Saturday's Seeger Sessions Band. I was in the queue at about number 250 with my eight-year-old daughter Megan and six-year-old Aisling, Sister Mary Barron, my sister, and my brother and sister-in-law Dominic and Marie.

We got in and took up a stance behind one of the barriers, beside the camera in the crowd. The kids sat on the barrier throughout the show.

Now they are really into SSB so I suggested Aisling waved to Bruce. I lifted her up when there was a low point in the crowd. She waved like crazy. Bruce picked her out and pointed and gave her a big smile. So then the *Live In Dublin* DVD comes out. At about 1.40 minutes into "My Oklahoma Home" there is the point and smile! My daughter thinks she's elected!

At the end of the show that night the cameraman came up and handed the set-list to Aisling, and told us how great it was to see kids at the shows and how much Bruce enjoys having them there as well.

Eddie Barron, Liverpool

BLOWN AWAY BY THE SEEGER SESSIONS
Aisling Barron, Liverpool, now nine, remembers a special moment

Dad, my sister Megan, and I set off. It was a cold, windy day and the boat was rocking like mad. I couldn't believe that today I would be going to my first music concert ever. I was six. When the boat stopped I was really excited. ⬇

Just as he started a moth flew straight into the spotlight in front of his face and hovered around the microphone. "Wild beasts have invaded the stage!" he said.

"You Can Look (But You Better Not Touch)" picked up the speed, before Bruce took a moment to give his usual thank-you "for coming out to the show tonight". "I know some of you've been following us around and we appreciate that and … I was telling the folks last night, this is where we started off our tour, here in Dublin and I'm glad we got a chance to come back. I wanna thank all you guys for supporting this music and this band. I wanna thank all these great musicians that I've been graced to have here on this stage [*cheers*]. This has been a lovely experience for me and this is the chance to thank everybody who helped us put on the show, all the guys in our crew and who make this possible every night of course [*applause*]. The whole thing sort of happened by accident but ended up being a very sort of happy and glorious accident for me and so this song sort of explains what our journey up here has been about, and I wanna thank you guys for taking it with us and we'll be doing this again in the future and God bless you and safe travels." The words introduced a performance of "When The Saints Come Marching In" which was played so smoothly it made the blood run cold. Then the party continued and closed at high speed

("We want you all to, please, rise from your seats now and join us. We wanna send you home with a little love in your life and a little light in your soul, are we ready now? Help us!") with "This Little Light Of Mine" running straight into "American Land".

The Sunday show on November 19 was a big bar band party. Most of the filming for the live DVD was in the can and Springsteen let loose.

"Atlantic City" was back as the opener. Then: "John Henry", "Old Dan Tucker", the return of "The Ghost Of Tom Joad", "O Mary Don't You Weep", "Jesse James", then Bruce's re-working of "Further On (Up The Road)" which allowed Marc Anthony Thompson to shine and "Erie Canal".

The Dublin weather was wet and windy that night and early birds had been let in to hear the sound check. It had included a tour premiere, which now followed for real. Dedicated to all those who had been "braving the elements", the band kicked into "For You". Like the century-old songs elsewhere on the set, this 35-year-old Springsteen song also got a freshness from being filtered through the new blend of musicians on stage.

Then: "My Oklahoma Home", "If I Should Fall Behind", "Mrs McGrath", "How Can A Poor Man Stand Such Times And Live" and "Jacob's Ladder". He took a minute to dedicate "Long Time Comin'" to his kids and followed it with "Jesus Was An Only Son".

The slide trombones, hammy theatrics of the singers and the pantomime of "Open All Night" followed, turning the feel-good factor right up ready for "Pay Me My Money Down" to bring the main set to its by now traditional raucous conclusion.

The encore highlighted this band's perfect blend of inspiring musicians, wonderful singers and spine-tingling arrangements: "We Shall Overcome", "Blinded By The Light", "When The Saints Come Marching In", "This Little Light Of Mine" and "American Land".

Fan Brigitte Tersek told *Backstreets*: "At the end of the show, Bruce thanked the audience for the three nights in Dublin, and said he was hoping to return again soon, only to get a humorous shouted response from someone in the crowd, 'Come back on Wednesday!'"

Summarising the amazing three-night stand Siobhan Long, of the *Irish Times*, said: "The Seeger Sessions is everything a great session band should be: powered by ensemble playing and sufficiently ragged-edged to let each player shimmy and slide, with a collective ear trained on the ultimate prize: constantly evolving incarnations of every song."

She said that having had a few months to absorb the music the fans who went to The Point "came not to just listen, but to worship at the church of Bruce the redeemer. And chances are, we'd return every week, if our preacher was so inclined".

My uncle took us to a hotel and we changed our clothes. We went for a walk and waited to go into the concert for ages in the cold.

When we were in the building and the concert started I was sitting on a red pole and the cameraman was behind us. I was really enjoying the music and when the song "Blown Away" came on my dad asked me to wave to Bruce. And I did. When he pointed back at me and smiled, the crowd who were in front turned around! For that moment I was on my dad's shoulder.

When the concert ended, someone tapped me on the shoulder. It was the cameraman. He gave me a piece of paper with something written on it. I said 'thank you'. It would have been rude if I didn't!

I ran to Dad and Megan. I realised it was a set-list and when I realised I was happy.

I liked the music because it is jumpy and makes you want to dance.

A TRIBUTE TO TERRY MAGOVERN

The last time I met Terry was November 2006 at the Merrion Hotel on the afternoon of the first of Bruce's three sell out shows of the *Seeger Sessions* tour at The Point before wrapping up the tour in Belfast.

I gave Terry a specially-designed whiskey bottle which I had customized to reflect Bruce's four shows in Ireland and which I wanted him to give to Bruce as this was going to be the first time I was going to see him perform in my homeland.

Terry loved the bottle and said he would give it to Bruce right away. He said normally I could give it to Bruce myself, but Patti and the family had arrived in Dublin the previous night for the finale of the tour and it was unlikely there would be time but he'd see what he could do.

Terry then asked me if I could prepare some more labels and send them to him when he got back home to Rumson as he was organizing the annual PALS fundraising concert and was going to get Bruce to autograph them so he could auction off the bottles at the event.

I said of course I would and explained to him how my late mother's cousin Michael, who lived in Dublin, was recently diagnosed with ALS (Amyotrophic Lateral Sclerosis) and had not been given long to live. Terry, a man of few words, appeared very moved and told me of his late fiancée's battle with the terrible disease and what he was doing to create ALS awareness through PALS and support group fundraising activities at home in Jersey.

Over the years Terry had given me VIP access to many Bruce shows (including all four *Seeger Session* shows in Ireland where I sat with family and friends of the band) and now I had the opportunity to do something very meaningful for him. I told him I was thrilled to assist in my own small way. He said simply, "Andrei, things always happen for a reason".

Terry Magovern also happened for a reason. Many reasons I believe. And there has never been a moment since his passing when I've seen or listened to Bruce that his formidable presence has been too far away from my thoughts.

Andrei Talbot, Toronto (originally from Dublin)

First saw the Boss in the "Dancing In The Dark" video many years ago and I was hooked. I didn't get to see him until 2006 in Belfast at the *Seeger Sessions* concert. It was absolutely fabulous. I went to Belfast on my own, queued all night for tickets. When I got there I was number 19 in the queue – I took a stool and book with me but didn't get it open as the craic was so good. Everyone was talking and telling their stories about previous concerts and the time just flew. The BBC came down and interviewed some people.

They opened the windows to the pay desks at 8.55am and everyone was very orderly and the man beside me in the queue asked me if I didn't need the four tickets you were allowed would I get two for him for his friend which I did.

It turned out he was sitting with his mammy next to us at the concert. This was my first time to see Bruce Springsteen – I had wanted to see him from the time he was in Slane. My daughter and myself went to the concert and thoroughly enjoyed it – couldn't believe he was so good as sometimes when you see someone they don't hold up to your expectations.

I was amazed at the *Seeger Sessions* concert, at the rate of the music. It was relentless and his stamina was amazing. The concert was more than I ever expected. On our way out there were posters on the walls that one of the radio stations were doing all night Springsteen music, in fact they had a recording of the concert so we played that all the way home to Derry.

Margaret Callaghan, Derry

She concluded: "This surely was folk music as it was meant to be: music by, of and for folk – delivered by the possessor of the most bodelicious booty in town."

Peter Murphy in *Hot Press* said it was "as if (Springsteen's) on a mission to remind everyone – his kinsmen included – that American culture need not equate with Scud missiles and Starbucks".

He said the last show was at times "reminiscent of the partisan trenchfoot camaraderie of the best Pogues gigs".

"It's carnivalesque stuff, equal parts Greek wedding, New Orleans funeral and Irish wake. Imagine a Depression era vaudeville revue that could encompass dustbowl ballads, Bolshevik calls to arms, zydeco, Big Easy marching jazz and ceilidh house," he wrote. "You know you've been to a bloody good Bruce gig when he can omit 'Born To Run' or 'Thunder Road' and nobody notices. Most of these young whippersnapper acts regard touring as a PR chore. Bruce, on the other hand, treats his job like a vocation."

Eamonn McCann in the same magazine observed how the huge bunch of musicians on stage "made like this night in Dublin was the night of their lives". It was "an occasion of stadium rock and Sandino's lock-in, a strictly traditional carnival, Irish-inflected, anti-conservative, gospel-rooted, the way America might sound coming up for the rising, all genders and ages and colours front-stage at the end, billowing out an engulfing storm of optimism and anger and fierce expectation of justice eventually triumphant …

"Every face afterwards was aglow with contentment," added the journalist and political activist. "But I wonder if many were sparked into action, come morning. Which I have to believe for myself was his hope."

The closing show of 2006 - November 21, in the Odyssey Arena, Belfast - was to be a family affair.

Twelve months previously, closing his solo *Devils & Dust* show in New Jersey, Bruce had brought his wife, kids and a whole lot of others up on stage for a special round-the-piano singsong of "Santa Claus Is Comin' To Town", joking "There's no gathering around the piano like this at home … That's about as warm and fuzzy as it gets. If I tried that at home I'd get looks like I'm insane."

Now at the Odyssey, after a family outing around Belfast (including a trip "up the Shankill and down the Falls" according to the *Belfast Telegraph*), Evan and Sam Springsteen took the stage to introduce their dad.

Bruce came out beaming and took the Odyssey on his own journey through the many musical directions he was now following.

The set began: "Atlantic City", "John Henry", "Old Dan Tucker", "Eyes On The Prize", "O Mary Don't You Weep" and "Jesse James".

Then his own "For You" ("Written and recorded in 1972 for my very first album when I was 11, I believe, and a very precocious genius") ran into a tour premiere of "Mansion On The Hill" (which had been sound-checked in Dublin).

The crowd hushed for this eerie tale of longing, the band evoking the distant lights and sounds of the mansion, unattainable to the young Springsteen.

In the crowd, opposing members of Northern Ireland's political scene – searching out solutions of their own – Gerry Adams (who later admitted to have Springsteen on his iPod) and Gerry Kelly, of Sinn Féin, and Ian Paisley Jr, of the Democratic Unionist Party, looked on. They were not known to be seen socializing under the same roof and their attendance made the news in Belfast.

The show continued with "Erie Canal", "My Oklahoma Home", "If I Should Fall Behind", "Mrs McGrath", "How Can A Poor Man Stand Such Times And Live", "Jacob's Ladder", "The River" and the scat-fight of "Open All Night".

Evan and Sam came back on stage for the crowd sing-a-long of "Pay Me My Money Down", and this time they were joined by sister Jessie and a number of friends. Parents Bruce and Patti – in the city of her mother's birth – looked very proud.

Prior to the trip to Dublin I had a Bruce encounter - rather two - at the Four Seasons in Paris, the George V.

First encounter was *Devils & Dust*, Paris 2005, with my friend Jerome Kersuzan, a French sommelier. We managed to catch up with Bruce on the way to the show, leaving the hotel, and got him to sign the tour booklet from *Tunnel Of Love*. He signed it, 'For Astrid', my wife.

During the *Seeger Sessions* tour, I was with my wife in Paris again, and this time we got lucky the day after the show, at the hotel. Bruce came straight on over to us and said, "What's your name, little fellow?" Our son Oscar was on Astrid's arm. He was one-and-a-half.

We then talked for a minute or two, Bruce asking where we were from, and us congratulating him on songs and arrangements. I told him I had seen some 30 shows over the years. He said, "I salute you", and made a bow. I said, "No, Bruce, I salute you."

We made our goodbyes, him waving back as he left - me feeling on top of the world. Well, I then went to Dublin for the *Seeger Sessions*, too. The idea was to get the photo I took in Paris signed.

After lunch Jerome went showering and I went to sit and wait for Bruce. Bruce came down and had photos taken with every single guy in the hotel, except me: I didn't bring my camera and Jerome was showering!

But I had my photo in my hands and Bruce signed it, 'To Astrid and Oscar'.

Bo Frederiksen, Luxembourg

We missed the three *Seeger Sessions* shows in Dublin as Emma was eight months pregnant, but we did make it to the show in the Odyssey Arena, Belfast, on November 21, 2006.

A few months previous, the old ritual of queuing had landed us three tickets, a GA for me and two very good seats, one for Emma and her escort for the night, her father-in-law (this was to be his first Bruce show - a late conversion to Bruce via the *Seeger Sessions* album).

I was particularly excited about this show, the first time I would see Bruce in My Hometown - pun intended.

I somehow managed second row, right in front of Bruce's mic and the long wait to show time commenced.

The band were introduced on stage by the Springsteen kids, and the band then absolutely tore into a version of "Atlantic City", which stands as the best arrangement of that song - one of his best ever (and I include the full E Street Band arrangement in that statement).

Again as in the *Devils & Dust* tour the atmosphere was set by the stage décor - lots of old style charm, chandeliers, and lanterns, framed by huge drapes. It's difficult to pick highlights from this show, as there were so many, from looking Bruce right in the eye a couple of times to the playing of "My City Of Ruins", "When The Saints Go Marching In" and "We Shall Overcome" - all of which seemed to have extra weight and poignancy played in a city with a history like Belfast.

Ciaran and Emma Gallagher, Belfast

The Dublin shows in November 2006 were on the most miserable days of the year especially on the Sunday.

I remember it as being a great weekend of Bruce and alcohol. Highlights were "Atlantic City", "Growin' Up", "Devils & Dust" and "Long Time Comin'" (November 17); "Bobby Jean", "Highway Patrolman", the new 'Irish' version of "The River" and the only ever performance of "Shenandoah" (November 18); while on November 19 we finally got to see the great new version of "The Ghost Of Tom Joad" with Frank Bruno Jnr sharing vocals with Bruce but the highlight of the night and the whole tour for me was the new version of "For You", splendid indeed.

By Tuesday morning we were all in the queue for the pit for the last show of the tour at the Odyssey Arena, Belfast. A great end to a great tour with "Mansion On The Hill" being the only unusual song of the night.

Kieran Lonergan, Mitchelstown, Cork

AN AUDIENCE WITH BRUCE

My first Bruce concert was Slane. I was 17, and kind of half into him, but certainly hadn't gone overboard.

My brother had *Born In The USA* and *The River*, which I had listened to quite a lot, and I had a cassette of *Born To Run* which on my crappy tape player didn't exactly faithfully reproduce the Spector-esque Wall of Sound they had laboured so hard to create! ⬇

"My City Of Ruins" opened the encore, followed by "Blinded By The Light" and "When The Saints Come Marching In", which was dedicated to Belfast. "This Little Light Of Mine", "American Land", "We Shall Overcome".

Springsteen and his family headed straight out to Belfast International Airport after the show to head back to the United States in time for Thanksgiving. He left the reviewers searching for superlatives to describe the show, the last of a tour whose shows were most often described simply as "joyous".

Brendan Crossan in the *Irish News* said the band "rocked the resplendent Odyssey Arena to a standstill". The "collection of songs – country, folk, blues, rock – rolled into one beautiful sound." He said *We Shall Overcome* was a great stocking filler but "you can't wrap what Springsteen has".

"One abiding wish from the Belfast crowd last night was for The Boss not to be a stranger in these parts," he added. "There's a problem at the Odyssey – the ceiling is too high to bang your brush handle off," joked Noel McAdam, of the *Belfast Telegraph*. "That was about the only thing missing from last night's barnstorming Bruce Springsteen gig."

The two-and-a-half hour show was "a magnificent madcap mix that was equal parts Mardi Gras and music hall" and was an "energy-packed concert of pure joy from start to finish". "The man once lauded as the future of rock and roll has for some time been embedded in the past, rediscovering and reviving rock and roll's gospel and folk roots and the music of folk legend Peter Seeger in particular," added McAdam. "Almost 40 years ago, they sang "We Shall Overcome" on the streets of Northern Ireland. Last night it was the climax of the concert."

The *Seeger Sessions* was not to every Springsteen fan's taste but there was no doubt about the power and pure fun of the live show. Countries with the story-telling tradition out of which Springsteen had grown, such as Ireland and Italy, in particular seemed to take the music to their heart. Long-time Bruce watcher, Joe Breen noted in the *Irish Times* – while making the *Seeger Sessions* project a highlight of the year – that it was a "remarkable statement by a remarkable performer". Who would have believed, he said, that an American rock star could have sell-out European audiences "join in on songs about unions, working, living, exploitation, dying, laughing. It's a remarkable sight and an amazing achievement."

Writing in *Backstreets* Jeff Vrabel, who admitted being concerned about the tour, said that each show turned out to be "a roaring, impossibly large jam session". "It was Bruce born on the bayou, part mourning, part hope, part celebration, part cry for rebirth – all metaphors you may remember from every other thing Bruce Springsteen has ever done".

Two fans in the same magazine summed up the tour wonderfully.

Robert Barany wrote: "I think Bruce has finally found the show he was always looking for. He has great singers (as in '92-'93, except now they get used properly); he has a horn section (as in '76-'77 and '88); and he has songs that twist and turn with numerous false endings (as in '73). He has a bunch of songs that are as American as the soil, all the bar band moves he has worked out over the years, and his own lyrics, which far surpass those of any of the songs he has borrowed. I wonder if he is trying to challenge himself for the next E Street Band tour, because it will be difficult for him to top the tour he has just pulled off."

And the Italian journalist and huge Springsteen fan Ermanno Labianca also wondered what was coming next. "The magic of this tour was experiencing a trip that took you in every musical direction. Like being on the same bus with Asleep at the Wheel, Hank Williams, Cab Calloway, Pete Seeger, Bob Dylan, Little Feat and the Chieftains. How was this possible? As long as you have a driver like Springsteen, anything is possible. What's next, Mr Bus Driver?"

Interesting that Robert felt Bruce might have been setting himself a challenge for the next E Street Band outing.

And fascinating that Ermanno used the word 'magic'!

So I loved the music I'd heard, and was looking forward to the gig, but I really had no idea of how much of an impact it would have on me. I remember one of the radio stations did a top 100 songs voted on by listeners about six months before Slane, and a Bruce song – I think it was "The River" – was voted No. 1. I was surprised – nowadays I'd be ecstatic! But it shows that, at the time, he was huge in this country, which accounts for the crowd at Slane.

June 1, 1985, a beautiful sunny day. I was with a crowd of mates on the hill just below Lord Henry's castle, and the gig was just mind-blowing. Nowadays I'd be able to sing along to every song, but in those days a lot of the lyrics went over my head. As they did with most of the crowd. During "Rosalita" he stopped singing for the "Gonna skip some school" bit, and no-one knew the words! Or hardly anyone. But it didn't matter – everyone was just having a great time.

Bruce was apparently a bit freaked by the size and drunkenness of the crowd. And he wasn't wrong. There were a bunch of girls in front of us drinking out of a big two litre lemonade bottle. Except it wasn't lemonade. One of them passed out about a minute before he hit the stage. She surfaced during the interval, asked why he hadn't been on yet, took a swig and then passed out again.

Anyway, that was it for me – totally hooked by the experience. I started buying up the back-catalogue (learning the words to "Rosalita", etc!) and went to every Bruce concert in Ireland after that (except for the Belfast leg of the *Tom Joad* tour – still trying to work out why not).

So, in recent years, every time he came to Ireland, I lobbed in an interview request. As a Political Correspondent, my work has absolutely nothing to do with music, but as someone once said to me, what's the point of having the inside track if you don't use it?

So I'd put in the request to the nice people in the record company, and they would politely tell me he wasn't doing any interviews, until, wonder of wonders, coming up to the first *Seeger Sessions* gig in The Point – May 5, 2006 – they said, "Maybe". I think the nice lady in the record company was as surprised as I was. So I double checked that RTÉ News would be interested in a piece (they would!) and sat back, fingers crossed.

Anyway, it was finally confirmed on the afternoon of the gig, and myself, cameraman Michael Lee and my colleague Aoife Kavanagh, who was helping me put it together, drove down to The Point, and were ushered backstage. We met Barbara Carr, who let us out into the arena to watch the sound check – which on its own was fantastic.

Then into a dressing room to wait. We could hear people chatting outside, Patti talking to someone about the kids and so on. Utterly surreal. And then he walked in, shook hands, sat down and we got into the interview. Most of the time you would expect a minder to sit in on the interview, but not in this case – Barbara Carr told me to try to keep it to ten minutes because Bruce had to get ready for the show, but I'm sure we were in there with him for more like 20. They say don't meet your heroes as they'll disappoint you, but needless to say that doesn't apply when your hero is Bruce Springsteen. He was thoughtful, engaged, funny, self-deprecating, warm, all the stuff you would hope for. And this from a man just after a transatlantic flight. That said, he's not much of a one for snappy sound-bites, which made editing a bit of a problem! But there was a nice line about New Orleans (just recovering from Katrina), about Bush (not very complimentary) and, naturally, I asked him a question about the Irish connection with the new music and the fans and all of that, so that got in too. Luckily Aoife was keeping notes and we were able to find the clips fairly easily.

After we wrapped up the interview he happily chatted for a bit, posed for photographs, signed autographs for us – Eamon Dunphy used to give out about sports hacks during the Charlton era as being "fans with typewriters": that was us! The piece got a great reaction and was absolutely justifiable from a news point of view. Honest!

Anyway, I walked down from The Point to the Harbour Master bar for my traditional pre-concert pint and chicken wings, absolutely walking on air. I doubt very much the encounter left any impression on Bruce, but it certainly left one on me. And the gig that night was fantastic as well. Having met the Boss once, I didn't imagine that we'd be hooking up for coffee next time he was in town, and indeed we didn't. The only view of him I got for the rest of the *Sessions* gigs was on stage – but that was pretty damn good! ⬇

But in the run-up to the Belfast concert in December 2007, to my very great surprise, the record company rang me to see if I'd like to do a repeat performance. Would I what? I'd like to think the incisive nature of my questions in the first interview opened new vistas for Bruce, that he felt an immediate empathy with me and valued my perspective on his work. Or it could be they had product to shift, he was doing interviews everywhere he went, and they knew I was interested! As it happened, I'd already seen a *Magic* show in Mannheim in Germany of all places, on the night of my 40th birthday. I had vowed that if he was playing anywhere in the world on that milestone evening, I was going. I had hoped for New Jersey, but Mannheim worked just fine. Anyway, in Belfast, there was me, cameraman Peter Doherty, my pal Brendan Mulgrew (the biggest Bruce fan in Ireland) and Brendan Wright of RTÉ's Belfast office, who heard where we were going and hopped in. The gig was in the Odyssey, a pretty good arena, although as it turned out there was a problem backstage with water on the floor of the little room we were doing the interview in – something to do with the ice rink the hockey team play on. We got it sorted out, rigged up some lights, then went out back to see the sound check.

Nice shots of a bit of banter on stage between Bruce and Steve, they ran through a couple of songs, then pronounced themselves happy. So we were backstage again, waiting for Bruce. Clarence walked by. Slowly. They don't call him Big Man for nothing.

Then Bruce arrived, but unfortunately there wasn't room for either of the Brendans, just me and Peter the cameraman and Springsteen, no minders again. As it happened I was a bit under the weather at the time with a stomach bug, which added to the unreality of the whole experience. But the interview was great, I mentioned I'd seen him in Mannheim, we talked about the show, the new album, Bush, all the rest of it. Really nice chat, and again a couple of good lines for the report.

Outside, Brendan Mulgrew was listening to Steve explain his theory of the Beatles ("they were lucky"). I got Bruce to sign an autograph for my boss, who had given me two gifts to present – a CD of Irish folk recordings (dangerous! I could be blamed for sending him on another Sessions tangent!) and an RTÉ drama radio production of *Ulysses* by James Joyce (dangerous! Could send him back to the rhyming dictionary and impenetrable lyrics like *Greetings* … !). I thought *Ulysses* might make an ideal Christmas gift for Jon Landau, but Bruce seemed interested in it and the music CD.

I considered myself extremely lucky to meet Bruce once – to interview him twice was unbelievable. I suppose a third time would be pushing it. But next time he's in town, I'll keep my schedule clear … So why is he so popular here? I'm not sure. He said he felt things changed around the time of the *Devils & Dust* gig in the Point, that there was a deeper connection from then on. If that's true it would perhaps point towards a political explanation, that his own position fed into the Irish distaste for Bush.

But then 'old W' was pretty unpopular throughout Europe.

Maybe it's because he is, at least in part, one of our own (in some fashion). He often talks about the Italian and the Irish in him wrestling for ascendancy.

Sharing a language helps, in terms of people getting the lyrics, while the musical influences aren't just on the *Sessions* stuff – there's a thread of Irish music at the heart of American music which led on to Rock and Roll.

Or maybe it's as simple as the amount of work he has put in over the years playing here. Each concert led to more conversions – just as Slane did with me.

**David McCullagh,
political correspondent, RTÉ**

René Van Diemen

**The Odyssey Arena
Belfast**

15 December 2007

Crowd: 10,000

Tickets: £49-£60

**RDS
Dublin**

22, 23 & 25 May 2008

Crowd: 110,000 over three nights

Tickets: 81.25 euro

In February 2007 Jim Aiken died. His death would be the first of three in the coming 14 months which would hit Bruce Springsteen badly.

Aiken had not just been the promoter who had started everything off for Springsteen in Ireland, he had become the rock star's friend.

On first hearing of Mr Aiken's illness, Bruce and Patti had sent a note: "Dear Jim, we have just got the news over here. We're crushed. Such a big part of the joy we feel when we come to Ireland is seeing that big grin of yours, when we come off stage. Patti and I send our love a thousand times over. Please call if we can be of any help in any way. All our love, Patti and Bruce Springsteen."

The *Irish News* reported that Aiken had always considered Springsteen's Slane show to be one of the most memorable achievements of his career.

On Mr Aiken's death, Springsteen dedicated the *Live In Dublin* DVD/CD recorded at the *Seeger Sessions* concerts in The Point at the end of 2006 to him. *Live In Dublin* capped Springsteen's adventure with a new group of musicians. But with the fiddles and banjos still ringing in his ears he was already turning his mind back to the E Street Band.

Back with producer Brendan O'Brien he was quickly preparing to put out his third new album in three years, and his first with the E Street Band since *The Rising*. *Magic* was released in October 2007.

And *Magic* truly was the E Street Band reunited, right down to Clarence Clemons' soaring sax on "Livin' In The Future". This was Springsteen filtering the chart-topping success of *Born In The USA* through the updated sound of producer Brendan O'Brien and the politics of George W Bush's America. "Girls In Their Summer Clothes" ruminated on the passing of youth, more than 20 years on from "Glory Days". The *Irish Independent* reported: "It says much for the man's reputation that a new Springsteen album is still a big deal." *Magic* was a "collection of wonderfully rousing songs urging the listener to seize the day and celebrate life". (The album would later make the newspaper's 2007 top ten.)

The newspaper's reviewer Neil McCormick noted a continuation in the themes from *Devils & Dust* and *We Shall Overcome*.

"An artist deeply tuned into the American psyche, Springsteen had almost acted as the musical conscience of his country and his output over the decade has chronicled a nation's increasing unease with itself," he said, adding that the themes were all brought together in the song "Long Walk Home", which opens amid a relationship between a man and a woman in which something has gone wrong but widens out to explore the gap between what the United States set out to be and what, under George W Bush, it had become.

Springsteen's manager Jon Landau called the song the "summational song on the album". McCormick added: "It is a truly great song, as anyone who heard it live can attest, and a key to his subtle marriage of the personal and political."

The hidden track on the album was "Terry's Song", a lament written especially for the funeral of Springsteen's close friend and personal assistant of many years, Terry Magovern. Terry had died on July 30 and Springsteen's pared down acoustic tribute spoke eloquently of his sense of loss. Terry had been a well-known figure at Bruce's side and would be missed by many fans as well as those in Bruce's close circle.

Magic ended on an intensely personal moment, but the tour which followed would be an ambitious one, both in scope and in message. There would be two legs in North America and Europe, plus a series of closing concerts in the States – a mini third US leg. Every night Springsteen lambasted the Bush administration for its assault on civil rights (over illegal wire-tapping, a drawback of the right to be tried by a jury and the fighting of an "illegal war") but the message was upbeat: it was, as *Backstreets* noted, "Rise up! Be strong! Better times are coming!"

Rehearsals for the *Magic* tour began in Asbury Park, New Jersey, in September 2007, and moved through North America and Canada, before arriving in Spain on November 25.

Odyssey Arena, Belfast 15 December 2007	RDS, Dublin 22 May 2008	
Radio Nowhere	The Promised Land	23 May 2008
No Surrender	Radio Nowhere	also included
Lonesome Day	Lonesome Day	
Gypsy Biker	Out In The Street	Night
Magic	Gypsy Biker	No Surrender
Reason To Believe	Magic	Trapped
Because The Night	Reason To Believe	Murder Incorporated
She's The One	Candy's Room	Darlington County
Livin' In The Future	Prove It All Night	Girls In Their Summer Clothes
The Promised Land	Darkness On The Edge Of Town	Jungleland
Waitin' On A Sunny Day	Because The Night	Glory Days
The River	She's The One	Dancing In The Dark
I'll Work For Your Love	Livin' In The Future	
Devil's Arcade	Mary's Place	25 May 2008
The Rising	Waitin' On A Sunny Day	also included
Last To Die	The River	
Long Walk Home	Devil's Arcade	The Ties That Bind
Badlands	The Rising	Spirit In The Night
Girls In Their Summer Clothes	Last To Die	Atlantic City
Kitty's Back	Long Walk Home	4th of July Asbury Park (Sandy)
Born To Run	Badlands	Growin' Up
Dancing In The Dark	Thunder Road	Racing In The Street
American Land	Born To Run	Rosalita (Come Out Tonight)
Santa Claus Is Comin' To Town	Bobby Jean	Ramrod
	Tenth Avenue Freeze-Out	
	American Land	

all photos René Van Diemen

The eleventh show of the first European leg was to be at the Odyssey Arena in Belfast on December 15.
Although Springsteen had twice played Belfast before, neither show had had the backing of the Big Man and the band. Demand for tickets, in what for the E Street Band was a modest-sized indoor arena, was huge.

Tickets were like "gold-dust", reported the *Belfast Telegraph*, for "Ulster's most anticipated rock reunion of the year".
It was reported that the 10,000 tickets for the Odyssey had sold out in five minutes, with 20 per cent of them going to fans in the Republic.
By the time the E Street Band arrived in Ireland, *Magic* had been at the top of the album charts for a month and had gone double platinum, and Springsteen said the band, now largely well into their 50s, was playing better than at any time in its history.
Ahead of the Belfast show Bruce spoke to David McCullagh of RTÉ to say the band was "raging against the dying light", playing at "100 mph" and "running like a freight train".
"It seems more important to do that now more than ever because I want the young kids coming to the show, going home and saying I've seen the heart-stopping, pants-dropping, earth-quaking, Viagra-taking, E Street Band at their best, you know.

BACKSTAGE AT BELFAST

When a friend of mine, David McCullagh, who is a broadcaster with RTÉ, secured an interview with Bruce in May 2006 when the *Seeger Sessions* tour was kicking off in Dublin, he offered me the chance to be his 'assistant' for the day. Too good an opportunity to pass up, I ended up passing it up! I couldn't get out of work to make the journey down from Belfast by the required time and so I thought I had messed up my best chance of shaking hands with Bruce and saying "thanks for the music."
Anyway the opportunity re-presented itself in December 2007 when *Magic* rolled into my hometown. What came to pass wasn't all that I hoped for originally but it is a story worth repeating.
I met David and we headed off, with the cameraman, to the Odyssey with me acting as the guy who hauls equipment back and forth.
Once in the arena we had to wait for a longer time than either of us had hoped but in time the members of the band began to amble down the corridor one by one. David had permission to record the sound-check, and while the E Street Band readied themselves for the arrival of their Boss we set up the equipment.
It was just us three people and Bruce's PR team (Barbara Carr and staff) standing in front of the stage in a completely empty arena. It was totally surreal to stand yards from the band as they warmed up themselves and their instruments. Soon enough Bruce arrived and it was very clear that the camaraderie and good humour among them is a

sincere feeling. Directed by Bruce they ran through "Radio Nowhere" a couple of times and worked on the bridge between a soulful end to "The Promised Land" and the beginning of "Waitin' On A Sunny Day". After 15 minutes or so they were gone.
Barbara Carr intervened personally to tell me I couldn't be in the room during the interview. In truth I think she had worked out I was nothing but a fan and in her eyes that was reason enough to exert some authority and that's fine – everyone has a job to do. It was a pity, but I was happy enough to be hanging out, taking in the sights and sounds of the E Street Band production gearing up.
As I stood in the corridor I shook hands with Max, Roy and Charlie and stood nearby while Steve regaled Max and Garry with tall tales from the '60s.
Every now and then I reminded myself that these were my guys, right here preparing to do a Belfast show. I didn't meet Bruce, didn't shake hands or utter my profound statement of thanks, but in the end that didn't matter: I had an afternoon on E Street to remember forever.

Brendan Mulgrew, Belfast

We were up front in the pit on Clarence's side. I was scared that I wouldn't get another chance to see the Big Man.
It was hard to believe that I was watching the E Street Band in my own capital city. The build-up in the days before from the local press was superb. ⬇

I want kids going home to their dad who saw us in the 80s, or their older brother who saw us, I want them going, 'I saw them at their very best', so it's something we take a lot of pride in."

"I always look to the crowd, I always look for faces that feed me during the night, and you always find that they're there … They're not listening to the show, they're living it, and you can see it in their faces. That's what we want to do. I don't go out there to play it, I go out there to live it, night after night …"

McCullagh told Springsteen about the astonishing demand for tickets for the shows in Ireland and asked him about his special relationship with Irish fans. "I felt something suddenly happen, starting with the *Devils & Dust* tour, and I don't exactly know if people felt like that over here, but you know we've always come and we've had great shows over the years here, but there was something about those shows that I did at The Point for me, I felt some deepening of the connection here.

"And then when we came back with the Sessions Band that seemed to really just … this was just a perfect place for us to play that music, you know, because it has so much Celtic influence in it. Those were very inspiring shows and we connected in a way that, I don't know, it just felt special.

Harry Scott

"The DVD we did in Dublin is one of my favourites, it's one of the best things we ever put out on film, so there's been some deepening of my connection here with people, so it's exciting to come back with the band now and feel some of that electricity and passion." He also spoke about his – and his wife Patti's – Irish heritage.

"It's great because where I come from, everybody, it's all Italian-Irish, like me, Patti. Patti's half-Irish and half-Italian, and I'm Italian and Irish, the whole neighbourhood, the Italian women married the Irish men, and that's all our part of New Jersey, my whole family, they're all Italian women and they all married Irish guys, so it's nice because you come back and you feel a little of that connection. It's just been great, it's turned into another very special place for us." During the interview Springsteen explained *Magic*'s mix of 1960s inspired pop melodies and its political message.

"I was sort of looking for a way to have a conversation about the events of the day, which is the way I see part of my relationship with my audience ... you are involved in an ongoing conversation about life, family, politics, just what's going on socially, fun, sex. I was kinda looking for a way to write about what had happened in the States since *The Rising* record, since 9/11 and talk about the developments, the road that the country took.

Years before in 1981 I had taken a ferry crossing from Belfast with my friend Rab to Liverpool where we got a National Express coach as poor students on our way with our £5.50 tickets to see this Springsteen guy. A train, a boat, a coach and a taxi in 1981, then 26 years later a taxi was enough, but well worth the wait.

Nigel Flynn, Ballymoney

Got into the pit and bumped into a couple I had met in Dublin in 2006. For me this is the best Springsteen show I have ever seen. Bruce and the band were on fire, the crowd were so into it, including the bride, groom and the whole wedding party who had their reception at a Springsteen show!

Hugh Rapson, Aberdeen, Scotland

I was at the Belfast gig of the *Magic* tour with my husband Hywel and our friend Andrew. Hywel and I were down the front near the stage. Andrew on the other hand had an excellent seat to the side near the front of the arena. We spotted him in the stand and kept in contact via mobiles and gestures whilst we awaitedBruce's arrival. As we neared kick-off time my mobile went and it was Andrew.
"Guess who I'm sitting next to ... Bruce's brother-in-law!"
My immediate response was for Andrew to ask him if he's the one from the song "The River". It turned out he was indeed the brother-in-law from "The River"!
Whilst we waited for the concert to begin

I could see Andrew and the brother-in-law having a good old chat ... apparently about Tom Jones as B-I-L is a big fan and what with Andrew being Welsh ...
The concert began and a little over half-way through the main set the opening sound of "The River" starts and Bruce explains that there is a very special person in the crowd tonight that he would like to dedicate the song to his brother-in-law Mickey.
Suddenly the spotlight pans around onto Mickey ... and my friend Andrew who has the broadest smile ever on his face!
Needless to say, Andrew being Andrew, he now has Mickey's number in his mobile ... and apparently Bruce's brother-in-law was the loveliest guy you'd ever wish to meet - even if he did want to talk about Tom rather than Bruce!

Ceinwen Richards, Llandybie, Wales

HATS OFF TO BRUCE
The only way to describe the build-up to this show is like being a kid at Christmas - I know that sounds sad, but it's true. I couldn't sleep the night before, I was up early that morning, and took December 14 off work "just to prepare", i.e. get shopping out of the way, etc.
After the usual rampage to get a good position, we ended up about six deep from the stage, although by the mid-point of the show we had been shoved up closer. This show was like a freight train, the pacing relentless; three songs in I was done in - raw throat, aching hands, sore feet - but I was loving it. ⬇

But I was also enthralled about going back to writing hopefully beautiful melodies with a lot of pop influences and a really rich tapestry of sound, and sort of classic guitars and rock songs and choruses, and I kind of fell in love with doing that again, probably the most since *Born To Run*."

And he explained the difficulty of dealing head-on with topical events such as those that had arisen during the George W Bush presidency.

"I don't like to write something that someone is going to hear seven years from now and feel it's dated, like an old newspaper, then you're a journalist. I'm not a journalist, I'm a songwriter and a musician, so whenever I go to write about something, that's a part of the events of the day, I try to find a way where if you listen you can interpret it personally, you can interpret it politically, there's multiple layers of meaning to the music, and those are the songs that last, and that you can sing for 20 years or 30 years, a hell of a long time."

He spoke about the "shocking turn of events" which led to the invasion of Iraq and the response of some fans to the politics in his music.

"I think that probably some of my politics are a little more in tune with being over here in Europe and here in Ireland," he said. "(In the States) you get the boxes of broken records (in the post), with the notes, but it's nothing drastic."

The encores as usual were total energy. "American Land", despite some fans disapproval of this song as a closer, well I love it. I feel a real connection and passion to this song - maybe I was an immigrant or something in a past life!

We, like many others in attendance, came prepared for Christmas with Santa hats hoping for an extra song.

As we only had one hat at home, Emma decided to buy one and chose a red Santa cowboy hat with white trim.

After "American Land", when the band was taking their bows, I threw the hat onto the stage. Steve Van Zandt picked it up and passed it to Bruce who was very impressed! We both almost had simultaneous heart attacks right in the pit!

It really was a magical moment. This sort of represented making that connection with my hero, that connection I had been searching for all those years ago when I was first getting into Springsteen. It also represented for Emma the end of her journey from having a boyfriend who was a Bruce nut to being a fully-fledged Bruce nut herself. We briefly looked at each other then started jumping and shouting something about Bruce wearing our hat!

He put it on and the band did a magical "Santa Claus Is Comin' To Town". Bruce kept adjusting the hat, you could see he thought he looked real cool in it. Bruce even took the hat with him and used it in Paris and London. What a show, what a Christmas present and what a night!

Every time I hear, "Do you believe in Santy Claus?!", I still get shivers …

Ciaran Gallagher, Belfast

On the *Magic* tour I promised myself to see as many concerts as possible.

This time I included a new city into my travel itinerary: Belfast.

Even though it had been complicated to get a ticket - a fellow fan helped me out - and the trip there from Cologne, where the previous show took place, wasn't that easy, I was looking forward to it so much.

After waiting in line outside with Jane, a very nice fellow fan from England, we got a place at the centre of the stage.

We got a very powerful show and being so close made it even more special. Bruce noticed us, looked at us and I could touch him several times. During "Born To Run" I was able to touch his guitar, too.

Ah, pure joy!

I travelled to Ireland again for the shows in Dublin. The Irish are huge fans, a great audience and Bruce loves to play in Ireland. What more could you wish for as a fan? As soon as my friend Susanne Nussbaum and I arrived in Dublin we went to check out the venue and took some pictures in front of a big poster of Bruce and The E Street Band, saying his shows in Dublin were sold out. Our anticipation was huge!

I made it to the front row at all three shows, each time a bit more central, a bit closer. I enjoyed myself very much, jumped and danced and towards the end of the last show, to my great surprise and joy, Jerry, Bruce's security guy, suddenly put the set list in a pocket of my jacket which I had put over the rail. What a darling! It made a perfect night even more special.

Mirjam Kunz, Switzerland

Evening Herald reporter George Byrne arrived in Belfast for the Odyssey gig and, while having a drink, bumped into a friend. "You won't believe it but I was talking to him on the phone yesterday," said the friend. Who? "Bruce, of course." Byrne explained that a female friend of his drinking companion had been in Burdock's chip shop on Werburgh Street, Dublin, the previous lunchtime when a hired SUV pulled up outside and three American men got out to join the queue.

Recognising one of them as Bruce she mentioned that her friend was a huge fan. "I'm sure he'd love to say hello," she said, so Bruce suggested she ring him. Byrne noted: "It's a very tough trick to maintain the balance between huge-selling artist and still being viewed by millions as representing the voice of the ordinary man but it's one that Springsteen has mastered over four decades in the business. There's a sense with Springsteen that his audience feel that they know him and while they wouldn't be totally shocked to find him wandering into, say Burdock's, they'd be very unlikely to give him any hassle."

A bag of chips was just the thing for those cold, dark December evenings. On the day of the show, as the early-birds stamped their feet in the queue outside the Odyssey, the band ran through a sound-check of "Radio Nowhere", "The Promised Land" and "Waitin' On A Sunny Day".

Ciaran and Emma Gallagher

Robert McMillen, of the *Irish News*, said: "Bruce Springsteen's concerts have become legendary not because of media hype but because of ecstatic word-of-mouth testimony from people who had witnessed arguably the greatest rock performer on Earth …"

As the time for the show approached the fans outside were funnelled between two lines of barriers.

"When the doors finally opened," wrote McMillen, "(they) flooded out like an uncorked champagne bottle to get nearest the Boss and the heat inside.

The atmosphere amongst them was like that of kids a quarter their age on Christmas Eve, nervously, excitedly knowing that Santa was coming later that night with a bag full of wonderful goodies."

There was an expectant hum inside the arena. The atmosphere crackled; then at 8.20pm the lights dropped, the band took the stage and Springsteen shouted: "Hello, Belfast! Is there anybody alive out there?" The crowd shouted back: "Yes!"

"Is there anybody alive out there?"
More cheers, louder this time.
And then the band ripped into the opening bars of "Radio Nowhere".

The *Magic* shows rocked from the moment the E Streeters came together on stage, having the energy and excitement of an encore from the very first note.

Belfast was beautiful in lights and Christmas cheer and the Glu-Wein was flowing in the market. The town is a transformed place from a Belfast I once knew a long time ago. The friendliness of the place is infectious, and boded well for the show. Once in the arena I found myself talking to a man who had brought his wife and three children. His first Bruce show had been in the Spectrum in 1978. The arena was full of such stories: fans were there from all over Ireland, Scotland, Wales and England.

Scattered Frenchmen and other Europeans brought home the point that fans of this music very much vote with their feet, and travel long distances. We were all there for the passion and inspiration that we seek in Bruce's music. It never lets up, it is magnificent each night. This night was no different with "Because The Night", "The River", an epic "Kitty's Back", and a quite exhilarating "Santa Claus Is Comin' To Town" leading the way for special mention.

The musicians laughed, smiled, played and sent out a powerful message of community. Being in the same 'room' as Bruce and his merry band is a special treat, anytime … Three nights in Dublin, and we saw three very different faces of Bruce. Night one gave us the professional crowd pleaser, delivering the required hits and energy to satisfy a stadium-size crowd.

Night two saw Bruce the Clown, interacting deep in the crowd, shaking up the set-list, drinking beer with the people, and "scaring small children"!

But night three was one of the most stellar and extraordinary and uplifting E Street Band performances of recent memory, possibly of the last nine years. On a cold, windy evening with threatening rain (which finally fell during the red hot encores), we were treated to a show that surpassed all expectations.

It was a night of authenticity and pathos, fire and magic, with Bruce in and out of the crowd, playing like it was the mid '70s, making silly hats look good ("You look good Steve, you look good!").

Bruce was in form that I could only dream of; inspirational, charismatic, focused and fully present like I have rarely seen.

All of us who follow these tours, who know this music so intimately, left the arena ecstatic and incredulous. "Did that really happen?" one German fan said to me. It most certainly did.

And what a community we were in Dublin! Besides the many Irish flags around the crowd, there were the Italian, Spanish, American flags, and flags from New Zealand and Greece, and many others. Folks had travelled far to make Dublin a true holiday destination for five days, and a more enriching, rewarding holiday experience I cannot imagine.

Karl Birthistle, Zurich, Switzerland (originally from Dublin)

From the very first strum of "The Promised Land" at 8.12pm on Thursday until the last beat of "Glory Days" at 11.05pm on Sunday, Bruce Springsteen was happy. ⬇

In Belfast, the band went straight into "No Surrender", "Lonesome Day", and "Gypsy Biker", an angry song for the dead in a foreign field, which ended with a blistering guitar battle between Springsteen and Steve Van Zandt.

At its end Springsteen, dressed like his band-mates entirely in black, took a break. "Good evening, Belfast," he said, to the obligatory cheers. "It's good to be in Northern Ireland." He smiled and indicated that his drive through the city had taken him past its new attraction outside City Hall. "I like the new Ferris wheel too. A town with a Ferris wheel – it's a good thing!"

He went on: "This is called "Magic". This is the title song off our last LP. This is a song about living in the past six years where, back home, we've seen the truth get twisted till it sounds like a lie, and lies twisted till they sound like the truth. The wheel of history is spinning round and round … so, I tell the folks every night – this isn't really about magic, this is about tricks …"

For "Magic", he and Soozie Tyrell were alone centre stage, Springsteen on guitar and Soozie on her violin. With Patti not making the trip to Europe, the duet would always feature Soozie. The crowd was hushed for the song and rewarded for their patience with the new – another new! – version of Springsteen's "Reason To Believe".

I know that's a strange word to use, but you could see it in his face; he was right there in his element, belting it out to a crowd who gave it right back to him.

He was having an absolute ball, so much so that he didn't want to go home after "American Land" on Sunday … When he went into "Glory Days", the place went wild. This is the Bruce Springsteen we've all read about, those legendary shows, those never-ending sets...for one night only, for old-time's sake, for his love of coming to Ireland, for that sunny day in Slane in 1985 … for whatever the reason we got the whole damn nine yards.

And we got a big smile and thumbs up from him as he left the arena on Simmonscourt Road. He hung out of the first van, towel over his head.

Damian Clarke, County Meath

At the Odyssey Arena, I got a spot up at the front, the last in the row at the left, beside the cameraman. Guess whose face Bruce would see first as he came skipping back to the middle? Mine!

I was wearing a Santa hat and shaking a red bandana. After "Gypsy Biker" he stopped, leaned forward and reached me his harmonica – I didn't take it immediately but instead asked in disbelief, "For me?"

My husband Noel Canavan who was standing behind me said something like, "Take it!" I didn't hear him.

Bruce leaned down even more, down towards me and smiled nodding his head to say "Yes".It was for me.

I reached up and Bruce slipped it into my hand. That wasn't the end for me because the joy lives on and on. I showed it to the crowd, they cheered for my luck. I'm a teacher and I showed it to the kids at school. I've played it in pubs with drunken Bruce fans.

Now, if that wasn't enough we then met him backstage in Dublin on the Sunday night of *Magic*. I've only ever missed two Irish concerts and our story is not over. Believe me.

Liz O'Céannubháin
Lavey, near Magherafelt

I just love Bruce. I was at the RDS concert on May 25, 2008, and it was fantastic from start to finish. He is the most amazing showman alive today.

It was a buzzing atmosphere, the excitement was electric. I was with my husband and my brother-in-law.

My husband Derek isn't an avid fan of Bruce and this was his first concert but myself and brother-in-law David are Bruce mad. Bruce came on the stage and my heart nearly burst with excitement - we were so close.

After Bruce played his first song my husband was singing along which I was surprised to see but he probably knows all the words to his songs as I never stop playing his CDs at home!

Sarah Campbell, County Wicklow

The song had now been turned into a full band, "Spirit In The Sky"-style anthem, telling its story of birth, life and death to a driving beat and with Springsteen striding the stage blessing the band with water. As with the solo *Devils & Dust* version of the song, Springsteen sang and played his harmonica through a bullet mic – the effect again was mesmerizing – but with the full band backing, it was less melancholy and had everyone on their feet.

From there, the tinkling piano introduction of "Because The Night" and the full-bodied solos of Nils Lofgren's guitar before "She's The One" completed a rocking triple pack.

"Woo!" said Springsteen at the end, his shirt already drenched with sweat. Then, putting his guitar down, he began to stride the stage, eyes down. "We're so glad to be here in your beautiful city tonight! This is a song called "Livin' In The Future", but it's about what's happening now back where we come from. How along with all the things that we love about America … over the past six years we've had to add to the American picture things like rendition and illegal wiretapping and the rolling-back of civil liberties, no habeas corpus, the right to defend yourself against charges in court. This is a song about sleeping through changes that you never thought you'd see happen in your home but that have happened.

Harry Scott

But the mighty E Street Band is here to do something about it!" The crowd cheered. "We're gonna sing about it, we're musicians …" He gave an ironic smile. "We'll see where that takes us. Max!"

A drum beat and into "Livin' In The Future" with Bruce walking the stage and rapping out the lyrics.

"The Promised Land" followed and then the upbeat "Waitin' On A Sunny Day", with the crowd – which included the then Taioseach Bertie Ahern – belting out the chorus at the tops of their voices.

Then two for the disappointment and triumph of love: "The River" – "to my brother-in-law, he's here tonight, he was the inspiration for that song" – and then "I'll Work For Your Love", preceeded by a little glance around the crowd from Bruce.

"Do we have any Irish lovers out there?" he said, with a knowing look. "Bring the lights up, come on, let me see! Do we have any lovers out there?"

Among the crowd were Paul Hull and his new wife Paula – he in his wedding suit and she in her gown. They had rushed straight to the show from the ceremony, and brought along the wedding party too.

They already had the spotlight shone on them before the show. Now the whole crowd cheered and their faces flashed up on the big screen.

"YOUR PASSPORT! I CAN'T SIGN THAT"

While walking by the Merrion in Dublin with two friends, one spotted Steve Van Zandt going into the hotel so we darted over and stood with many others hoping for a glance of the greatest bloke in the world or anyone else from his fantastic band.

After a while my friends had to leave to check in to their hotel but I stood around for a while … just in case. And to my surprise along walks Roy Bittan. A crowd gathered around him and he gladly signed autographs and posed for photos. All the other clever Bruce fans had things for him to sign - record sleeves, tickets, etc. I realised I had nothing for him to sign. Then I had a brainwave: I'll get him to sign my passport. Feeling kind of chuffed with myself for having such a brilliant idea, I got next to Roy and asked him to sign it. I asked him to make it out to Roy as, I told him, "I am also called Roy", and he said something like, "Another Roy? There's a lot of Roys", and he signed my passport.

Half an hour passes by and lo and behold Garry W Tallent walks out. It's my lucky day. I calmly waited my turn and presented my passport, with another page already turned over for him to sign – I'm so smart at times!

Garry realised it was a passport and said, "Your passport? I can't sign that!" And he handed the passport back.

My chin was in serious danger of having a chin-wobble moment. But quick as a flash I turned over the other page and said, "Howay, Garry, Roy's signed it."

So Garry shrugged his shoulders and said, "Okay", and signed it. As I walked away Garry looked at me and I knew what he was saying in his head, "What a ******* daft clot!", and he's right.

I was thinking I might have a bit trouble getting in or out of Milan for my next Bruce show that June … The day got even better, as a bit later Nils and Max came out. The crowd was getting bigger by then and I didn't get the chance to add to my passport/autograph book, but got a couple of canny pictures.

Then the Big Man came out, and the crowd went crackers.

Clarence put his hand out to the crowd, and I managed to shake the great man's hand. Sparks did indeed fly! What a bloke!

Bruce is right: you wanna be like Clarence, but you can't.

Roy Young, Newcastle

"YOU'VE GOT A GREAT COUNTRY THERE"

I was originally going to Finland to visit my girlfriend Tanja.

Since I would be there at the time of the concert Tanja felt it only "fair" to get me a ticket (unknown to me) since she and her mother were going anyway.

I was only told the day I arrived. I was blown away at the possibility of seeing the Boss live. Little did I also know that we would be right up at the front!

The concert was to start at 8pm sharp and did it ever. He didn't waste a single second of the clock. ⬇

Paula later explained: "We'd already booked our wedding entertainment when Paul rang me to say he had good news and bad news: the good news was that Bruce was coming to Belfast but the bad news was that it was on our wedding day. At first we were in a bit of a dilemma – but when we sat down and thought about it, we realised there was no dilemma. We had to see Bruce."

As Shane Hegarty, of the *Irish Times*, quipped: "Some people were willing to sacrifice anything to catch Bruce Springsteen and the E Street Band's return to Ireland."

The new Mr and Mrs Hull, who would later receive a gift from Clarence Clemons – his maracas – now got Springsteen's good wishes from centre stage: "Let's hear it for them. God bless, good fortune, good luck, this one's for you …"

After "I'll Work For Your Love", the mood became more reflective for "Devil's Arcade" with its images of lost limbs and lonely hospital walls, but then built up pace again for a four-pack which closed the main set: "The Rising", "Last To Die", "Long Walk Home" and "Badlands", which of course had the whole crowd punching the air.

Opening a six-song encore, Bruce gave his usual thanks for coming to the show before adding: "We're gonna do this one for all the Irish lasses." The crowd cheered. "And for one special one in New Jersey … Patti sends her love …

At one point he shouted out: "Now I wonder, just outta curiosity, is there anybody not from Finland out there?"
And I of course shouted up (to his surprise), "Yeah, I'm from IRELAND, Boss!" Well, he jumped down to the front to see me and with an out-reached arm he grabbed my hand and said: "Hell, yeah, so nice to meet an Irishman again. You gotta great country there."
I was absolutely speechless. All I could say was, "Finland is better", to which I got a thousand cheers and I could feel hands patting my back in praise.

Brian Fox, Galway, on a special moment in Helsinki

On the Thursday night in Dublin, my husband Brian and I attended with his brother and wife. Brian's brother Peter was one of the lucky ones who had seen Bruce in Slane back in 1985 and this was his first time since - he wasn't disappointed! "Because The Night" was a particular highlight for me that night. Nils' solo was electrifying. I also adore "Badlands" live and Brian and I jumped up and down with the rest of the crowd whilst that belted out.
On the Friday I met fellow fans Sinead and Stephen Quinn for my first pit experience. We started queuing at 3pm and couldn't get over how polite everyone was. No pushing, robbing places, etc. The gates opened at 5pm and we just walked to the front of the stage. People were sitting, chatting in the sun - such a relaxed atmosphere. I met a lady from Chicago who was there for two nights on her own.

When the concert eventually started it was mind blowing. It was without a doubt the best concert I have ever attended (my 6th Bruce gig).
Thank you, fellow Bruce fans, for making it such a wonderful night. Thank you, Bruce, for yet another performance where you gave 110 per cent.

Tracy Hegarty, Limerick

I was born in Ireland, to a single mother, who by law couldn't keep me back in 1949. I was adopted by Americans and grew up in Missouri and California. I was so lucky. I had a great life, great parents, great education, etc. After they died when I was only 22, I moved to Colorado.
I've been in Colorado ever since, with my husband Steve and our daughter Caitlin.
In 2003, my family and I took a trip to Ireland, to show our daughter the country. Before we left, I told my family that I needed to find out where my birth mother was buried. (A nun tried to track her once, and found out she had died).
I began to research where I was from and found out that the Beauparc on my birth certificate was an area near Navan. We got a map of County Meath and I literally stuck my finger in the air and told my family wherever it landed, we'd stay at the nearest town. My finger came down near Slane. Well, I remembered that Bruce played Slane Castle and we had to stay there. Little did we know that we were right next to Beauparc. In church records at Beauparc I found my mother's entry and it provided me with her married name. ⬇

we have three teenagers now, so somebody's gotta make sure the house doesn't burn down …"

"Girls In Their Summer Clothes" began the encore slowly but then

"Kitty's Back" was a highlight for many and a heart-warming "Born To Run" and a joyous "Dancing In The Dark" carried on the pace.

"American Land", written for the Seeger Sessions Band, had survived the move back to E Street – and had its heart played out in its spiritual home, Ireland. As the song drew to a close, Springsteen shouted out the band introductions to huge cheers. He counted them off, just the names until "in for Danny Federici, Charlie Giordano". During the tour the poignancy of this moment would become deeper for fans.

Danny had started the tour but had not come to Europe. For some years he had been fighting cancer and had stayed in the United States for treatment. Since Madrid, *Seeger Sessions*' alumni Charlie Giordano had been drafted in as an honorary E Streeter. He was quickly a popular figure, leafing through the huge Springsteen songbook on the organ and taking on the accordion for "American Land" but fans naturally wished to see Danny back.

With the introductions done, Springsteen wound himself up for a big finish – a feature which would become

Iggy Hughes

Iggy Hughes

Tina Gill

a favourite on the tour and would spawn new T-shirts across Europe: "Belfast! You've just seen the heart-stopping, pants-dropping, hard-rocking, booty-shaking, earth-quaking, love-making, Viagra-taking, history-making, legendary E STREET BAND!"

A last chorus of "American Land" and then an extra song which had naturally found its way into the set during December. As Christmas hats of all shape and design were tossed onto the stage, Bruce picked a red felt cowboy hat out for himself and asked the Belfast crowd: "Do you believe in Santa Claus? He is almost here … I think I see him", and into a barn-storming "Santa Claus Is Comin' To Town" to close the two-and-a-half hour show. (Springsteen's ragged version of this song had long been a radio favourite but this was the first time the E Street Band had played it live in either the UK or Ireland.)

"Judging by the reaction," wrote Shane Hegarty, of the *Irish Times*, "the audience must have felt as if all their Christmases had come at once."

Eamon Sweeney, of the *Irish Independent*, was thinking along the same lines. "For a capacity crowd in the Odyssey, Christmas has come early," he said, adding that parts of the show were simply "awesome". "In time-honoured tradition, "Born To Run" completely brings the house down," he noted, "inducing a communal bout of delirious bedlam." Nigel Gould, of the *Belfast Telegraph*, said Springsteen had "held a spellbound Odyssey Arena in the palm of his hand".

"(The band's) sheer exuberance at playing together was palpable. Dressed in black, they prowled the stage with the passion of musicians half their age.

Music aside, though, Springsteen and his rabble-rousing crack team, are consummate entertainers - without the frills."

Springsteen was a "magnetic showman". "Both he and his band were outstanding - bequeathing the Odyssey one of its best gigs ever," said Gould.

"From the opening 'Radio Nowhere', toes tapped, hands clapped and arms swayed. And dancing in the aisles - by grown men who should know better.

Some wore Santa hats and a bride turned up with her bridesmaid. No ordinary night.

"Musically, the kitchen sink came out: lighters-at-the-ready stadium anthems, killer choruses, swirling keyboards, mad harmonica, scorching riffs, blistering sax and Springsteen's distinctive whisky-throated vocals."

The *Irish News* noted the absolute warmth of the Belfast crowd toward Springsteen and the E Street Band, noting that the show deserved its place as the fastest selling event in the history of the Odyssey. "If the Springsteen experience ever returns to the venue," it predicted, "it is a safe bet that the record will be broken again.

When we got back to the B&B, the owners met us at the door saying, "We just talked to your aunt and she wants to meet you." A big family reunion ensued. I was made to feel so at home and the new family was shocked to see that I looked just like my mother. I left Ireland with an aunt and cousins galore, but most importantly a sister, brother-in-law, nieces and a nephew. My sister and I promised that we would see each other every year and have done so since. I must say that I am a huge Springsteen fan. And I became a huge fan of the TV show, *The Sopranos*. I loved Steve Van Zandt as Silvio.

2008 was our turn to go to Ireland and since Bruce and Steve have such a big part in us meeting, my sister and her family got us tickets to the concert at RDS on May 25, my birthday.

Knowing this, I told Steve Van Zandt my story through emailing his record company. I was excited when his secretary emailed back that Steve wanted to meet us and hear the story again! We were invited to the E Street Lounge before the show. Steve was so nice and funny. He greeted us warmly, handshakes for everyone. I briefly reminded him of our story and he said, "That is really weird". He graciously posed for pictures and signed an autograph.

Every time I told him how much I enjoyed some of his work, like *The Sopranos*, the music, the radio show and how he is saving rock and roll, he got sort of embarrassed and smiled and thanked me so much. We met Nils too. The E Street Lounge was not what I expected.

It was in a horse barn at the RDS. I told Steve that I never thought that when I finally met him it would be in a barn. He laughed and said, "Only the best for our fans!"

Mary King, Colorado

These shows were about joy; they celebrated life. Sure, you can argue, all Bruce shows are about that, that's nothing new – but this time Bruce was oozing it big time.

The very first song, "The Promised Land", seemed to be fitting. I got the feeling Bruce had decided to use those famous lyrics of the song to cut the pain from his heart regarding the passing away of blood brother Danny; he was using the one and only powerful medicine he's always used to heal and get whole again: his music. I loved "No Surrender", "Trapped", "Jungleland", "Girls In Their Summer Clothes", and my husband Burki sure loved "Murder Inc". Our friend Heidi had made a sign "Murder Inc" for him the previous night, holding it up lots of times, but Bruce didn't seem to notice it.

We believe (you can *always* believe) that perhaps Stevie or Soozie did spot it on Thursday and told Bruce about it – could be, why not?

It was very noticeable again during the whole evening that Bruce was so happy, enjoying playing his music, enjoying the responsive Irish crowd, enjoying being there in Dublin, enjoying being alive. Watching him was absolutely heart-warming.

Beate Rossbach, Munich, Germany

It was simply a magnificent occasion, not just for the bride and groom who left their wedding reception to dance in the aisles but for everyone lucky enough to be there."

The newspaper's reviewer Robert McMillen noted: "If Incitement to Dance were a crime, Springsteen would be doing 20 years in Sing Sing. The thing about his songs is that you can enjoy them at whatever level you want – just as great tunes or you can dig deep into the lyrics to find the political anger just below the surface."

McMillen described the Belfast audience's connection to the old songs too, to the longing for escape that characterized much of Springsteen's earlier work. "We didn't have Harley-Davidsons and turnpikes in Belfast in 1975 but we ached to be free like the characters in "Born To Run"; we were looking in the mirror when we heard the life story of the characters in "The River"; and, although he didn't sing it [at the Odyssey], we've all had a "Hungry Heart" at some stage and so Springsteen wrapped up the personal and the political in soaring music that brought us to places we don't visit too often."

Both the *Irish News* and the *Irish Independent* made the show their gig of the year. The parting words of Robert McMillen, in the *Irish News*, summed up the feelings of every Irish fan that December. "This was a joyous concert, profound and uplifting.

I am a Bruce fan since *Darkness On The Edge of Town*. I have been at every concert in Southern Ireland since 1985 (including Slane).

One of the days queuing at the RDS in 2008 I met and chatted to an English fan. He related a story to me about meeting Bruce. He hung around a stadium he was playing at and eventually met him and got an autograph and picture.

But he said to us he could not think of anything to say when he actually met him except, "Bruce, I love you, man". We all had a great laugh with him and he shook his head and said, "Where did my brain go?" Anyway, we went into the concert and there was a jetty out into the audience at which I was standing.

And lo and behold along comes Bruce to get in touch with the crowd - he is really rocking - and as the music played he began to shake hands with everybody and indeed I shook hands with him …

… And of course I felt I had to say something - but the only thing to come out of my mouth was, "Bruce, I love you".

I immediately cringed and thought of the English lad I had met outside - and hoped for that moment that he was nowhere near me. Just goes to prove - we are in awe at greatness!

Don Harper, Dublin

My friends and I queued all night for the *Magic* tour for Belfast and Dublin and there is a special enjoyment of the show when you know you have earned your ticket.

I met various members of the band in the Merrion in Dublin and they seemed a pretty down-to-earth bunch, happy to talk with fans about previous shows, about Danny Federici.

Soozie Tyrell was actually surprised we knew who she was when we congratulated her on a great show - I guess that's the type they are.

Stephen Devine, Belfast

TEENAGE KICKS

My mum Eilish got me into Bruce at the young age of four, after which I was hooked. I was 16 at the time of the *Magic* tour and bought a ticket for £300 on eBay, using my dad's credit card of course.

I was at the May 25 gig and it was a spectacular experience. When Bruce came out onto the stage and started into "No Surrender" I knew this was something special.

I was in the pit with my cousin, and just to be that close to the E Street Band for me was extraordinary, never mind being that close to The Boss himself. The 'Big Man' Clarence was on our side and I am sure he gave us a wink. I nearly got a touch of Bruce but unlucky for me my arm was not long enough!

When Bruce then roared, "Is there anybody alive out there?" a shiver went up my spine as I watched him start into "Radio Nowhere". "Spirit In The Night" for me was one of the greatest performances of the night, the crowd loved every minute of it and Bruce was giving us everything we wanted. ⬇

May in the RDS just can't come quickly enough." Veteran journalist and political activist Eamonn McCann reviewed the show for *Hot Press*. A long-time Springsteen fan, he was ecstatic. "I first saw the man maybe 30 years ago," he said. "Truly hasn't changed a bit. Or else for the better. Really."

McCann said Springsteen's husky voice "drenches the lyrics in compassion", and he picked out "Gypsy Biker" as a highlight, memorably describing it as a "beautiful rage against the machinery of death". "We pile out to collude in exotic cigarettes along the fairy-lit Lagan and argue whether this was really the best gig ever," wrote McCann. "Maybe. "Cleansed in a way we haven't felt since we believed in confession. *Wholly* communion at the Odyssey, Belfast. *Magic*? A miracle.

"We dashed for the car, just because we felt pell-mell, hit the M2, headed for the Sperrins, Glenshane Pass and home. 'Tramps like us,' breathed the Cork blond, 'born to run.' "Born again. I'm truly desperate for tickets for the RDS." Two more shows in Europe followed, with Springsteen taking the same cowboy hat to Paris (it was brought out from backstage at the Bercy while other hats rained down) and then London. It was not until the end of February that the tour resumed with a two-month tour of the US and Canada. On March 20, Danny Federici made an emotional appearance with the band in Indianapolis.

"Badlands" was brilliant, it shattered Dublin to its core, no wonder people seven miles away were ringing complaining about the noise, but how could you complain, it's Bruce?

What better way to finish than with "Glory Days"? The RDS was electric.

Afterwards people were walking around shocked wondering if what they had just seen was real. Many were saying it was the best concert ever, and who would I be to disagree?

Eamonn Kerr
Antrim

We've gone to see all the shows in Ireland for the last few years due to the fantastic Irish crowds and because Bruce clearly loves playing there.

Over three days in Dublin in May 2008 we met all the band, had photos taken and got things signed. I must say they were all very gracious. Unfortunately Bruce had used the back entrance and was avoiding the large crowds.

Anyway on the Sunday my son Oliver met Bruce coming out of the elevator (in the Merrion) and we got our 1975 copy of *Time* magazine signed - it looks awesome.

Now after the show Oliver and I went down to the hotel bar for a last few drinks before leaving the next day. It was pretty amazing to be standing at the bar chatting to Max for a good 20 minutes or so. He was very relaxed, no-one pestering just talking and listening. Also in the bar was Roy, Soozie and Nils. A short time

after arriving one of Bruce's entourage approached Oliver and said he saw Oliver waiting patiently outside and that Bruce was in the bar with friends and that he would introduce us before he left. Oh, my God, was this happening? He introduced himself as Tony.

Oliver was shaking in anticipation and I wasn't far behind. After about an hour we saw Bruce stand up to leave, saying goodbye to his friends, then Tony called Oliver over and we are both stood in the middle of the room as Bruce casually walked over.

He smiled at Oliver and said something along the lines of, "I remember this young man from this afternoon".

We talked for a couple of minutes about nothing, I suppose, then Bruce shouted, "Has someone got a camera? We need to get a picture of this".

Of course Oliver produced our camera and Tony took a picture. Then Bruce said get another one.

Bruce then shook our hands and wandered around the room saying hello to a few other people and posing for more photos before going to his room.

The next day we used the pool and gym before heading back to the elevator. Who should walk out of the elevator heading to the gym? Yes, Bruce. He said, "Morning fellas!" Sort of wish we had stayed in the pool a bit longer.

Surreal.

David Evans
Wrexham, North Wales

He had known Springsteen since the late 1960s when they were teenagers trying their luck as rock 'n' roll musicians. He was one of the founders of the E Street Band; "one of the pillars of our sound", as Springsteen described him.

However, on April 17, 2008, less than a month after his special appearance he succumbed to cancer. The E Street Band and its fans had never had to deal with such a blow. Danny had always been there; when the band came together, they were always *all* together. The band postponed three shows as they dealt with their grief. Springsteen had lost his Irish friend, Jim Aiken; his confidante Terry Magovern; and now one of his oldest pals in the world in a little over a year. "Danny and I worked together for 40 years," Bruce wrote on his website. "He was the most wonderfully fluid keyboard player and a pure natural musician. I loved him very much."

The E Streeters had to move on without Danny, although his memory would be evoked many times during the shows to come.

The Dublin shows would be the first of a European leg which would see them crossing Scandinavia and the western half of the continent between May 22 and July 20.

The show had developed significantly since Springsteen's first visit.

David Evans

John and Tina Gill

John and Tina Gill

Iggy Hughes

The spring set-lists in the United States had been changing nightly with Springsteen testing the band with some of his choices and realising on one occasion that he didn't remember the song he had chosen to play. "A little panic is good for the system," he said at one point. The fluid set-list also incorporated Springsteen's new penchant for taking signs for requests from crowd members. This saw the development of ever more elaborate signs and banners – one fan wrote "Glory Days" on his face – which peaked at the final show in Barcelona when a fan smuggled in an electronic sign with a request for "I'm Goin' Down" running across it.

Springsteen's plan to bring up a dancing partner for "Dancing In The Dark" returned too – 17 had made it up on stage in Dallas. And you didn't have to be Courtney Cox either – men and in particular children regularly got a look in. (Springsteen shows were featuring a higher number of younger fans than previously, due in part to his being cited as an influence by so many new bands, including Arcade Fire, The National, The Hold Steady, The Killers and the dance rock group Kharma 45, who are originally from Derry.)

In fact, everything had been cranked up a notch *again* for the outdoor shows. The guitars of Nils Lofgren and Steve Van Zandt, alongside Springsteen's had been turned up to eleven.

René Van Diemen

There was a story going around about a group of Derry teachers who went to the Springsteen concert in Dublin. Apparently they were in some restaurant after the concert and the manager came over and said that the table they were sitting at is the one Bono usually sits at when he comes in and he had phoned for a table. He asked if they would move to another table and the meal would be on the house. They moved. Bono came in and being backward like all Derry girls they went over and asked could they get their picture taken with him.

They said he was really nice and got photographs taken. After he left the manager came over to them about getting the pictures taken with Bono and said well you had a famous photographer and they said who, and he said well you had your photograph taken with Bono by Bruce Springsteen … and they didn't even recognize him!

Margaret Callaghan, Derry

The day the *Magic* tickets went on sale was sheer panic. Up to queue at 8.30am, tickets on sale at 9. And then … shop not opening until 9.30am! Ridiculous. I stay queuing while my father stays online. Panic is setting in; word quickly spreads through the queue that the single night on sale is sold out. Word then spreads of a second night. I ring my father, he got tickets! Friday, May 23, second night in Dublin. Thank God! In the end of course there was three nights in total but I was happy. ⬇

all photos René Van Diemen

A dream had been realised. The day came. 'The greatest group of musicians in the world' walked on stage. *Bang!* straight into "Night" and the deal was sealed. There was a fantastic atmosphere hanging around and I was certain this was going to be a gig to remember. One of the major highlights was "Mary's Place". Whilst the roadies were setting up the stage myself and my *compadré* Peter couldn't help but notice the bowl of water being filled beside the drum kit. Was Max bringing his pet dog onstage with him? What was this? Well, we soon found out.

During the instrumental break, Bruce went back to the kit, took a cloth from the bowl, and proceeded to saturate his jeans. No, he couldn't, he wouldn't. The man is over 50! Well lo and behold, off to stage right and – WOOOSH! – a Springsteen-shaped blur flies across the stage, down onto his knees, and the crowd went insane!

Throughout the gig Bruce's interaction with 'Big Man' Clemons really kept the spirit alive. It was like watching two guys just jam for the first time and not care about the outcome. It was all about the fun. The blistering solos from Van Zandt and Lofgren were ear-bleedingly good. And what can be said about the pounding drums from Max Weinberg except wow! And of course the remainder of the band cannot be forgotten. By the end of the night my feet were killing me but my spirits were high. What an incredible night it had been.

Niall Hetherington, Kildare, Ireland

172

Lofgren was a small bundle of energy, twisting in circles on his longer solos. It was impossible to believe that soon after the tour he was booked in for a double hip operation, even though now finally and sadly fans were having to face up to the awful fact that E Streeters do grow old and like poor Danny they do pass on.

Van Zandt is in many ways Lofgren's opposite. Well-built, largely stationary, but with a face that pulls a thousand expressions, always picking someone out in the crowd, exchanging a laugh with other members of the band, shuffling over to Springsteen to share a mic. And then Springsteen at the centre. Terrifyingly fit. Shirtsleeves rolled up. Running from one side of the stage to another and sliding ten feet. Going down on his knees at the microphone and then springing to his feet.

Springsteen and the E Street Band flew in to the city airport and stayed at the Merrion for the duration. The street outside the hotel was lined with a varying number of autograph hunters throughout the stay, with fans catching glimpses of the band as they came and went after the shows, and as they went out shopping, particularly on the Saturday which would be their day off. Springsteen was on the cover of *Hot Press* and featured in all the major newspapers during the week.

When you've racked up over 30 concerts, it's very easy for us hard-core fans to think that we can predict what will happen in a Springsteen show. We start to think we know what's coming next. And quite often we do. But therein lies the danger. Bruce likes to keep us on our toes; probably for his sake as much as ours.

I was there with my girlfriend for all three of his shows in Dublin. There's something about an Irish crowd, both north and south of the border, that seems to bring out the best in Bruce and his band. Having already seen a couple of shows on the *Magic* tour in Milan and Tampa I felt I knew what to expect. And for the first two nights Bruce rocked the house as only he can. The only drag being at the end of the night taking ages to exit the venue when the hotel is only a five-minute walk away. And is seeing "American Land" performed live for the umpteenth time really that essential?

"Shall we go now?" I said to my girlfriend. "American Land" had just started up. We know the routine. And besides, we all know that on this tour Bruce finishes the show with "American Land". It's not like he's going to do another song or anything. The nights of elongated encores belong back in the 1980s and beyond … "Only if you really want to," she said. "I don't mind but it would be nice to beat the crowds".

And so we started to make our way from out of the pit by the right of the stage where only an hour earlier I had held my girlfriend up, missing my chance of shaking Bruce's hand, figuring that he'd rather be singing to a good looking woman than some bloke with sideburns and a silly grin on his face (he did a whole verse of "Mary's Place" which made her night).

Leaving the venue I had a strange feeling in my gut that I was committing a cardinal sin. But still we carried on walking. And as "American Land" blasted out behind us and we walked down the road with ease I felt that I was right to resist my inner-fan-like urges to savour every single moment in the company of Mr Springsteen. But as we left the venue and the point of no return back inside … *"Ramrod!"*

"Bollocks," as we say here in England. The one time I leave early to beat the crowds he plays one more song!

A shame, but not essential. We carried on walking. Back to the hotel. Into the lift. Into our room. And as I close the door I can hear a sound coming through the window … surely not?

HE'S STILL PLAYING! "This must be the longest version of "Ramrod" in history," I'm thinking to myself. But as I strain my ears I realise this isn't "Ramrod" I'm hearing. It's … "Glory Days"! "******* Glory Days"! Now "Glory Days" is probably my favourite Springsteen song ever. It was the first song I ever learnt to play on the guitar. I still remember the moment when I figured it out. I just sat on my bed playing that opening riff over and over again, dreaming of being on stage in front of a squillion people. Ahhh, the dreams of youth … Suffice it to say I LOVE this song. And there he was. On stage. In Dublin. Playing "Glory Days". And there I was. In my hotel room. Listening through an open window. ⬇

all photos René Van Diemen

Fans walking in Grafton Street – where Springsteen took a wander himself – could see special displays of his records in the music stores. At one point he had 12 albums in the Irish top 100 chart.

Since his visit to Belfast he had also been named Best International Male at the Meteor Irish Music Awards.

While in town, Springsteen was seen walking around town, buying CDs. He also took time to order organic cheese from Ralph Haslam, of Birr, Co Offaly. The Dublin shows, for May 22, 23 and 25, 2008, had been announced before the band's arrival in Belfast the previous winter. The tickets – well over 100,000 of them – were snapped up immediately. In Derry fans queued up all night outside one record shop for a handful of tickets.

Louise Hogan, of the *Irish Independent*, reported: "Fans launched an early morning raid as around 38,000 tickets for his first scheduled concert at the RDS next year went on sale. The May 22 concert was sold out within 15 minutes of internet sites and ticket offices opening at 9am.

"Aiken Promotions then announced a second date, and it took just 20 minutes for all the tickets for Bruce Springsteen and the E Street Band's concert on May 23 to be snapped up. "At 9.40am, Aiken Promotions then launched a third date, on Sunday, May 25, and tickets were all gone by 11.30am."

all photos René Van Diemen

So, to all fellow fans who think they think they can leave before the end of a show because they know what's coming next I say, "DON'T!" Don't move an inch. Don't even *think* about it. Because do you know what? He'll out think you. Every time. Dublin, you taught me a valuable lesson.

**Mark Wright, singer,
"Real World: The Bruce Springsteen Project"**

A MAGIC MOMENT IN DUBLIN
I attended Bruce's Sunday night concert in Dublin - well, the first hour, I should say… I am a recent Bruce convert but my husband Tommy has attended all the Irish concerts since Slane. I had seen Bruce live once before and thought he was fantastic, so despite being 39 and with a baby due on Tuesday, May 27, I made the trip to the RDS on May 25. The niggling pains started while walking from Paddy Cullen's over to the concert but, as the births of my previous two babies were quite long, I presumed I'd have loads of time and at least see the concert out. We got to the RDS and time passed. I thought Bruce would never come on stage. Then, as soon as he did, my contractions started.Initially, I was reluctant to take pain relief as I wanted to monitor the situation, and by the time I popped two Nurofen tablets, I may as well have been taking Smarties. An hour in to the show … in the middle of "Because The Night", I informed my Tommy that I thought I was in labour …
➡

Sinead Watters, of Aiken Promotions, said: "It was the best record. He is the fastest selling artist we've worked with." The tickets were priced at 81.25 euro for general admission and 91.25 for seating. The wild sale had resulted in joy for some, but disappointment for many more and the message-boards were alive with people venting their frustration and disappointment at missing out.

The demand was even more remarkable given that, as the *Irish Independent* explained, some of the country's major summer music events were suffering slow sales, with artists like Westlife, Bon Jovi and Radiohead all having seats unsold for shows. Springsteen was an exception, the newspaper reported, adding: "Some heavy-hitters can still cause a stir at the box office, no matter what the economic climate, but they have become the exception, rather than the norm."

The afternoon of Thursday, May 22, was cool with the threat of drizzle in the air. "We brought the New Jersey weather with us, I guess!" Bruce said as he kicked off the new leg of the tour.

The RDS was the largest venue of the *Magic* tour so far. Springsteen had called up the big stage and put two huge screens either side. One was topped with the Stars and Stripes, the other a Tricolour.

It was still light at 8.10pm as Springsteen stepped out into the Dublin evening; the crowd went wild.

Springsteen, the sleeves of his black shirt rolled right up, ready for business, put the harmonica to his lips and the band ripped into the first of a 26-song set with "The Promised Land". During the final solo Springsteen came right down onto one of the platforms stretching into the crowd and the thousands of fans in the pit surged forward.

"Radio Nowhere" and "Lonesome Day" followed, before Springsteen lifted the party atmosphere with "Out In The Street". "Gypsy Biker" maintained its dark feeling, despite the size of the venue, and then the pace slowed as Soozie and Bruce shared vocals on "Magic" – "here's to the end of eight years of mismanagement."

Patti Scialfa had not travelled to Europe – although she would arrive in Spain later with the couple's three children. Bruce told the crowd: "Patti's at home. The cookies have been taken out of the oven. The Guinness is being poured. My favourite clothes are being sold on eBay. No, we've got three teenagers, one of whom is graduating."

The next section rocked. "Reason To Believe", "Candy's Room" (an audible shouted to the band by Springsteen), a piano-pounding "Prove It All Night", "Darkness On The Edge of Town", "Because The Night" and "She's The One" showed the E Street Band, despite a three-week break, were quickly winding up to top speed.

Springsteen's political speech before "Livin' In The Future" continued into this the third leg of the tour, with Clarence's sax once again helping the song soar. (Ed Power in the *Irish Independent* called the song "as sweet a ditty as you will ever hear about the suspension of habeas corpus by the US Supreme Court.")

The house-party atmosphere returned with "Mary's Place" and "Waitin' On A Sunny Day". The crowd kept singing at the end of "Waitin' …" and were shushed by Springsteen before "The River". The spotlights dimmed for "Devil's Arcade", and the band finished the main set "The Rising", "Last To Die", "Long Walk Home" and an air-punching "Badlands".

The encore was one for the old fans. "Thunder Road", "Born To Run", "Bobby Jean", "Tenth Avenue Freeze-Out" (with Southside Johnny) and "American Land".

Hot Press noted that, "Even by Brooooooce's exalted standards, it was a killer gig".

Reviewer Stuart Clark added: "The shitstorm quality of tonight's show has everything to do with Bruce being flanked by the E Street Band, who may be a bit flabbier round the midriff, but still know how to wring every drop of melodrama out of one-act-Springsteen-plays like 'The River', 'Badlands' and 'Because The Night', which is well and truly claimed back from Patti Smith …

all photos René Van Diemen

His reaction was full of thought and consideration, but his face said it all: "Not *now*!" Anyway, we left by ambulance and headed to The Coombe Hospital, where the nurses kindly opened the windows so that we could catch the rest of the concert. Declan was born at 11.10pm, just as Bruce left the stage ... Another fan had been born, but thankfully not in the RDS.

Dara Clarke, Kilcullen, County Kildare

"HARMONICA PLEASE, BRUCE!"

The spring European leg of the *Magic* tour began in Dublin. My husband John and I were fortunate to get tickets for all three concerts.

At the end of Thursday's show we heard that a queue had already started for the Friday night. It was crazy to join a queue so early but if you want to get to the front you had no choice. There was a roll call every two hours. This system is unofficial, but it works very well. Everyone is given a number, we got numbers 20 and 21. There were tents, sleeping bags, deck chairs preparing for a long night. There were taxis coming and going, the local pizza delivery van was busy.

During the day I spotted Kevin Buell, Bruce's guitar technician walking through Ballsbridge. I stopped him and said, "Hi, are you Kevin?" He seemed pleased that I knew his name. We discussed Thursday night's concert. He put his hand in his pocket and gave me one of Bruce's plectrums. ⬇

"Giant video screens aside, there's no 'show' other than nine best mates acting out their wildest bar-room band fantasies …

"Honest to God, this really was the Pet Sounds of gigs." That was one heck of a conclusion. But it was how a lot of fans felt after the first show. They had no idea that Springsteen was only just warming up.

Friday would see the party turned up a notch further with Springsteen changing more than one third of the set and playing nine songs not played on the opening night. The rumour that Bono, who was in the audience, was going to make an appearance on stage turned out to be unfounded.

"Good evening, fine citizens of Dublin," said Springsteen striding out on stage behind the band. "We're so glad to be in your beautiful city tonight. Are you ready to be transformed? Are you ready to be re-born? Is there anybody alive out there? Is there anybody alive out there?" The crowd cheered every line but Springsteen still acted like he could not hear. "IS THERE ANYBODY ALIVE OUT THERE!?"

"Yessss!" cried the crowd, and the band responded with a blast of a drum and guitar which sounded like the engines of a hundred Harley-Davidsons firing up in a tunnel, and we were flying down a New Jersey freeway for "Night".

A brief break as Springsteen again asked, "Is there anybody alive out there?" and then into "Radio Nowhere", a hard-rocking version of "No Surrender", "Lonesome Day" and a stunning version of "The Promised Land" during which Springsteen came down into the crowd. Hands reached up from the pit and, as with the Thursday, Springsteen gave away his harmonica at the end of the song.

This was already a Friday night to remember. "It's good to be back in Dublin. We had a great night the other night. Who was here last night?" The question was met with a huge cheer and most people in the pit seemed to raise their hands. "Get outta here, come on!"

Springsteen laughed and looked at the band. "Alright, we'll switch it all up for you tonight."

Soozie and Bruce sang "Magic" in its now familiar arrangement, and then the keyboard opening of "Trapped", the powerful, but rare, live favourite which gave way to "Murder Incorporated".

The crowd was bouncing now as the band swung into "Darlington County", "Prove It All Night", with Nils Lofgren playing yet another ever-evolving solo and spinning on one foot, and "She's The One", with Springsteen running his guitar down his microphone stand before hurling it over his shoulder to be caught by his guitar technician Kevin Buell at the back of the stage.

"Alright now," Springsteen said, taking a breather with a walk to the corner of the stage. "How we doing over there?"

He said that these plectrums are unique. They are larger than normal and since Bruce sweats so much they have sand paper on them, for grip. He told me that the band and all the crew were going to an all-night bowling alley (in Stillorgan) after the concert. A passer-by took our photograph, another one for the collection.

The gates opened at 4.50pm, we got second row centre stage where there was a small platform into the crowd. This was an ideal place to get close to Bruce.

Over the years we noticed that Bruce handed harmonicas to people in the crowd. I longed to be one of those lucky people. Before we left home John surprised me with a colourful sign that read, "Harmonica, please, Bruce!" It was worth a try.

The concert began at 8.15pm. "The Promised Land" was song number five, and towards the end of the song he came right down in front of us. We were within touching distance. As he played the harmonica he was looking at my sign. John said to me, "Tina, it's now or never." To my astonishment Bruce made eye contact with me. As he finished the song there was a tremendous surge forward, all hands were reaching for the harmonica, but to my utter delight he placed it into my hand. He held my hand for a few seconds as I said, "Thank you, thank you, thank you." It was a dream come true, I jumped for joy. I felt I was the luckiest girl alive that night. From now on "The Promised Land" will be my favourite Bruce Springsteen song.

Our friend Mark was standing five rows behind us. He captured this precious moment on his mobile which I will treasure forever. After the concert lots of fans asked to see the harmonica, and some got their photo taken with it. It now takes pride of place on our sitting-room wall. There are two people on earth I always wanted to meet. I met Bruce Springsteen, the other person is the CEO of the National Lottery.

Move over Jim Carrey, there is only one Bruce Almighty.

Tina Gill
Quigley's Point, County Donegal

My friends and I arrived around lunchtime on the Thursday and after queuing got a good spot at Steve Van Zandt's side right beside where one of the new perches stuck out of the stage. It was a standard enough set list but being our first outdoor Springsteen show in five years we all had an excellent night. The next day we ended up in the same spot in the pit. The set included some real treats such as "Trapped", "Murder Incorporated" and "Prove It All Night" with the new Nils Lofgren solo. The Sunday show surpassed any we had ever seen before. It was a real tribute to Danny Federici who had of course passed away by then, with a big concentration on the early songs. We all left on a high. My other great passion is travelling and I've often thought of Bruce along the road. Not just in obvious places like New York and Asbury Park but once on a rattlesnake speedway in the Utah desert and recently at Khe Sahn in Vietnam. ⬇

He took a look around some of the signs in the pit. "From New Jersey?" he said, responding to one banner and laughing.

He wiped his brow. "Alright, this is called "Livin' In The Future" but it's about what's happening now back home. Along with all the things that we're proud of, we've had to add to the American picture over the past eight years things like rendition and illegal wiretapping and rolling-back of civil liberties, no habeas corpus, which is the right to defend yourself against the charges brought against you. These are all things that when I was a little kid, people always told me that happens someplace else, it didn't happen in the USA … Well, this is a song about sleeping through changes that you never thought you'd see … help me tell the story, Max …"

After the pop and politics of "Livin' In The Future", Springsteen lightened the mood.

"Are you ready for a house party? Come on, that's all I wanna know …" Leaning on the microphone stand, Springsteen sang the opening lines of "Mary's Place", a song from which he rang out every last drop of energy.

The sun had shone on Ireland that Friday but the evening was cold, a fact which Springsteen, although he had been running around the stage like a teenager, acknowledged as he introduced "Girls In Their Summer Clothes":

"I guess it's a little cool for this one," he said. Jumping down from the stage during the song Springsteen began shaking hands with fans at the front. One held up a lager in a plastic glass and before he knew it Springsteen had whipped it away. He climbed back on stage, singing the final verse, and as the song ended, stood in the centre of the stage, raised the glass and drained it (to shouts of "Down it!" from the crowd): "To the Irish girls … I owe somebody a beer now," he laughed.

The band then changed tone for "Devil's Arcade", "The Rising", "Last To Die" and "Long Walk Home", before a "Badlands" which would have lifted the roof had the RDS had one.

Beginning the encore, Springsteen said: "Thank you very much, Dublin, thank you, Ireland, and thanks for all the support for all the music we've made. We've had such a great time, over the past 10 years, particularly, you guys have just really supported us. We appreciate that very much."

The piano and violin broke through the Dublin night, and Springsteen sang out the 10-minute "Jungleland".

The crowd, in the stands and on the pitch, bounced through "Born To Run" and the fun continued into "Glory Days". During the final verses, Springsteen and Van Zandt hammed it up for the big screens.

"Hey, Steve!"

"Yeah?"

When my friend Donal gave me that cassette tape of his 'Best of Bruce' all those years ago who would have guessed what it would lead to? All the friends we've made. All the miles travelled.

Sleeping on floors, in cars, early mornings, late nights, whatever the future brings one thing Donal and I agree on is … IT'S ALWAYS WORTH THE HARDSHIP!

Kieran Lonergan, Mitchelstown, Cork

LOCAL HERO

In May 2008, my wife, Caroline, had given me a present to go home. She was pregnant with our second daughter, Amia (both Amia and our two-year-old Kayla were born to the sound of Springsteen's music) and she got me tickets to all three *Magic* shows in the RDS and booked me into Dublin's Merrion Hotel.

I was not going to go because she was pregnant, but she simply said, "Go enjoy." I walked into the Merrion and checked in and who was standing beside me? Roy Bittan. I had met Roy before. There was a lot of history between us - me and the band. I dated one of Springsteen's nannies, Hilary, on and off back in the late 80s-early 90s.

In fact, during the *Human Touch* tour my brother, Thaddeus, had been in LA with me for the shows and we had gone up to Springsteen's house to pick her up one night. When she came out through the gates she was carrying a ginger ale. My brother asked, "Is that from Springsteen's fridge?" He was so excited he still has the bottle to this day in a little shrine in his house! Anyway, back to *Magic*. Having seen Roy Bittan it dawned on me that the band must be staying in the hotel too.

I got to my room and changed clothes and hit the gym to get ready then to meet up with my four brothers to go to show number one. (My brothers Damien, Nicholas and David live in Dublin so Thaddeus kipped with me.) We got back to the hotel late after a great show and Bono and The Edge were in the bar. The next day, leaving my room on the way to the second show, I ran into Little Steven. He was staying three doors down from me. We chatted about New York and his wife took a photo of us together.

The next day there was a break in the shows so I went to the gym. I walked in and was on the treadmill when I heard this American voice talking about bowling and, yes, it was the unmistakable voice of Bruce.

Springsteen was working out right beside me and he was with Tony Strollo, his fitness guru and all around great guy! I just kept running and tried to channel my brother Thad to come down, and then got off after about 45 minutes and began my sit-ups and weights.

All of a sudden Springsteen walked over to me and said, "Hey, man, are you ever gonna stop!" I turned around to him and said: "Bruce, this is all your fault!" "My fault?" he said, amazed.

I said, "If not for you, I would not be here working out, trying to get rid of the jet lag. I would not have a wife pissed off with me and pregnant back in New York and I wouldn't have to come all the way over here to meet up with all my brothers!" ⬇

"Is it quitting time? ... Is it going home time?"

"No!" shouted the crowd.

"Is it sleepy-time?"

"NO!"

A pause.

"Is it *sexy*-time?"

This time the crowd cheered.

Springsteen went on. "Maybe it's Guinness time."

The crowd cheered but Steve gave a shake of his head.

"No?" said Bruce. "Then, Steve, what I wanna know is ... what time is it, Steve?" The crowd shouted.

Van Zandt looked like he was studying his reply to Tony Soprano before eventually stuttering out in his thick accent: "Oh, it's Boss-time!"

"Dancing In The Dark" followed with Springsteen bouncing through the song. When the time came to find a dance partner, Bruce saw a little girl and waved at her to come up for a dance. For a moment she was frozen on the big screen as she seemed too overwhelmed to come up on stage and she turned back to her parents. Smiling, Springsteen came back to the centre of the stage and pulled up an Italian man and they shared a little boogie. "Thank you, my friend," said Springsteen at the end, before announcing: "I now scare small children!"

The crowd went wild for "American Land" but when the "E! Street! Band!" came up on the big screen in bubble writing (1960s *Batman* TV show style)

the screen got struck on the E.

A capital E seemed fitting though. For Entertaining.

On the Sunday, as *Backstreets* reported, Springsteen and the E Street Band "put pedal to the metal and blew the doors off".

"No Surrender, "Radio Nowhere" and "The Ties That Bind" signalled Springsteen's intentions.

He then surprised the crowd with "Spirit In The Night", kicking off the song with a "Can you feel the spirit?"

As the crowd grabbed his legs, he bent over backwards and lay on the stage.

The guitar battles of "Gypsy Biker" began a quake which rumbled through "Atlantic City" and "Reason To Believe".

But then more surprises from the Springsteen songbook, in honour of Danny Federici. "Danny's name was Federici, but he was adopted," Springsteen told the crowd. "That red hair and freckles ... I'm sure he was Irish."

He sang "4th Of July Asbury Park (Sandy)" and thanked the fans for their condolences on his friend's death.

Before "Growin' Up" he told a story, repeated at various lengths throughout the tour, of how Danny had got arrested "after parking his car in a tow-away zone with a huge marijuana plant on the front seat".

Springsteen explained: "And so the police come and they tow it away.

So he comes home and says, 'Bruce, Bruce, I'm going to go down to the

police station and I'm going to tell them that my car was stolen.' I said, 'I don't know if that's gonna work.' 'No, no. No problem.'

"He goes down to the police station and *boom!* straight into the slammer!"

Bruce laughed. "That was my man, my friend." Next, it was Nils Lofgren's turn to shine, continuing his apparent mission to never play the same solo twice on "Because The Night" and joining with Springsteen and Van Zandt for the guitar-fireworks of "She's The One". Springsteen's introduction to "Livin' In The Future" again laid into the damage he felt was being done to America by its administration, then the party continued into "Mary's Place" and "The Promised Land", before a change, with the *Magic* regular "Devil's Arcade" dropped in favour of a classic from 1978, "Racing In The Street", whose beautiful melody filled the Dublin air. It hushed the arena, said *Backstreets*, in what was an "astounding communal moment".

"The Rising", the political double-shot of "Last To Die" and "Long Walk Home", and "Badlands" closed the main set.

But there was a lot more to come.

"Tenth Avenue Freeze-Out" and "Born To Run" opened the encore, with the spotlights surfing across thousands of up-stretched hands.

Springsteen peered out into the darkness. "Is the band ready? Are the people ready? Is the *band* ready? Are the *people* ready?"

Yes! was the cry as Springsteen played the opening riff of "Rosalita" and he and Steve Van Zandt turned up the goofiness.

"Dancing In The Dark" saw Bruce again turned down for a dance by a young girl. "If this keeps happening," said Bruce, "I'm gonna be cited for child abuse!" The band launched into "American Land" but instead of being the night's closer it served as an aperitif for more fooling around.

"One more for Dublin," said Bruce, before proving that either he could not count or he just did not want to go home. "Ramrod" was played for laughs, with comedy hats being donned, and "Glory Days" brought the show to a wild finish after two hours and 45 minutes.

The three-night-stand represented a remarkable achievement. Each show reached a series of peaks, with every high always being followed by yet another. The songs, some 36 years old, sounded as if they had been written yesterday and had just been perfected by the band in the afternoon's sound check.

The two songs after "American Land" on the Sunday were proof that Springsteen simply did not want his visit to Dublin to end (although the same might not be said for some local residents as all three shows broke the city council's "acceptable noise levels" and resulted in a 50,000 euro fine for Aiken Promotions).

He cracked up!

"So you came back from New York but you are from Ireland originally, as I can hear. Why did you go over to New York in the first place?" So I told him the story about my mother buying me a radio and hearing that song "Incident On 57th Street".

I said, "It was all to do with a guy called Bruce Springsteen and Daisy from *The Dukes Of Hazzard* that made me make my way to the promised land!"

He laughed and said, "Good ole Daisy Duke!"

He asked all about my family. I told him about my brothers and sisters (who I didn't know at the time were coming to see me at the last concert with nieces and nephews, as I was flying back the next day) and all about my dad who was still teaching Irish dancing at 82.

He said, "I want to meet your dad. Never mind that, I want to meet your whole family!"

Bruce wanted us all backstage before his final show in Ireland!

I told him my dad only likes ceili music but I would call him and see if he wanted to meet the man we tortured him about all through the years!

He cracked up again.

Anyway, when I had first seen Bruce at the gym, I'd left my brother Thaddeus a message to get his ass down for a workout. He magically arrived in his workout gear and there I was ... talking to Springsteen!

Thad said, "Iggy, did you tell him about the ginger ale bottle?" with a smile as wide as it could possibly be.

We told him the story of the ginger ale bottle and he said, "Hey man, you owe me a ginger ale and tomorrow night when you come see me make sure to bring me that ginger ale! I was wondering where that got to!"

My brother went into the locker room and then so did Bruce and I carried on working out, grinning in disbelief.

The next thing I see Bruce and my brother in the pool – they're racing! I thought, "This is unreal!"

Ten minutes later I am done. I opened the door and Bruce is walking out. He said, "That brother of yours is something else, but I think I just clinched him in a race at the end."

I have owned bars and restaurants in New York City for years and I am very used to dealing with all walks of celebrities ... but here I am talking to Bruce Springsteen, an idol if I ever had one, and it was as natural as talking to your best friend.

We lost our mother Kathleen Hughes in 2002. She was hit by a car and after 14 days in a coma, she passed.

Then Bruce came out with *The Rising* and the songs "You're Missing" and "Empty Sky" brought some solace and togetherness to us all after her death (we love and thank you, mom).

Bruce and I talked about kids. I told him again about my wife being pregnant with our second child. He said, "That's such a special time, it meant so much to me that time of my life."

I was feeling like I was holding him up but he kept chatting and said he was going to go for a walk later. ⬇

In *Uncut* magazine, Gavin Martin, who had been in the Merrion on the Thursday after the show as the "ever-voluble" Van Zandt, Nils Lofgren and Garry Tallent mixed with Bono and the Edge, said of the shows: "Leaner and meaner, Springsteen in 2008 has cut the flab of his 80s mainstream heyday. His sense of proportion – and self deprecation – could provide a salutary guide to any rock gladiator preparing to re-enter the arena." Martin also noted in *The Mirror*: "By staying true to original principles he still inspires uncommon devotion."

David Cheal, of the *Daily Telegraph*, wrote: "There are bands, there are stars, there are singers, there are songwriters. And there's Bruce Springsteen. This tireless bundle of feverish energy is still head and shoulders above anyone else in the world of popular music. Whenever I see him on stage, everyone else fades into the background; all those so called globe-conquering acts are thrown into sharp relief by the glorious wall of sound and waves of emotion that pulse from the man and his band.

"He has a heart as big as a planet, he makes music that's pure joy, and he does it for hour after hour."

"He never tires of playing in Ireland and his Irish fans never tire of hearing him play," added Ireland.com.

Actor Jonathan Rhys Meyers had recently told *Hot Press* that *Born In The USA* had been the first album he had bought and that Bruce was still on his iPod, and at the RDS another Irish export to Hollywood had been seen having the time of his life. "Smiling like a preacher who has sought, and found, the promised land, Colin (Farrell) even jumped around to 'Rosalita' and 'Born To Run'," wrote Barry Egan in the *Irish Independent* (footballer Damien Duff was also dancing in the VIP area).

"There's a universality, a depth of humanity, to Springsteen's lyrics and music that resonates with just about everyone over 27 who realises manufactured teen bands are not the future," said Egan. "That's no disrespect to Westlife, who deserve their success, but their music can never say anything about our lives the same way that Springsteen's does.

Bono, Larry and the Edge were watching from backstage on Thursday night. I couldn't help thinking what thoughts were flashing through Bono's head as he watched a jeans-and-shirt-clad Bruce perform "Thunder Road" on a stripped down and gadget-free stage, holding 40,000 people in thrall in just the bare songs. No bells, no whistles. Just the E Street Band."

That connection with the audience, Egan noted, manifested itself in not only bringing joy but also a powerful sense of community which 23 years on from Slane, Springsteen could still do, even in large outdoor arenas such as the RDS.

Egan, inspired by Springsteen's performance of "The Rising", told the story of Joanne Cregan, from Churchtown. A friend of his sister, she had perished in the North Tower of the World Trade Center.

"Sunday night's rendition of "The Rising" had Colin Farrell's boot heels tapping with a suitably melancholic verve to the 9/11 masterpiece and Bruce smiling sadly like a preacher in excelsis. And somewhere in heaven, Dublin girl, Joanne Cregan, was looking down approvingly on proceedings."

I said, "Maybe you will have a real beer!" He said, "I had a beer onstage last night for the first time in a long time, and it was good, man!"

"Bruce, you can't possibly tell me that was good. It is draft shite!"

"After an hour-and-a-half of singing your lungs out, believe me, it was good," he said. We parted ways and I walked into the steam room where my brother Thaddeus was. We just looked at each other and burst out laughing.

Then I said, "I see you had a little race with him, Thad?"

He replied, "Iggy, I think I just nicked him in the end." I laughed and told Thad that Bruce felt the same way.

We became hysterical. It started hitting us a little bit - the two of us just met Bruce!

Back in my room, the phone rang. It was Tony, Bruce's trainer and friend. He said: "Iggy, how many do you think there will be tomorrow?"

Thad then broke me the news that my sisters and nephews and nieces would be there. "A few,' I said.

"It's no problem, Iggy. He wants to meet them."

Anyway, so now I have a surprise of my own for my sisters and nephew Christopher and nieces Lauren and Alanna and Natalie. I, of course, had to act surprised to see all of them when we met outside the RDS. Then we told them they were going to meet Bruce. We went backstage - this was 15 minutes before he was due to go on stage.

My sisters were getting excited. He came out of his trailer and said, "Wow, Iggy, big family!"

And my sister Siobhan turned around and said, "Hey, Bruce, you did not expect *The Waltons*, did you?"

Bruce started laughing and said, "With *The Dukes Of Hazzard* and *The Waltons*, these Irish people sure know American TV!" We had bought Bruce two very beautiful books about Ireland and we all had written stories in them about how much his songs meant to us. My brother David handed them to him (David wrote a beautiful thing: part of it was, "Unfortunately our mother is one of those "Souls Of The Departed", as is now Danny and we offer our condolences").

Bruce said, "You guys did not have to bring me gifts", but then turned to my brother, Thad, and he said, "Thad, where is that ginger ale I have been waiting on?"

We were in stitches! The guys said 'time to go' but Bruce said, "Hang on, I am not ready yet." So Bruce took his time and talked with all my sisters and nieces and nephew.

He then took a shine to Natalie and said, "I finally get a brunette in the crew!" I was trying to take everybody's photo and Tony said, "Get in the picture Iggy, I will take it." So there in the photo there is me in front of my family and some friends and Bruce right in the background!

He even shouted after me, "Iggy, you didn't get a picture."

I said, "Don't worry." I knew the Irish crowd was waiting for him.

A few of his guys came out to us about a half hour later and said, "Well, Iggy?" and I said, "You guys just made me the local hero." I said, "I hope we weren't too much?" And they said, "Are you kidding? He was in there reading all the notes you wrote in the books. What did you write? We could not get him out as he was enjoying it."

"We all just wrote messages about what he and his music meant to us."

My dad, Peter, sadly never came that night to the concert, but did come down to see me and sat outside my brother Nick's house, with Nick's wife Mary, and heard the whole concert as the house is just minutes from the RDS. He had worried that it would be too loud and also, which I found out later, he thought we were having him on about Bruce wanting to meet him. We always have a laugh with him, but he did regret not going.

There is nothing more I would have loved to have than a picture of my two favourite men, my father and Bruce Springsteen.

Iggy Hughes
New York (formerly of County Tyrone)

RDS
Dublin

11 & 12 July 2009

Crowd: 80,000 over two nights

Tickets: 86.25 euro

In an interview with *Rolling Stone* early in 2009 Bruce Springsteen recounted a conversation with his wife Patti.

"You are in a manic state," she had said to him, "running like crazy from, let me think, death itself?"

The memory made Springsteen laugh. "It's a funny thing to say," he added. "But I've got a deadline! And that fire I feel in myself and the band – it's a very enjoyable thing."

So enjoyable, that fans of an artist who had once had to wait years for new material were now no longer sure where one project ended and the next began.

Working On A Dream, the album released on January 27, 2009, had actually been started immediately as the *Magic* sessions concluded.

"Towards the end of recording *Magic*, excited by the return to pop production sounds, I continued writing," Springsteen wrote on his website. "When my friend, producer Brendan O'Brien, heard the new songs, he said, 'Let's keep going.' Over the course of the next year, that's just what we did, recording with the E Street Band during the breaks on (the *Magic*) tour. I hope *Working on a Dream* has caught the energy of the band fresh off the road from some of the most exciting shows we've ever done. All the songs were written quickly, we usually used one of our first few takes, and we all had a blast making this one from beginning to end."

The year started feverishly.

Simon Nicholl

Madeleine Harbison

Ian O'Connell

Ian O'Connell

There was not only the release of an album, there were also the small matters of an appearance at new president Barack Obama's inauguration (Springsteen had campaigned again – and this time not turned out on the losing end) and a half-time show at the Super Bowl.

There was also a Golden Globe for the theme song to Mickey Rourke's comeback movie *The Wrestler*. The song would be an extra track on the album. Patti's comments strike a note with the themes of *Working On A Dream* which used soaring melodies and 60s harmonies to create an upbeat lament on the passing of time and a celebration of the one thing that eases the anxious mind of the mortal: love.

It is the passing by of time's winged chariot, rather than a 69 Chevy, that can be heard on the album, from the twinkling of fading stars in "This Life" and the wistful remembrances of "Tomorrow Never Knows", to the birthdays of "Surprise, Surprise" and the closing of the day which runs through the lament for Danny Federici, "The Last Carnival". These central themes are brought together in the ticking clocks and passing seasons of "Kingdom of Days", a love song for Patti. Springsteen has always faced hard truths head-on in his music, whether he be the rich man owning up to earning his living in a poor man's shirt or the duplicitous, troubled husband of "Two Faces".

Therefore, it came as no surprise to fans to discover this was one rock star who could quite seamlessly work the appearance of grey hairs into his work. Joe Breen made the album the CD of the week in the *Irish Times*. "The album lays down a mark for a new era of hope, realism and solidarity while openly celebrating the sense of change with a striking bounce in the playing and the music. It's no accident that it goes on release during Inauguration week." Tickets for a single show at the RDS went on sale at 9am on Friday, January 30. A second show was added during the morning. The shows were set for Saturday, July 11, and Sunday, July 12, 2009.

Bruce and the band arrived in Dublin early in the week, checking in to the Merrion, and flying out to Denmark for the show on the Wednesday. On Friday, a number of fans gathered outside the hotel and were rewarded with chats with all the members of the band as they went out shopping and sight-seeing. Bruce himself signed autographs for a short time as he returned to the hotel early in the evening.

With the E Street Band were backing singers Curtis King and Cindy Mizelle, who had been recruited from the Sessions Band to the live show to add further depth to the pop melodies on the new record. Saturday started dry but the forecast promised rain and would not disappoint.

11 July 2009

Intro: The Fields Of Athenry
Who'll Stop The Rain
Badlands
Cover Me
My Lucky Day
Outlaw Pete
Out In The Street
Working On A Dream
Seeds
Johnny 99
The Ghost of Tom Joad
Raise Your Hand (instrumental)
You Can Look (But You Better Not Touch)
Seven Nights To Rock
For You
Thunder Road
Because The Night
Waitin' On A Sunny Day
The Promised Land
The River
Kingdom Of Days
Lonesome Day
The Rising
Born To Run
Hard Times Come Again No More
Tenth Avenue Freeze-Out
American Land
Bobby Jean
Dancing In The Dark
Ramrod
Twist and Shout

12 July 2009

also included
No Surrender
Night
Hungry Heart
Youngstown
Darkness On The Edge of Town
Spirit In The Night
Sherry Darling
Proud Mary
Prove It All Night
Trapped
Radio Nowhere
American Skin (41 Shots)
Jungleland
Rosalita
Glory Days

Two thousand fans were already in the pit queue by midday and from 1pm the queue was a solid one. (The queue had been started by one of the hardiest of all Springsteen's English fans way back on Wednesday.) Even as the skies darkened and the rain began to bucket down, more came for the 3,500 places stewards said were permitted in the pit. The hawkers' cry of "Five euro, your heavy duty poncho" filled the streets around the RDS and as show-time approached few with standing tickets chose to resist the lure of the waterproof gear.

By 8pm most were wet-through and only one thing was going to lift spirits. Shortly afterwards, the rolling notes of an accordion rung out and Nils Lofgren wandered on stage. It took a few seconds for the opening sounds of "The Fields of Athenry" to penetrate the wind and rain to the far reaches of the stadium but the cheers quickly rose, gathering and growing as each member of the band strode out, their faces large on the two big screens each side of the stage.

Then, with Bruce at his mic, the band kicked into a traditional opener for nights of bad weather, John Fogerty's "Who'll Stop The Rain", which pushed "Badlands" back in the set.

The first half of the night represented a blend of the old and the new: "Cover Me", "My Lucky Day", "Outlaw Pete", with Bruce donning a cowboy hat

all photos Greg Lewis

halfway through, and "Out In The Street". "Working On A Dream" included Bruce's full spiel regarding the E Street Band's duty to "rock the house here in Dublin", although the album from which it came played only a small role in the two shows.

At the set's heart was the muscular "Recession pack" of "Seeds", a reworked "Johnny 99" and a full-band "The Ghost of Tom Joad", each tackling the economic meltdown which had affected Ireland as much as the US.

As "Tom Joad" closed, the band kicked into a lively instrumental version of "Raise Your Hand" and Bruce began his run around the stage collecting request signs from the outstretched hands in the pit.

First off came "You Can Look (But You Better Not Touch)", then a cover from *The Rising* tour, "Seven Nights To Rock", and an old favourite "For You".

"Thunder Road" was, as usual, at once moving, majestic and inspiring, and during "Because The Night" – with Bruce and Nils sharing the guitar licks - a faint rainbow appeared above the stage. Although it did not signal a change in the weather, Springsteen did point to a thin strip of blue sky before launching into a rousing sing-a-long of "Waitin' On A Sunny Day". The song had been the subject of a request on a large flag and, despite the continuing rain, had rarely been sung so fervently by so many thousand voices.

"The Promised Land" moved into a sparse and beautiful version of "The River" and "Kingdom Of Days" was dedicated to Patti, at home with the couple's two youngest children.

"Lonesome Day", "The Rising" and "Born To Run" closed the main set but the band stayed on stage to spare the soaked crowd and went straight into an encore beginning with "Hard Times Come Again No More", a rousing version of Stephen Collins Foster's composition from 1854, previously covered by Johnny Cash and Bob Dylan, and a mainstay of the *Working On A Dream* tour.

Clarence's nephew Jake, who has played on records by Dave Matthews and Will Smith, joined his uncle on sax on "Tenth Avenue Freeze-Out" and on "American Land" Bruce's son Evan added an additional guitar.

Hammering hard on his guitar as the song turned into an Irish Ceili, Bruce slipped over as he jumped from one part of the stage to the other. As Nils rushed over to see if he was alright, he got up and went back to his starting point to make the leap again.

In honour of the fall, the "legendary E Street Band" acquired the additional title "ass-breaking" during Bruce's holler out to Dublin. Bruce told the crowd it was the second time he had fallen during the song. Whereas "American Land" began as a show closer, it now formed an aperitif for the fully cranked-up climax to the encore.

I have been a fan of Bruce since 1981, the year my father died suddenly of a heart attack. I was 15 and I loved the song "The River" and bought the album and as I listened to it I found some of the lyrics very comforting. "Two Hearts" just summed up how I was feeling at the time. That album and his music was my therapy. I went to see him in 1985 in Slane Castle. I still have the blue shirt I wore at that concert. It was fantastic to be in the middle of so many Bruce fans singing all my favourites.

I went to see him as often as I could when he came to Ireland and always bought his albums when they came out. I saw him in RDS in 2008 and cried because I didn't know how long more I would be privileged to see Bruce and the amazing E Street Band live. So, in 2009, I decided I would go to the two concerts and book into the Merrion Hotel. The first night I was lucky to get into the pit and it was electric. The following morning I was fortunate to get my photo taken with Nils Lofgren, Charles Giordano and Roy Bittan.

The second night I stayed back in the pitch and soaked in the atmosphere and once again cried at the wonderful rendition of "Jungleland". Clarence Clemons is amazing.

That night, back in the bar of the hotel, I finally got to meet Bruce. I shook his hand and said what I had always dreamed in my head I would say if I ever meet him. I said I was a big fan since 1981 and I thanked him for his amazing music and how the album *The River* was my solace after my father's sudden death.

He listened and took it all in and he said it was great to hear that and thanked me and gave me a kiss on the cheek. I asked would it be okay to get a photo and he said sure.

Oh, my God! I was in floods of tears and on cloud nine. My lifetime dream had materialized and I could not believe it. I was like a teenager.

There is an amazing aura about him and he looks fantastic and is so laid back and natural. I was told you should never meet your idol but I am so glad and fortunate to have met him. Thanks Bruce and the E Street Band for the memories and the wonderful healing music and lyrics.

Ann Marie Kennedy, Limerick

My first time to see Bruce Springsteen and the legendary E Street Band was on the 11th of July 2009 in the RDS. It was a very rainy Saturday, nevertheless it didn't stop people queuing up outside for hours before the gig.

The screens and amplifiers swayed in the wind when Bruce and the band took to the stage, opening with Nils Lofgren playing "The Fields Of Athenry" on the accordion then blasting into "Who'll Stop The Rain". The highlight of the night for me would be when they played my all time favourite song, "Thunder Road". Another highlight was Bruce holding a massive sign that read "Waitin' On A Sunny Day" and as the band played the rain stopped and there were blue skies above the RDS. The evening closed three hours and 30 songs after the band hit the stage with a final climax, "Twist and Shout". ⬇

"Bobby Jean" rocked, "Dancing In The Dark" had the whole audience singing along and a shortened-version of "Ramrod" featured in response to a request sign which Steve held up. It said: "Bruce, ramrod me tonight". "I can't do that," Bruce smiled. "But I can play a bit of the song!"

Forty-thousand voices then made the two stands rock in a foot-stamping version of "Twist and Shout" with its "La Bamba" chorus. 'Follow that' was the thought of many as they drifted into the cold, wet night. However, Sunday would not be a case of following Saturday's show. It was a case of blowing it right out of the water.

After Nils' opening, the show went straight into a high tempo with "No Surrender", "Badlands" and "Night", and with Bruce in energetic form, the band seemed to be raised to a new level. "Dublin!" shouted Bruce. "Are you ready for round two?" "My Lucky Day" and "Outlaw Pete", along with its title track, were to be the only offerings from the current album. "Hungry Heart" began a mass sing-song which continued into "Working On A Dream", with Clarence again taking the whistling solo. "The big man whistling," Bruce announced, by way of introduction.

The Springsteen speech was expanded from the night before. "Like I said last night we didn't come all that way just to have the fish and chips at Burdock's," rasped Bruce, "although that would be a reason to make the voyage.

For me it didn't end there. My E Street-filled weekend ended on Sunday when I met the legends Little Steven Van Zandt and Professor Roy Bittan in Tower Records where Little Steve's radio show was broadcasting live. It was a fantastic weekend that I will never forget.

Ciarán Kilbride, aged 15, Dublin

I started my journey travelling to see Bruce live in Ireland in 1985 when I was 17 and the journey continues. The *Working On A Dream* tour has been particularly special to me as friendships were renewed and more friends were made from O'Donoghue's to Bewleys and to the best place of all, the pit queue – waiting in line for up to 10 hours each day was magic. That probably sounds crazy to tens of thousands of people but the best t-shirt I saw this year summed it up: 'It's a Bruce Springsteen thing – you just wouldn't understand.'

I lost everyone I was with on the first night because I went to wave to friends in the stand. But it didn't matter and I happily joined other fans and even ended up front row. My lovely friend Ceinwen, whom we met in 2008, stood beside the guy who introduced me to Bruce's music almost 30 years ago. The rain poured down all night but it was a minor hiccup and no-one cared. Front row night 2, as well, and I got a phonecall. The voice said, "Hi Sinead, it's Nellie from Chicago – where are you?" Nellie was on her own in 2008 and we had a great night with her.

Bruce never fails to deliver amazing shows to his fans and keeps them fresh by adding something exhilarating each night – don't think anyone saw "41 Shots" coming. I call it my 'Strange Little Bruce World' because somehow by fate we have made the most amazing friendships and know they will continue for as long as we have that one thing in common. Ceinwen, Hywel, Michelle, Paul, Tracey, Lorcan, Adrienne, John, Eamon, Andrew, Roy, Nellie, Declan, Gordon are just a few that I would have never met only for Bruce in Ireland.

Thank you, Bruce – you make my world special every day.

Sinead Tyrrell-Quinn, Ballina, Co Mayo

I have been a Bruce fan since 1975, when I was 14. Having cousins from NJ fuelled the fire and so I was delighted to see the Boss in Slane and on (almost) every Irish occasion since. During Steve's appearance at Tower Records on the WOAD tour, I got to speak to him about his "Checkpoint Charlie" track as he autographed his album for me, to Charlie about his Irish trips and to Curtis about his first trip to Dublin in 1987 with Duran Duran. I just said 'hi' to Roy and Gary.

The guy beside me in the pit on Sunday, July 12, was on his 50th concert. He and his wife and child were from England and were staying in the Merrion Hotel.

Their 13-year-old daughter swam in the hotel pool at the same time as Bruce. The daughter has seen 38 concerts - starting when she was five.

Tom McCormack
Clonskeagh, Dublin

"We didn't come all this way just because the Dubs won the Leinster final, though that would be a reason to make the voyage. We didn't come all this way just to suck up some Guinness in O'Donoghue's or Long's Bar, though that would be a good reason to make the voyage.

"We didn't come all that way to be graced with the presence of Mr Brian O'Driscoll in the hall here tonight, though that would be a damn good reason to make the voyage. We didn't come all this way just to see all of these beautiful Irish women out there, although that would be a good reason to make the voyage.

"We came here tonight cos we want to build a house right here on this field, out of hope and faith and joy. We're going to build a house out of music and out of spirit and out of noise. And the mighty E Street Band are here to lay down the music on you. But, Dublin, we need you to bring the noise!"

A huge wave of noise swept through the showground towards the stage and the band went back into a final chorus: "Sing it like you mean it!" Bruce hollered.

With the sun on the band members' faces, they then ripped into the Recession-inspired section of the set, with "Seeds" and the new train-ride melody of "Johnny 99", this time joined by "Youngstown" and "Darkness On The Edge of Town".

Springsteen's music had always had significance in my life, from my student days when he took Hammersmith by storm through to the tours – *Born in the USA*, *Tunnel of Love*, *The Rising* …

His music always evokes a strong emotional response, whether of elation, happiness, sadness or despair. His ability to capture and articulate the voice of protest against injustice, the anger arising from the misuse of power or the everyday pain, anguish or joy that we all recognize from our own lives, knows no bounds.

So, I have always loved his music, had a blast at his shows, but did not identify myself as a true fan.

Queuing all night for tickets? Not me. Travelling the world to see him play? Never. Yelling out "Brooooce!" at his shows? No way, far too cool for that!

Then the *Seeger Sessions* came along. Everything changed, I would follow them to the end of the earth or the moon if I could afford the flights.

Seeing so many musicians on stage having so much fun was amazing. Their energy and drive was incredible … very powerful. Such a unique experience. They could tackle anything, traditional, contemporary, big band, gospel or haunting solos. I was mesmerized.

I thank Bruce for bringing together this wonderful band of musicians, not only did I enjoy the shows but the experience made me revisit music I had enjoyed in the past (I even dug out and sorted my old vinyl LPs). More than anything I got to know the music of Cindy Mizelle and Curtis King Jr – they are so talented in their own right.

Curtis's vocals on "Eyes on the Prize" in Dublin sent shivers down my spine, his duet with Bruce on "Love of the Common People" a surprise treat. Cindy's vocals are so powerful and pure – they could shatter glass - and the fun she has with the other females on the Dublin DVD is great to see.

Cindy and Curtis have both worked with a wide variety of artists and it was fun to track them back within my existing record collection.

You can imagine how happy I was to discover that the both of them had been spotted at the rehearsal shows for the *Working On A Dream* tour so I followed the concert reviews with great interest. To see both shows in Dublin was a real treat, despite the freezing wet weather at the first show.

Bruce yet again gave a spectacular show but for me this was really special as the vocal support from Cindy and Curtis took it to another level – particularly on "Hard Times" and the harrowing "American Skin".

Missing out on the final *Seeger Sessions* Dublin shows is one of my regrets so it was a wonderful experience to see the *Working On A Dream* tour in Dublin (a beautiful and friendly city) and to meet Curtis and Cindy – such wonderful people with so much talent.

Let's hope the Seeger Sessions Band rides again soon, albeit in a different way, as Bruce sure never stands still!

Moira Storrar
East London, England

Steve and Charlie led an extended "Raise Your Hand" as Bruce raced to and fro collecting bundles of request signs, including "Spirit In The Night", a "summer song" "Sherry Darling" and "Proud Mary", a second John Fogerty cover of the weekend which had everyone singing along. During "Spirit" Springsteen laid out flat on one of the platforms as fans reached out for him and 40,000 cheered. "It's so peaceful down here," he joked.

Bruce and Nils came together for a scintillating guitar duel on "Prove It All Night" and the band was note perfect on both the quiet but brooding verses and the shout-along chorus of "Trapped".

Bruce's acoustic guitar took a hammering during "Waitin' On A Sunny Day". During the song's instrumental break, Bruce whipped it off and prepared to make his usual throw to guitar technician Kevin Buell. But with Buell out on stage and Bruce two platforms below, Bruce hesitated and then threw the guitar too high so it bowed through the air and plunged down onto the stage. As he trotted off to come down to the edge of the crowd, Bruce shouted, "Sorry, Kev!"

"The Promised Land" had Bruce standing, harmonica to mouth, at the edge of the crowd while "Radio Nowhere" proved what a rousing rock song it is, wherever it comes in the set.

Greg Lewis

Niall Hetherington

Tom McCormack

Tom McCormack

Ann Marie Kenneddy

Then a surprise. "American Skin (41 Shots)", which had appeared in the soundcheck, held the crowd spellbound, although it was apparent that not everyone knew it.

"Lonesome Day", "The Rising" and "Born To Run", which, as on the previous night, made the RDS shake with pure joy, again closed the set.

Springsteen and the band left the stage to a roar from the crowd and when they returned it would be for a blistering six-song encore which would take the party well into the night.

Steve's guitar and Clarence's sax nailed a tremendous version of "Jungleland", with Springsteen's voice on the closing section crystal clear and the final cry making the blood turn cold.

"American Land" rocked, with everyone on the pitch or in the stands jumping up and down. There was no slip tonight, Bruce having been reminded of his previous mishap by a sign which he had earlier read out: "Caution, slippery when wet - we don't want you to break your ass tonight."

With the band introductions completed, Bruce then turned to his left: "I need the glory of Little Steven." Steve stepped forward and joined in with the opening chords of "Rosalita", and Bruce jumped on the spot as he sang out his heart to Rosie.

"Glory Days" was joyous, concluding with an extra-special "Boss time" exchange which befitted a hardrocking night at the RDS.

"I think we got to be moving on now, Steve. I think we've got to be moving on. I do believe it's quittin' time."

"I don't wanna go home," countered Steve.

"There's a curfew, y'know," Bruce chided him.

"I don't care."

"I'm telling you there's a curfew."

Steve stamped his foot. "I don't care about the curfew."

"Well, Steve, if it ain't quittin' time, I just wanna know …" Band stops. "What time is it?"

A pause. Then Steve: "It's curfew bustin' Boss time!"

A doll-shaped request for "Girls In Their Summer Clothes" had appeared on stage and Steve took time to beat Bruce over the head with it.

But, although the clock ticked past 11pm, Bruce had far to go.

He hammered down hard on his guitar during "Dancing In The Dark" and then a final, energy-filled "Twist and Shout".

As one "La Bamba"-shaped chorus blended into another Bruce cried out, "We ain't going home. We got no place to f***ing go. Except back to the f***ing hotel."

Then, "Steve, is it a bird?"

"Nah."

"Is it a plane?"

"Nah."

"Is it Superman?"

"Nah," getting more confused.

"Is it Batman?"

Sunday, July 12, 2009, in Dublin had begun just like any other day … A trip to the Little Steven "Tower Records a Go Go" Underground Garage recording, a chat with E Streeters Charles Giordana and Curtis King in the street outside the hotel and getting thrown out of a supermarket for getting my photo taken with Clarence's nephew, the "Little Big Man" … "You can't take photos in here. Errr, who was that big man?"

Then we made our plans for another trip to see the Greatest Show on Earth. Sunday gig's was simply the best ever for me. I need say no more.

Afterwards, I set off back to the hotel and, with no voice left and hands sore from clapping, went along with Mrs A's idea that we should just have a quiet drink in the bar.

So there I was propping up the doorway when Max, Roy, Soozie and the lovely Cindy came in … with *him*. "Oh, my God," I stuttered aloud, "it's the Boss."

Staring, I moved aside, and he smiled and walked past me into the bar.

The next couple of hours or so were a blur. I was in a state of shock. At about 2.30am, Bruce stood up to leave and I plucked up the courage to make my approach. "Excuse me, Mr Springsteen." He turned round, smiled and said, "Hi."

Mrs A then stepped in as she could see I was struggling to speak. She had a few words and shook his hand while I got my voice back.

Bruce then flung his arm round me and I just did the same, so there we were: the Boss and some jabbering Geordie basket case cuddling each other.

I said exactly what I'd always wanted to say to him, thanked him for all he has given me for the past 30-odd years and that I hoped he'd continue to do so for a few more years yet!

After a few more laughs he went on his way.

Actually meeting him ranks alongside my wedding day and the birth of my children (and my little dog, of course) as one of the most emotional moments of my life.

And he's such a lovely bloke, so friendly he could even be a Geordie!

Gary Aston
Newcastle Upon Tyne

Springsteen has earned every bit of his fame and fortune and as a musician he is adamant that we are rewarded for the part we played in getting him where he is. When I saw him literally sit into the crowd in the RDS and allow his guitar to be battered by the crowd during the "Born To Run" 'breakdown' it was clear, the live show is *ours* and the Boss is just happy to be a part of it. I've been to over 50 gigs in my life so far but the four Springsteen shows I've been to have still never come close to being beaten.

Saturday 11th July 2009: After an hour's worth of queuing in the pouring rain myself and my father landed a spot right up at the soundstage at the barrier, couldn't ask for more. The mood was set straight away with Nils playing "The Fields Of Athenry" on the accordion, one of the nicest touches I've ever seen a band include in their live show. ⬇

"No."

"Is it ... [meaningless words]?"

"Er, is it *what*?"

"Is it *Dublin*?"

"Ah, yeah!"

Laughing, Steve again gave Bruce a beating with the doll. The band, unsure whether Bruce had finished, then found him going into another "Hey, baby".

Finally, he brought it to a crescendo by shouting "Louie Louie" and going into a few bars, before back into "Twist" to close.

"We've lost our minds!" cried Bruce before going into a mad flurry of guitar swinging which saw it encircle his neck like the sails of a windmill.

The RDS show lasted three hours and six minutes – both it and Saturday's show would have the promoter reportedly facing fines for breaking the city curfew. It was high energy from start to finish. "Born To Run", like The Clash's version of "I Fought The Law", packs energy into its few minutes, as if each note were some explosive gas barely contained in a bottle. Sunday's set somehow extended that energy across a whole show.

Steve Van Zandt made a few extra-curricular appearances during his Dublin stay.

Ian O'Connell

On Sunday, he hosted his radio show from Tower Records and introduced the bands The Urges and the Len Price 3.

On Monday morning he appeared on Ireland: AM on TV3: "This really is one of our best audiences in the world," he told the presenters. "We've just got a great relationship with Ireland."

Asked about how he coped with doing three-hour shows, he said: "We just follow [Bruce's] lead. He's just in great shape. He keeps himself totally together and we try and keep up – that's about all we can do."

On Sunday, they more than kept up with their energetic leader. They combined as one to produce a show which all who witnessed it, and all who compare it with Springsteen's Irish appearances over a quarter of a century, will remember for years to come.

It was just a great bit of respect and effort for the country and audience and really gave the Irish crowd an instant connection to the band. By the end of the 31-song, three-hour marathon of a gig we were soaked but satisfied. My father turned to me on the way out and asked, "How is he gonna do that all over again tomorrow?" The Saturday show was, at least I thought at the time, the single greatest gig experience of my life. The songs were there, the atmosphere was there, everything was perfect. After six hours sleep I arrived at the RDS with my friend, and fellow musician, Peter, at half-ten on Sunday to begin queuing for a pit pass. Walking into the queue we were branded numbers 609 and 610 and so we were confident we were going to be in a good spot. Armed with my 'I Caught A Cold Here Last Night, I Need "FIRE"' sign we took our seats on the grass for the long wait until the gates opened at five. Before we knew it we were standing three or four rows from the stage to the right of the centre podium.

We were treated to some real gems during the request slot (my sign was unfortunately missed!). "Spirit In The Night" saw Bruce float amongst the crowd and truly have a ball singing, pity our timing and volume was so out, prompting Bruce to remark, "That's terrible", much to the laughter of the band and crowd.

On came "Trapped" and an even better "Waitin' On A Sunny Day" where Bruce succeeded in getting one of the many children in the audience to sing the chorus, a memory she is sure to cherish for the rest of her life.

Moving into the night came the song we had the privilege to hear in the sound check but I never thought I'd hear it live. The performance of "American Skin (41 Shots)" was worth the ticket price alone. On the trek back to Kildare, myself and Peter could barely speak. What words could sum up what we had just experienced?

I'll be happy with the memories I can take from one of the greatest weekends of music in my entire life. May the E Street Band continue to create the wonderful miracles they do so well.

Niall Hetherington, Sallins, Co Kildare

Irish Weekend Friday: Alarm goes at 3.30am. I head to Bristol Airport. Meet members of the Greasy Lake internet forum on plane. Arrive at Dublin Airport. Get a map and go to O'Donoghue's for a Guinness. Go back to the hotel and meet up with friend named Funkster. We head back to Temple Bar on a bus and meet Dean in a bar called Thunder Road.

Later, we head back to O'Donoghue's to meet up with lots of other Lakers. After another trip to Temple Bar, it goes all wrong. I jump in a taxi and it takes me to the wrong hotel - right out at the airport. One and a half hours later and after spending 80 out of the 90 euro I have left, I get back to my hotel. Saturday: Head to Temple Bar to meet Dean and just as the bus stops I realize I have left my concert ticket back at the hotel. Dean, being the hero he is, tells me to calm down and we jump in a taxi. We miss the pit queue and decide to head to the Badlands party. ⬇

We spend the rest of the day drinking and meeting Lakers, mostly from Wales. Show was fantastic. 31 songs. Sunday: Queue up. Get pit wrist bands. Wow, he really does pull out all the stops for the Irish. Monday: Head to airport to get flight for Glasgow and Bruce's Tuesday show. Am one of the first in the queue for the flight. Turn around and it looks like every person is a Bruce fan. The nice people I sit next to on the plane say you need a Bruce shirt just to get on the flight!

Chris East, of Exeter, England

A good friend of mine, Eithne Wynn, had brought several yellow ponchos for us to bring along to the concert. It's not that we are overly fashion conscious but we decided to put one to better use. We had already planned to make a banner for the concert and considering that it was a yellow rain mac what better omen than to make a banner for "Waitin' On A Sunny Day"? Jo Buckley quickly put her artistic talents to good use and I scoured the web to find a smiley photo of Bruce. Tent poles were supplied to hold it in place. We arrived at the very front of the pit at 5pm and the heavens opened.

I handed out a few spare macs to people who were ill-prepared and already drenched and joked that in return they would have to help me with the banner.

With the help of my sister Emily, newly acquainted friends and fans from Limerick, Helen O'Sullivan and Anne Marie Kennedy, a couple from London and a big gang from Cork, we raised the banner and the crowd around us began to sing "Sunny Day".

We knew then it was going to be a great night. Conscious that our friends Marion Coleman and Jo Buckley were back further from the pit, we raised the banner so that they may see it on the big screen.

Each time it was raised in the rain we got a big cheer and a song. When the concert began Bruce came close for several songs and we knew he would pay us a visit again. We held the banner high in the air screaming, difficult in the wind and rain, and then Bruce came over. He looked at it quizzically and then saw the photo of himself in the middle of the sun, shook his head and laughed. We screamed, "Take the banner, Bruce. Please, please!"

And when he did the cheer from the pit was loud. He placed the banner along with all the others and as time went on we thought that it had been left at the back of the stage and forgotten about.

Then to our surprise he took the banner and, struggling against the wind, held it in both his arms high in the rain. The crowd went wild. Just at that moment as if the gods were looking down on us, the sun broke through the clouds and Bruce pointed to the sun. What a moment! The crowd was uplifted and sang the song with Bruce. The banner gang in the pit was overjoyed. Moments later I received a text from Jo at the back of the stadium, saying, 'We rock!', and we did that night!

Madeleine Harbison
Ashbourne, County Meath

11 July 2009: Bruce Springsteen is howling because he understands. It's the end of "The River" and our hero has chosen to extend the song's mournful coda with a primal howl.

He did the same to "Cover Me" an hour or so earlier. The rain has been coming down for hours. Dublin is wet and cold and the RDS crowd couldn't care less. Why? Because the man they paid to see (and his band) are putting in a shift. They're here for business, not just fun. And we all believe him ...

Bruce Springsteen turns 60 in 2009, but his artistry still burns so bright that he can tap into the spirit of the times in each nation he visits and hold a mirror up to the thousands before him. The Italians love him for it. The Spanish too.

But, in Ireland, Springsteen is the prodigal son coming home in the wild Atlantic rain. And he's here to use the good and bad times we're all facing during this time of global recession and turn them into something tangible. Something we can feel. And, when he throws himself into the crowd, something we can touch. Times may be tough - hey, they may even get tougher - but we've got each other tonight.

Nobody wins unless everybody wins? And the dogs on Main Street howl because they understand ...

Alan O'Hare
of the Liverpool band, The Trestles

Ian O'Connell

Greg Lewis

Simon Nicholl

Ian O'Connell

Authors' Story

The road was dark when we started our book.

Shortly before we headed to Ireland for the *Magic* shows in 2008, Moira suffered her second miscarriage in the space of six months.

Despite the heartbreak, we never considered cancelling our trip. We knew the energy, excitement and companionship of the pit would be better than any therapy, rest or comfort we would get from anywhere else.

Coming away from Dublin, we knew that many around us had felt the same highs, the same elation.

We knew there must be many stories worth telling.

And so this book began.

I have been into Bruce for more than 25 years so it was strange to be now treating him as 'work'.

We spent hours in the National Library in Dublin, had old newspaper cuttings and disks sent through the post from fans and began to have stories and photos emailed and posted to us.

We began to re-live old concerts.

Reading about *Devils & Dust*, in particular, took us back. There is something special about *all* Springsteen shows, we all know that, but *Devils & Dust*, at The Point was so … intimate. It was just Bruce, a guitar, a piano and a pump organ.

Sure, there were a few thousand fans in the building that night but it felt like we were all sat *at his feet*. We had almost never made it at all. The show fell four days before our wedding day and I'd made a bad start on all those promises for married life by having failed to get us tickets.

Then as we sat with the hotel's wedding planner a couple of days before the show my mobile rang. Someone had seen my appeal for tickets and had two for sale.

I paid over the odds but what the heck. We drove somewhere out into the wilds of County Derry and handed over our cash. We were in.

Moira had seen Bruce before but I am not sure she actually got my obsession until that night.

Alone on stage, playing and chatting through his songs, laughing about his troubles, his inadequacies, Bruce had never been so seductive.

Our story is about more than a love for the music. It's personal. And that is what Bruce does: he gets into your life. Many of the fans who have told their story in this book have found Bruce and his songs to be loyal companions through the years: he's been there through the hard times for them and he helps them celebrate the good.

He writes in such a personal fashion that you don't have to be from New Jersey, you don't have to have worked the Mexican border or in a Pittsburgh steel mill, to get it.

As a writer he marries the importance of the political with the essence of the personal in a way that few, if any, can match.

Some here have met Bruce. Other fans maybe can be pretty jealous of that. But we all feel like we know him.

Personally, ever since a local radio station used to play "The River" virtually every morning, I have pretty much thought of him as a friend.

It's presumptuous certainly; kind of strange even; but I just know you know what I'm talking about.

Colm Mooney

... and Authors' Note

All who contributed to this book have been generous with their patience and time, and with their willingness to share so many special stories.

Many remained in touch with us throughout the writing of the book and, although we do not have the space to thank them all here, their support and friendship is much appreciated.

We've been lucky enough to meet some of them along our journey and to be Facebook friends (yes, I'm afraid so) with many more. They are a great bunch.

We would also like to thank contributors and the moderator of the Greasy Lake internet forum and the many posters to the Backstreet BTX forum who supported us. Special thanks to Lakers Ceinwen and Hywel, Sinead and Stephen, Lars, Deano and Chris, and also to John and Tina Gill.

Many people were kind enough to help us source photographs for the book. We cannot thank them enough.

We were given a tremendous boost by meeting René Van Diemen and Harry Scott at the Rotterdam Convention organised by Jan Rodenrijks in 2008. René's photos from the *Magic* shows were an inspiration.

Please check out René's work at *www.springsteen.nl/photos*.

Harry very kindly allowed us to use shots from the Seeger Sessions and the Magic show in Belfast.

Our picture credits page lists the names of everyone who has photos in the book. Many people spent time searching and scanning photos for us, including Justin Evans, Thomas Quinn, Jocelyn Kelly and John Markey. We also received many more photos from other contributors to the book and we were sorry we could not use them all.

Thanks also to Carol Lee, Terry Thorp and Paul Hayden, *Irish Times*; Lisa, of Maxwell Photography (Maxpix).

Three people put in a tremendous amount of time to help us proof-read the manuscript. We are extremely grateful to Dan French and Mike Saunders for not only picking up on our mistakes but also for being hugely supportive of the project. Their encouragement kept us going. Mary Sharkey also went through the manuscript for us and her task was even more difficult: she is not even a Springsteen fan! That is dedication.

Andrei Talbot, born in Ireland, now living in Toronto and a Bruce fan since 1975, designed a promotional leaflet for us that he sent to Bruce's management to tell them about the book. His commitment and messages of support also kept us going.

Thanks also to our friend Andrew Canham, from Cardiff, who did a great job designing the website which accompanies the book, and to Phil Cope and Darren Dobbs for working so hard on the design of the book.

In researching the Springsteen family tree we had tremendous help from the staff at the New Jersey State Archives.

We would particularly like to thank the journalists who covered the shows featured in the book, and the editors who allowed us to quote from their work, in particular, the editor of the *Irish Times*.

One final thank you: to Bruce and his bands of musicians.

Postscript: Our road brightened shortly before this book went to press when our son Evan was born in June 2009.

Greg Lewis and Moira Sharkey
August 2009

Terry Conroy

Simon Nicholl